Cable Television
and the FCC

Don R. Le Duc

Cable Television and the FCC

A Crisis in Media Control

Temple University Press
Philadelphia

Temple University Press, Philadelphia 19122
© 1973 by Temple University. All rights reserved

Published 1973
Printed in the United States of America

International Standard Book Number: 0-87722-062-X
Library of Congress Catalog Card Number: 72-95885

Contents

Preface

Cable television might be described as a regressive mass medium because it is attempting to return electronic communications to the wire from which broadcast innovation freed it several decades ago. Yet if the cable "revolution" should succeed in overturning the present broadcast structure, the public may benefit from the availability of a far broader range of electronic media services. This claim might seem paradoxical to the extent that the unique attributes of the cable challenger are seen as emerging from its "wire," but eminently reasonable if its distinctive promise is defined more accurately in terms of its expanding channel dimensions.

Public support for cable television has arisen not because of the closed-circuit nature of its distribution technique, but because its coaxial linkages can deliver a far greater number of channels of communication than television stations can transmit through an overburdened broadcast spectrum. The competitive strength of cable, then, seems based upon the same fundamental human urge, an apparently insatiable desire for ever more extensive communications service, which has spurred the evolution of each successive mass medium since the advent of the industrial age in Western society. It may be that industrialization, in diluting the strength of oral tradition, instilled in modern man a craving for the certitude that was once drawn from countless springs of communal and kinship custom—a thirst no narrow and mechanized message channel has had the capacity to quench. In this context the cable medium could represent the first communications force capable of ending man's Tantalus-like quest; its vast array of channels offering the diverse, variant, and thus more human message bonds which mass-produced units of entertainment and news have supplanted but have failed to replace.

vii

If there is any truth in this metaphoric description, the cable controversy appears to have a significance ranging far beyond the particular issues the operators of cable, the broadcast industry, and government have faced during the past two decades. If cable is only a prototype for future systems offering ever wider options in communications functions, and if public demand continues to swell in response to this expanding promise, the pressure exerted upon the governmental agency standing between such a potential and its realization seems likely to increase in almost logarithmic progression during the years ahead.

The Federal Communications Commission was not designed to withstand this type of stress, and unless its capacity to integrate innovation into existing communications services is augmented, some future wave of media technology may suddenly break free of its narrow restraints to sweep away every vestige of governmental control over this vital evolutionary process. While there is no need for an agency whose protective policy toward the industry it regulates frustrates the public's desire for communication, there seems to be a growing need for an impartial mediator to protect the rights of those members of the public who can exert no effective economic pressure, and to prevent technology alone from dictating the quantity and quality of future media services.

Because communications and law are both processes, the basic nature of the interactions between the cable medium and its regulator should be revealed most clearly through historical perspective. In this manner it should be possible to isolate any constantly recurring patterns of administrative behavior indicating that some characteristic of the regulatory process itself could be dictating the agency's response to the stimulus of technological competition.

Thus, while each specific agency action relating to innovative challenge might be explained in terms of its own unique facts, a comparison of a substantial number of decisions concerning similar types of challenges over an extended period of time might reveal significant parallels in approach and resolution transcending any explanation involving coincidental consistency, the tactics of a particular coalition of opponents, or the attitudes of a specific administration. Such an inherent bias, an irrelevant factor consistently influencing all deliberations concerning this type of challenge, would remain unaffected by changes in either agency personnel or industry factions. Therefore, unless any structural bias against technological competition revealed by this study is remedied through modification of the agency's regulatory process, each future advance in the potential of communications delivery may be foredoomed to a series of restraints no less severe than those already experienced by the cable medium.

No single study can provide the foundation for a comprehensive set of remedial proposals, but this work may at least offer a basis for discovering whether certain nonevidentiary elements may have contaminated the objectivity of the commission's procedures in evaluating the interests served by new communications techniques. While nothing can guarantee the wisdom of regulators making such crucial decisions, it may be possible to purify the process by which such wisdom is obtained.

This behavioral approach to communications regulation is derived from my background as an attorney for an administrative agency and is based in part upon research conducted during the preparation of my dissertation, "Community Antenna Television as a Challenger of Broadcast Regulatory Policy." However, this study has actually been drawn from a broad reservoir of encouragement and inspiration extending more than a decade into the past. Among those to whom I am most deeply indebted are Professors John L. Phelan, Department of History, University of Wisconsin; Calvin W. Corman, School of Law, Rutgers University; and Gaines Post, Department of History, Princeton University, whose examples of scholarship stimulated my earliest interest in legal research; former Wisconsin Insurance Commissioner Robert Haase and Brown County Judge James Byers, whose perceptive administration of law reveals the difference between justice and legalism; Professor Walter B. Emery, Department of Speech Communication, Ohio State University, whose writings made me aware of the challenges involved in broadcast regulation; and former *Journal of Broadcasting* editor Professor John M. Kittross, Temple University, who has constantly encouraged my efforts at communications publication.

I should also like to thank those University of Wisconsin faculty members who reviewed my dissertation and offered valuable suggestions for its improvement: Department of Communication Arts professors Charles Sherman, Ordean Ness, Russell Merritt, and Winston Brembeck; and University of Kentucky journalism professor Dwight Teeter.

Broadcast consultants and attorneys were, without exception, eager to give me the benefit of their special insight and knowledge. Special thanks are due communications engineer Archer S. Taylor; former FCC chairman and NCTA president Frederick Ford; and my fellow Federal Communications Bar members Grover Cooper, John Cole, Bruce Lovett, John Summers, and especially Erwin Krasnow for their invaluable assistance.

I am also greatly indebted to my students, at both the University of Maryland and Ohio State University, whose keen interest and searching questions have tested the validity of every premise advanced in this work.

The general historical outline employed in the first chapter of this study was originally published in *Annals of the American Academy of Political and Social Science* (Vol. 400, 1972), while the basic system of analysis advanced in chapter 2 was based upon an article first appearing in the *Federal Communications Bar Journal* (Vol. 23, 1969). I should like to thank the editors of both journals for generously agreeing to the use of such material in this text.

Finally, there are two persons whose influence upon this study cannot be adequately described within the formal style of an acknowledgment, but who know, I hope, how much is owed to them. The first is Lawrence Lichty, Department of Communication Arts, University of Wisconsin, my major professor, whose enthusiasm for broadcast scholarship encouraged me to leave the practice of law five years ago to begin anew as an apprentice. Throughout the tedious process of revision, as renewed federal activity began transforming major policy discussions of earlier drafts into historical footnotes, and as a sudden outpouring of cable literature threatened for a time to cover every topic of significance, the incentive for continuing came from the example set by this tireless and dedicated scholar.

The other is my wife, Alice, who not only has helped but has understood, and with rare feminine grace once again put aside her dreams for mine as I wrote this study with hours we might have shared.

I

The Cable Controversy: Expanding Channels vs. Restricting Regulation

The Radio Act of 1927 represents one of the earliest major efforts of the federal government to resolve a pollution problem arising from misuse of a natural resource. Between 1921 and 1927 that portion of the radio frequency spectrum allocated to broadcast stations became so heavily saturated with competing signals that interference-free reception in most metropolitan areas of the United States had become virtually impossible. To prevent further over-burdening of the nation's broadcast channels the Congress created a new regulatory agency, granting it trusteeship over this vital resource to insure that all future access to radio frequencies would be consistent with a policy that conditioned usage upon service in the public interest.

For almost a half-century the entire structure of broadcast regulation has rested upon this single base of authority, the privilege of spectrum access which provides both the legal justification and the administrative procedures essential for supervision of this type of electronic mass communication. Through licensing standards founded upon this power the Federal Communications Commission (FCC) has labored diligently to establish and maintain a nationwide system of locally oriented radio and television stations, with each licensee offered an exclusive territorial right to disseminate programming on a specifically assigned set of frequencies.

Cable television posed the first serious challenge to this traditional structure; its vast potential for program delivery granted it the capacity to flood broadcast markets previously protected from outside competition, and it flowed through wired channels not dependent upon spectrum access for their operation. By 1965, as public support for these wired systems continued to mount, the

1

FCC felt compelled to act in order to prevent further erosion of the program-distribution functions of local stations. Although the commission could not prohibit the operation of nonspectrum devices, it could protect its broadcasters, and thus the control structure they supported, through restrictions upon cable carriage of broadcast signals bypassing these local-station outlets. Yet this tactic, however well adapted for safeguarding established program-delivery channels, would seem to inhibit rather than encourage a broader flow of communications services to the public.

All federal regulatory decisions relating to cable have involved some variation on this single theme of public interest, balancing the value of communications service furnished by the existing industry against the potential value in newer techniques challenging its predominance. Thus a case history of commission deliberations weighing this factor seems to provide a unique perspective for determining whether a series of cable actions, each apparently justified in itself, might betray in its totality a pattern of regulatory behavior consistently sacrificing broader service goals to maintain industry stability.

The fact that the Radio Act of 1927 and its successor, the Communications Act of 1934, reflected enlightened conservation of the spectrum resource when enacted is, of course, no guarantee that their underlying premises remain constructive or even valid today. The nature and extent of the societal functions performed by broadcasting have expanded substantially during the intervening years, responding to an ever increasing demand for communications services. Radio now claims the largest potential audience of any medium, reaching 99 percent of all American households, while television, with 97 percent penetration, has been ranked in recent surveys as the most widely used medium for news information, as well as the most popular source of entertainment. Yet this increasing public dependence upon electronic media comes during an era when private users of spectrum, outnumbering commercial broadcast stations by a ratio of almost one thousand to one, are pressuring for broader access to this already overburdened resource.

In essence, then, industrial growth may have operated to transform a progressive policy into regressive restraint, and thus

polluted the very resource it was created to protect. If this
evaluation is accurate, the dimensions of the current communications
controversy extend far beyond cable television to encompass a
much more crucial and fundamental issue, the ultimate ends to be
served by a continuing federal role in the evolution of electronic
mass media.

The past two decades of cable growth seem far more a symptom
than a cause of the television industry's difficulties, with wired
systems simply responding to public demand not satisfied by the
less efficient dissemination technique of the local broadcast station.
Yet cable appears to be only a precursor of future media systems,
its threat only a small-scale simulation of challenges soon to be
mounted by the more effective wave-guide or laser-linked networks
capable of delivering messages directly to each subscriber's home.
Therefore, even if recent commission efforts to negotiate an
accommodation between broadcasting and cable should prove
successful, such a settlement will represent only a temporary
resolution of those major questions of communications policy raised
initially during this cable era.

The first chapter of part 1 will outline the primary economic,
political, and social issues emerging from cable television's
challenge, as well as the probable impact of existing policy in these
areas upon future communications innovation based on the cable
model. The second chapter will examine the structure and operation
of the FCC in an effort to isolate the factors which seem to
dictate its attitude and behavior toward technological advances in
the field of communications.

Clearly, innovation, even when enhancing the capacity of
message delivery, may not be universally beneficial for society, and
there could well be cogent and compelling reasons for preserving
the established industry from challengers offering nothing more
than increased dissemination efficiency. Thus, the underlying
question in determining whether a critical situation exists in
communications control is not whether the commission has
consistently opposed change, but whether, operating in an era of
communications revolution, it has retained the capacity to evaluate,
rather than react instinctively to, challenge; and to formulate policy
encouraging the maximum service consistent with its broad public

interest mandate. If the interests of the public appear to have been paramount in determining its course of action, the agency would seem worthy of preservation despite any short-term loss in the potential of communications delivery. However, if through bias inherent in its structure, the primary motivation for restraint has been protection of the clientele industry, then the agency has already imposed an unjust burden upon vital commerce in communications, a burden which will become increasingly intolerable if public demand should continually be denied even broader ranges of communications services in the future.

1 The Cable Challenge and Regulatory Response: A Two-Decade Overview

During the past few years an ever expanding chorus of expert opinion has hailed the advent of a new stage in the history of mass communications, the cable era. It sees cable as a medium destined to revolutionize the existing broadcast mass-message delivery process through its capacity to act as a conduit for individual opinion and specialized communications service.[1] Yet, in a manner typical of the arguments of disciples, the studies and reports of the proponents of cable tend to blur crucial distinctions between potentiality and actuality; they predict the imminent emergence of a nationwide eighty-channel coaxial system, while the cable television industry of the early 1970s remains firmly rooted in the present, if not the past. Its average operator still furnishes less than a dozen channels to some 2,300 subscribers.[2]

This marked divergence between recent projections of the rate of cable evolution and the present pace of the industry's growth has resulted from the tendency of research groups to place undue emphasis upon technological advances in the field while overlooking existing legal and economic restraints upon expansion. A decade of almost constant improvement in coaxial and microwave equipment has provided cable owners with the potential of expanding system capacity from twelve to forty-eight or more channels while substantially extending the effective range of their wired coverages. These innovations, however, have as yet had little impact in improving either the breadth or the scope of existing cable services, with no more than 25 percent of the industry's 3,000 systems now performing a greater number or variety of communications functions than those already possible in 1963.[3]

5

The Nature of the Cable Medium

It is vitally important to distinguish between the projected and actual capacities of cable systems today, for channel capacity influences the nature as well as the quantity of messages delivered to their audiences. "Cable television" is, in actuality, a deceptively uniform term which describes without differentiating among the three distinct forms of wired service it encompasses. Cable can mean the true "community antenna," a four- to six-channel operation simply enhancing the clarity of existing television signals; the typically twelve-channel "CATV," augmenting local transmissions with broadcast programming imported from other markets; or the modern "cable-TV," whose twenty-four to forty-eight channels and two-way circuitry provide a communications network for a broad spectrum of private information as well as general entertainment services. Thus, while all cable operations share a similar multichannel, audience-supported, closed-circuit technique of delivery, neither societal value nor competitive impact can be defined by this commonality.

In this more accurate functional sense, then, the cable industry still straddles its evolutionary stage of antenna and program importing and therefore remains predominantly an auxiliary broadcast service rather than a distinct medium in its own right. One basic reason for this reluctance of CATV operators to assume the responsibility of cable-TV functions has been the lack of a sufficiently large audience to justify incurring the high costs of broadband construction or conversion. The cable industry claims an audience of over 7 million subscribers, more than one television family in ten, but cable coverage can be described more accurately as massive saturation of the one-tenth of the nation's television homes accessible to it. The remaining 90 percent of its potential audience is located in one of the major, or "top-100," markets where federal restraints upon signal importation made CATV penetration virtually impossible prior to April 1972.[4] Cable leaders contend that the federal policy of protecting major-market television stations from wired competition not only denied the cable industry revenues essential for conversion to more comprehensive communications service but also lessened the incentive for cable-TV construction, while CATV remained artificially restrained from reaching its potential growth in these markets.

Since 1970 the FCC has been attempting to formulate rules to furnish this incentive through some technique which would grant major-market signal-importation rights in return for gradual conversion to "cable-TV" operation.[5] These proposals have been labeled "pro cable," but a substantial number of cable operators view them as being simply "anti-CATV." They argue that a requirement conditioning expansion upon extensive capital investment in an industry whose largest ownership group serves less than one television household in 100 seems roughly equivalent to granting local trucking franchises solely on a basis of national cartage activity or authorizing nonscheduled airline service only after a carrier's purchase of a sizable fleet of Boeing 747s.[6]

The claim of covert regulatory opposition in the guise of apparent encouragement is obviously debatable, but it is difficult to dispute industry figures indicating that the growth of the cable audience since 1969 has come about largely through more intensive saturation of existing service areas rather than through expansion in new areas of opportunity. Even if the commission, through its "Third Report and Order" of March 1972 extending urban-cable signal-importation rights, should stimulate the development of nonbroadcast services envisioned in recent public and private studies, these services will still have to evolve under the condition of compatibility with existing broadcast services in these markets. As the FCC itself declared in its letter of intent projecting these cable functions, the wired systems may supplement but may never supplant the established spectrum structure they challenge.[7] Thus, despite optimistic projections of a new cable era just ahead, it seems highly unlikely that cable, whatever its ultimate delivery efficiency, will ever attain the status of a dominant medium on the basis of service alone.

The Cable Challenge to Broadcast Markets

Most communities in the United States of major and even moderate size have had specific television channels reserved for their use since 1952 when the commission established its present system of allocation and assignment.[8] At that time almost 55 percent of the nation's most valuable space in the lower-frequency spectrum was allocated for television transmission, a resource generously employed to insure interference-free operation by the more than two thousand stations expected to serve some thirteen hundred communities. Unfortunately, the willingness of broadcasters to construct and operate such stations was influenced not by the commission's community-oriented programming standards, but by a far more compelling, economically oriented, "market" standard—the number of television homes included within the allocated coverage area.

Television advertising is predominantly national in origin. For this reason a system measuring television viewing on a community-by-community basis would not be as valuable in discovering the extent of nationwide exposure to particular sales messages as broader-based regional reports encompassing the entire national audience. To furnish this more comprehensive perspective, a private audience-analysis firm has divided the nation into some 270 "broadcast markets," with each station's commercial time rate dictated by its effective coverage of television homes within its designated market. These rates, reflecting economic rather than political borders, determine the station's profit potential by setting the maximum range of revenues it can hope to receive from network, national spot, and even local advertisers. Since these rates are solely a function of its market audience, a television broadcaster has no economic incentive to devote any greater portion of time to coverage of local issues of interest to his assigned community than to coverage of issues important to any other locality within his market. In essence, then, despite the FCC's liberal grant of spectrum space dedicated to support of community-oriented television, the overriding significance of market-based economic considerations has eroded its efforts, leaving only its massive allocation machinery intact.

While this allocation design has been largely ineffectual in creating a "local television" pattern of broadcast service, it has had a substantial if unintended impact upon the diffusion of television signals across the nation: the emphasis upon local dissemination has denied many regions the ability to receive the programming of all three major television networks. The commission's plan, envisioning independent broadcast entities supported primarily by local advertising revenues, had ignored network coverage patterns. The costs involved in television programming, however, demanded an unduplicated population base of at least twenty-five thousand viewers for even the most limited operation of a network affiliate, and far more to support any degree of local programming, so that by 1960, only 515 television stations were on the air, and less than one-third of the nation's 263 markets received the programming of all three major television networks.[9] While the FCC seemed oblivious to the dominant appeal of these network services, the cable industry was not, and wired systems expanded to fill the vacuum in spectrum coverages arising in large part from the commission's restrictive goals for local licensing.

Since broadcast revenues are earned by exposing audiences within a designated market area to sales messages delivered by its stations, community antenna systems simply carrying signals beyond the borders of existing markets had no real impact upon the profits of television stations. By the middle of the 1950s, however, a few of the 450 systems then serving some three hundred thousand subscribers began to penetrate existing market contours, using newly approved microwave relay devices to import network programming not otherwise available in that market.[10] These earliest CATV operators did constitute at least a minimal threat to the audience base, and thus to the revenue potential of stations in that market, by allowing cable subscribers to view additional channels which reduced the proportionate share of exposure to local television each market station could claim.

The commission tended to ignore broadcasters' complaints concerning this threat during the 1950s, in part because complaining stations were unable to show that this market problem had any adverse effect upon their ability to provide community-oriented broadcast service; and also, perhaps more significantly, because the agency still viewed cable as a temporary aberration destined to disappear as broadcast coverage expanded.[11]

By 1965, however, the FCC was finally forced to accept the fact that the broadcast market structure then supporting 569 commercial television stations would never furnish the full array of spectrum coverages necessary to supplant cable without regulatory intervention. In fact, the cable industry, which had swelled to more than thirteen hundred systems serving some 1.2 million subscribers, appeared likely, through its technique of flooding markets with network and syndicated-film programming, to undercut the economic base of existing stations and make future broadcast growth impossible. Thus the commission, responsible for the community-based, local program orientation of television control, was compelled to base its cable restraints upon the need to protect the broadcast industry's markets and functions of national-program distribution.[12]

The FCC and Spectrum Controls

Congress has never enacted any legislation granting the FCC specific regulatory jurisdiction over cable television activities. In 1959 the agency opposed a proposal to provide it with limited authority, arguing that the magnitude of the threat did not justify the administrative burden entailed.[13] Seven years later the commission acted to contain the cable challenge without requesting congressional authorization; it contended that it was simply exercising its existing power to protect broadcast service from injury arising from unfair competitive use of its programming. While the FCC held no mandate to insure the economic prosperity of its stations, it did have the right to intercede, according to one federal court decision, when the end result of destructive competition among communicators would be to "damage service to an extent inconsistent with public interest."[14]

The agency had actually been restricting microwave importation of programming to cable systems which seemed to threaten the economic stability of competing television stations since 1963 when a federal court had sustained the commission's authority to use its common carrier power in this fashion.[15] In April 1965 the FCC simply extended this power generally over all microwave-served cable systems and in a companion "Notice of Further Inquiry" refused approval of any further microwave services in top-100 markets until its deliberations in this area were completed.[16]

Although the commission established procedures for obtaining such importation approval in March 1966 and created a new broadcaster-controlled program to handle these requests in December 1968, the practical effect of the "freeze" and its subsequent modifications was to make cable operations in major metropolitan markets virtually impossible. Cable could not hope to attract subscriber support in markets already offering full network coverage off-the-air unless it could augment this service with additional film and other syndicated features from other areas. Lacking this appeal, its chances of success were far too marginal to stimulate the capital investment necessary for costly urban construction.

For a time between 1965 and 1969 there seemed to be a distinct possibility that through copyright controls then being considered by both the Congress and the courts the FCC might be relieved of its obligation to act as the sole guardian of major-market television stations. If either branch of government had brought cable carriage of broadcast signals within the terms of copyright protection, broadcasters could have limited cable competition without further administrative intervention. However, Congress failed to broaden the provisions of the Copyright Act of 1909 to include cable carriage, and the Supreme Court in June 1968 held that cable carriage of broadcast signals under existing law did not constitute copyright infringement.[17]

Thus isolated in position, the FCC in December 1968 created by administrative decree virtually the same type of broadcast control over cable's signal usage rejected by Congress and the courts.[18] At the same time the commission declared its intention to open its first broad-scale inquiry into the nature of cable and other advanced forms of electronic mass media in a unique attempt to range beyond its historic role as a broadcast regulator. In effect, then, while raising the barriers against cable penetration still higher, the FCC seemed interested at last in gaining the capacity to evaluate the promise as well as the peril inherent in communications innovation.

Yet despite this apparent concern for a broader approach in weighing the relative advantages represented by competing media systems, the commission, issuing its "Third Report and Order" after three years of such study, cautioned that, although it was relaxing its long-term restrictions upon signal importation by major-market cable systems, this effort "to get cable moving" would be conditioned upon the agency's ability to do so "without jeopardizing the basic structure of over-the-air television."[19]

This a priori assumption concerning the necessity of perpetuating the spectrum television structure may be increasingly difficult to justify in the years ahead, however, not only because of the commission's obligation to encourage the maximum media service consistent with public interest, but also because of its equal responsibility to manage the spectrum resource in a manner fostering its most efficient usage. Each television signal, because of the extremely complex electronic message it must deliver, demands a range of frequencies almost six times the breadth of the entire Standard Broadcast, or commercial radio, band. Therefore, to preserve a domain large enough to accommodate all present and projected television stations, the FCC was compelled to dedicate more than half of its most valuable spectrum space between 30 MHz and 960 MHz to television services, while governmental exclusive or shared channels occupied another third of this band space.[20] As a result of this disproportionate burden imposed upon the spectrum resource by some one thousand television broadcasters, the agency has been forced to cram nearly four million "Safety" and "Special" radio facilities, such as aviation, fire, and other emergency or industry services, into an allocation occupying less than 5 percent of this frequency range. While the growth of television stations has reached a relative plateau during the last few years, these private services are expected to increase by one-third during this decade, but, unlike commercial broadcasters, they cannot substitute cable for spectrum message delivery. It has been estimated that land mobile-broadcast operations contribute more than $20 billion annually to the Gross National Product, and that the cost of each television channel in access denied these services ranges from $1 billion to $5 billion each year in expenses imposed by the need to employ alternative methods of communication.[21]

This disparity in range and value between frequencies reserved for the television industry and those available to other enterprises seems justifiable only if television broadcasters use this generous grant to offer the public substantial amounts of otherwise unobtainable communications service. In actuality, however, more than 80 percent of all television programming is delivered to local stations by national distribution sources without need of spectrum, primarily through network line and microwave relay, or directly from film-syndication organizations. Thus this rich resource of frequencies yields no more than three or four hours of local programming to the flow of entertainment and news which might otherwise reach the public each day without occupying vital spectrum space.

Each of these criticisms of the commission's policy of television allocation has been met by spirited counterarguments from the broadcast industry. In respect to restraints upon cable's capabilities of program dissemination, these spokesmen contend that restriction preserves rather than depletes communications services available to the public, by protecting the economic capacity of broadcasters to prepare programming that cable can deliver but cannot create. They maintain that television now provides the public with entertainment and news services valued at more than $100 billion a year, a vast audience benefit that cable expansion would endanger. They also argue that estimates of land mobile-spectrum costs omit this public service factor inherent in broadcast usage and tend to minimize the total economic value of an advertising and marketing structure which generates, among other payments, more than $1 billion a year in employment income, $3 billion in receiver sales, and $3 billion in advertising revenues.[22]

Yet even if the validity of all of the broadcast industry's contentions could be established beyond question, any attempt to draw from this evidence justification for a continuation of the preferential treatment accorded television broadcasters might still be subject to serious challenge, if not by rival media, then by a public denied their services. The commission's dual mandate to encourage existing and potential communications services does not allow it to pursue one objective and ignore the other.[23] Therefore, to assess the true merit of the present federal spectrum policy, it seems essential to balance against the value of communications functions the FCC has protected the value of all potential communications services it has thereby restrained.

The Promise Inherent in Future Communications Systems

Each broadcast station operates a single channel, supported by mass advertising, with one-way local distribution of predominantly national programming. Cable and all future systems have the capacity to short-circuit the local station's exclusive control of program distribution and, in doing so, to alter the fundamental relationship between the mass communicator and its audience. The new techniques, which are multichannel, subscriber supported, and two-way, are potentially far more flexible in responding to the specific needs of their audiences, with each distinctive attribute allowing another dimension of broader, society-based service.

A broadcast station, because of its continuously competitive struggle for the largest share of the audience in its market, cannot insert significant but limited-appeal programming into its prime-time schedule without irretrievable loss of advertising revenues to its competitors. In contrast, multichannel systems, relying upon audience support for a total package of communications services, need not be concerned with the broad appeal of any one channel as long as each in itself attracts additional subscribers to its system.

The closed-circuit, subscriber-supported technique of funding programming is also far more efficient in matching production expenses to viewer interests. It allows a small segment of the population to pool revenues in order to obtain material either too expensive or too specialized for general broadcast dissemination. The programming of "prime-time" network television is dependent upon viewing in an average of from ten to twelve million households in order to achieve a profitable return from the use of broadcast time, but a one-dollar weekly payment by an equal number of cable subscribers would furnish a production budget exceeding the present weekly film expenditures of all three television networks combined.[24] On the other end of this audience scale, a viewing group of fewer than one thousand subscribers could, by making a similar payment, provide a sufficient financial base for production of a variety of local cultural, educational, or other special-interest programming.

In addition to the capacity to create programs at both national and local levels, cable and all future types of multichannel systems will offer the promise of direct access by members of the public to the audience of the electronic mass medium, either through channels dedicated to public use or through facilities available for leasing. Those who now challenge the objectivity of licensed broadcasters are limited in relief to "fairness" complaints evaluated by the FCC, but in ending the restraints imposed by single-channel operation, the multichannel systems can also end the need of private citizens to depend upon either the goodwill of professional communicators or the concern of government in order to exercise their right of free speech by means of electronic mass media.

The value of multichannel, audience-supported systems of communication extends beyond their capacity to allow more effective use of programming revenues, however, or even beyond their unique ability to act as a forum for public debate of issues of local or national concern. Because these techniques have the capability of ending limitations upon the dissemination of electronic messages imposed by a scarcity of spectrum channels, they could broaden both ends of existing coverage and service patterns. Operating as a community-oriented facility, for example, cable has both the channel space and the circuitry control to match the audience needs of almost any potential user. Thus, candidates for minor political offices, local businesses interested in limited sales campaigns, and others in a community with only minimal funds and narrow dissemination needs might for the first time be encouraged to seek access to electronic communications by the offer of a favorable time and channel at an audience-based rate they could afford. Yet while local delivery circuits serve these interests within communities, a far more specialized set of channels, providing individualized access to a vast array of national and international information and culture, could link their citizens with the world.

It is the two-way circuitry of these systems which will make this last function possible and which may ultimately have the most profound influence upon the future role of electronic mass media in our society. A fundamental characteristic which distinguishes "mass" from personal communication is the absence of direct "feedback," or the ability of the communicator to gauge audience reaction to his message. Most cable systems are now being constructed with the capability for at least limited two-way transmission, which allows a subscriber to respond to a particular inquiry. These circuits are being installed primarily for monitoring proposed television subscription services, but they offer cable the capacity to perform a much broader range of functions in the future.

While citizen groups have recently been demanding some role in the selection of media programs, the individual capability for program selection may eventually have much greater significance in making programming responsive to public desires. The ability to receive information from audiences would in itself immediately transform CATV systems of program delivery into efficient mechanisms for conducting marketing research and launching direct-sales campaigns. Such a conduit for surveys, catalogue purchases, facsimile newspaper and magazine delivery, computer services, and countless other economic transactions involving information exchange might soon become so lucrative that the systems could offer programming free of charge simply to gain household access.[25]

At the other end of the chain, members of the audience would no longer be simply the passive recipients of mass communications messages but would participate actively in their selection and dissemination. The television receiver would be in direct contact with its medium for the first time in the history of mass communications, and each family would be able to use this contact to select and program a broadcast schedule best suited to its needs.

Thus, direct feedback could well result in the reversal of the traditional roles of mass communications, making the communicator little more than a common carrier in a communications process controlled by each individual subscriber. In such a humanized atmosphere broad governmental control may no longer be necessary, except perhaps for the type of supervision of rates and service exercised over other private communications carriers.

These projections of communications functions now being sacrificed through efforts to protect the existing spectrum-based broadcast system are based solely upon technological capacity aleady available. Yet, as in any similar innovation, both the ultimate social value achieved by these systems and the willingness of industry leaders to seek such public-interest objectives depend not so much upon the scientific potential involved as upon the economic incentive and, in this instance, the quality of government guidance as well.

Societal Issues Involved in Communications Revolution

There seems little question that cable television, because of its broader economic base and greater distribution efficiency, will eventually replace a major portion of the spectrum delivery system, unless prevented from doing so by continued governmental restriction. To the extent that wired dissemination will thus result in the levying of charges for programming previously delivered free of direct charge, some would argue that the American public will be denied a basic right to broadcast entertainment. Yet it is important to remember that the present American broadcast system was not preordained, or consciously fashioned to reflect our national values, but simply evolved through historical accident from a flaw in the technique of broadcast distribution which made direct audience support impossible.[26] Lacking the ability to restrict reception to those paying for the service, broadcasters operating in a nation without a tradition of governmental support for such activities could only turn to commercial enterprises willing to provide programs in order to attract audiences to their sales messages. Business in the United States is no more obliged to furnish the public with free electronic entertainment than it is to support the performance of plays, the publication of books, or the distribution of other forms of art.

There are also fundamental reasons for challenging the contention that the existing system operates without cost to the public. Although the question whether broadcast advertising adds to or decreases the cost of each item sold is still without clear resolution, there is no question that television service is being subsidized through its broad access to the radio spectrum, a dedication costing the economy at least $1 billion a year in efficiency denied its "next best users." Therefore, even if broadcast advertising, in itself does not result in raising consumer prices, the use of spectrum frequencies for such commercial services imposes a higher cost upon a wide variety of goods and services ultimately paid for by the public.

In addition, the American public now invests almost $3 billion a year in television receivers to obtain the limited number of programming channels available in most markets. Considering the magnitude of this investment, it seems only fair that the public be granted the option of paying an additional $5 a month to expand the breadth and range of services available through these receivers. In effect, then, all efforts to maintain the widest possible public access to "free TV" must of necessity be based upon restrictions denying others the widest possible access to communications services. Stated in this fashion the question confronting the FCC is at least more clearly described, if thereby made infinitely more difficult to resolve.

Other questions must be raised and answered, however, before the commission will be able to measure accurately the potential capacity of wired systems to serve public interests, and these questions introduce two additional difficulties to its task. The first involves the likelihood of broad discrepancy between the potential of these new systems and their probable level of performance, while the second concerns the true societal value of these projected functions in the event that full technological capacity is realized.

In view of past experiences in the evolution of radio and television there is certainly valid cause for challenging the assumption that an electronic mass medium will naturally seek to furnish the highest level of services consistent with its technological potential. Since mass communicators operate as businesses, economic rather than scientific or philosophical considerations dominate their decision-making processes. It can be argued, however, that economic motivation may now dictate expansion in the variety, if not the quality, of communications service, simply because each channel augments system revenues only when in operation. The commission might therefore have a unique opportunity to couple this economic incentive to public needs, making expansion conditional upon each system's offering a certain quantity of financially unrewarding but socially valuable programming to its audience. This has been the theoretical basis for the "Third Report and Order" of March 1972, which grants relatively generous rights of broadcast-signal importation to cable operators in top-100 markets in return for commitments to construct systems of at least twenty-channel capacity and to dedicate certain of these channels for specific local, nonbroadcast services. Unfortunately, this five-year experimental proposal has been flawed by the commission's emphasis, now traditional, upon market rather than audience considerations, with each community's complement of broadcast and nonbroadcast channels dictated solely by the accident of its competitive impact upon existing boundaries of television advertising. Thus, to comply with the new rules, the smallest village on the periphery of a major market must insist upon a twenty-channel system, while cities outside major markets remain without FCC support for augmentation of either limited broadcast or nonbroadcast services. In addition, the commission has delegated primary responsibility for supervision of these emerging nonbroadcast services to state or local authorities and has retained only the absolute control necessary to restrict usage of broadcast signals. In these circumstances, than, it seems fair to question whether the FCC has as yet begun to encourage the development of true broadband communication systems, or whether it is simply employing these nonbroadcast requirements in a new effort to discourage rapid cable growth.

While most research considering the societal implications of increasing the flow of electronic media messages has concluded that broader audience access will result in a more enlightened, aware, and concerned public, there are experts who feel that, even if media systems should operate at full-channel capacity and provide a wide range of services, the public may not want or should not have such expanded service made available to it. Some believe that no attempt to provide a broader base of communications alternatives will be successful because only a limited number of viewers will select anything but professionally created national programming. Others are concerned about the cultural fragmentation already attributable to broadcasting and feel that cutting one of the few remaining threads of commonality, the shared television program, will only heighten this tendency toward disunity and disorganization.[27]

The FCC might thus be completely justified in deciding, after weighing these conflicting findings, that wired systems, although potentially more efficient in disseminating messages, were not as effective as existing systems in serving primary public interests. Because serious questions concerning the need for free television service, the additional benefits to be derived from wired systems, and the probable effects of these new communications functions upon society still remain unresolved, the immediate release of all cable restraints would seem no more compelling evidence of the commission's concern for public interest than continued restriction of their activities.

In essence, then, before taking action the mediator for the public in the vital field of mass communications must have a comprehensive understanding of societal needs and media's capacity to satisfy them.[28] Any regulatory agency lacking such understanding would be incapable of safeguarding, much less championing, the rights of the public it represents.

The Future of Communications Regulation

The "cable controversy" is no longer truly representative of the crucial communications questions which faced the FCC during the mid-1960s and seem likely to reemerge within a matter of years. In June 1968 the Supreme Court affirmed the authority of the commission to restrict CATV activities threatening the viability of broadcast service, and by the end of 1969 broadcasters had gained control of cable systems serving more than one-third of the industry's subscribers.[29] Therefore, any leniency displayed by the FCC now that the cable industry is being assimilated into the broader system of electronic media would seem to have little relevance in determining its probable attitude toward the next communications challenger operating outside its regulatory control.

Future challenge appears inevitable because cable, like broadcasting, has certain inherent flaws within its delivery mechanism which newer techniques will exploit to stimulate a seemingly insatiable public appetite for communications service. The cost of the construction of trunk lines now limits cable diffusion into sparsely settled regions of the nation and necessitates a huge capital investment for entering urban areas already heavily saturated with wire connections. Devices for transmitting high-frequency signals now offer the promise of extending the effective range of cable systems by allowing subscriber circuits to be linked by inexpensive microwave relays rather than by costly and less flexible coaxial trunk lines.[30] Yet in this promise there may be a peril for the future of cable. Coaxial systems have begun replacing broadcast stations because of their superior carriage capacity, but these narrow-band microwaves, or "quasi-lasers," mark the first step toward techniques of spectrum delivery equaling the efficiency of wired systems without need of cable.

Wave-guided or true laser transmissions could bypass cumbersome wired circuits to deliver an infinite number of messages directly to individual homes. At least the earliest forms of these innovations seem likely to be ready for commercial use by the end of this decade, and all questions concerning the relative value of "free" and "paid" audience access, and the benefits of various communications functions possible with each type of support, will be reopened. Cable interests will undoubtedly demand FCC intervention to protect the media structure from such destructive competition, but in view of past history in this field, there is no reason to believe that restriction will be any more successful in that era than in this, or that any regulatory reaction based primarily on industry pressure will ever achieve any consistent society-based guidelines allowing communications evolution without continual crisis.

It is difficult to project the ultimate extent of technological development in a field where wired dissemination now challenges a broadcast technique which made it obsolete nearly three-quarters of a century ago, but it is not difficult to predict that public interest and support will continue to furnish a powerful incentive for such innovation in the years ahead. Nor does it seem difficult to prophesy that the FCC will remain incapable of channeling this inventive force spurred by public demand into productive media services without extensive administrative delays accompanied by lengthy freezes and restrictions.

Yet to declare on the basis of past regulatory conduct that the commission lacks the capacity to encourage an expansion of services of the electronic media is in itself a rather meaningless generalization, labeling an effect without understanding its causes. The "commission" is, after all, only a collective term describing the activities of some fifteen hundred civil servants, headed by seven relatively short-term political appointees. Its chain of command is amorphous, with commissioners, like feudal barons, commanding the loyalty of only a few hand-picked subordinates; the staff members, segmented by specialization, owe their allegiance not to their temporary overlords but to the greater majesty of Congress and the Civil Service law. Therefore, if there has been a rather consistent pattern of regulatory opposition to cable innovation, its causes appear to lie within the structure of the agency rather than within the attitudes of particular commissioners, especially since the cable controversy has transcended several eras of divergent agency leadership.

The following chapter will attempt to isolate any irrelevant structural elements which may have affected the objectivity of the commission in assessing and satisfying the public's communications needs during the first two decades of the cable era. From this analysis it should be possible to evaluate the capacity of the FCC, as presently constituted, to supervise similar expansion of the electronic media in the future. If past decisions have been influenced by bias inherent in the traditional regulatory process, there is every reason to expect that subsequent administrators, no matter how enlightened, will be foredoomed to perpetuate patterns of control restricting the expansion of communications channels. In that event the only difference between the crisis described in this case study and future communications crises would be one of magnitude, since public demand and communications capacity each attain larger dimension with every passing year.

2 The FCC: Traditional Ruler in an Era of Communications Revolution

While the basic powers and responsibilities of the FCC are expressed in the Communications Act of 1934 and in subsequent amendments, the commission, like any administrative body, is actually subject to a far more extensive set of influences, both legal and political, when conducting its deliberations. Its procedures, for example, are controlled in large part by the provisions of the Administrative Procedure Act of 1946, its personnel policies dictated by civil service rules, its decisions often modified by judicial review, and its general authority severely limited by its status as a congressional agency. Thus, in order to isolate all significant factors inherent in the commission's administrative process which may have influenced its attitude toward cable innovation, it is necessary to consider both the agency's specific regulatory responsibilities in the field of communications and its more fundamental obligations as an independent commission in the federal regulatory structure.

The Regulatory Mandate of the FCC

The Communications Act of 1934, in creating the FCC, declared that its primary objective should be "to make available, so far as possible, to all people of the United States, a rapid, efficient Nation-wide and worldwide wire and radio communication service with adequate facilities at reasonable charges."[1] Ths general objective describes a standard for two distinct and separate regulatory roles assigned the commission: its authority over communications common carriers as set out in title 2 of the act, and its differing responsibilities with respect to users of the radio spectrum, as described in title 3. The FCC's function of regulating common carriers closely parallels that of other federal agencies such as the Interstate Commerce Commission or the Civil Aeronautics Board

23

—supervising industry rates and services to insure reasonable charges and adequate service without impairing the economic stability of the regulated industry.

However, when acting as a broadcast regulator under title 3, the FCC, in a manner unique among federal industry regulators, is involved, not in the pricing aspects of the clientele business operation, but only in maintaining the intrinsic value of the service it supplies the public. Because economic factors are almost irrelevant to the issue of spectrum usage in the public interest, the commission has been granted virtually no authority to intervene in matters relating solely to industry revenues, except in the unusual circumstance where a financial crisis might otherwise imperil the quality of broadcast service furnished a particular audience.

Since the FCC has been able, through the unusual nature of its regulatory assignment, to avoid direct power over and thereby responsibility for the financial well-being of its broadcasters, it should have exhibited an unexcelled capacity for evaluating innovation without excessive concern for its economic impact upon the regulated industry. If, instead, its actions have been similar to those of the ICC or the CAB when facing this type of challenge, the cause of its behavior seems more likely to be found in the elements it shares with these agencies than in its own unique mandate.

The FCC as an Independent Commission

The independent commission was once an innovative response to the problems of governmental control in an industrial era. Legislatures found themselves lacking both the time and the techniques necessary to allow them to enact all the detailed regulations required by complex and highly technical industry practices. In addition, statutes did not provide the degree of flexibility demanded by experimentation in new fields of governmental social control where the precise rule of law to be enforced was not apparent. For this reason legislatures delegated rulemaking powers to agencies created to regulate particular industries and also delegated to them the powers to enforce compliance with the rules, make modifications when necessary, and adjudicate controversies arising out of their application. Common-law scholars objected to the intermingling of executive, legislative, and judicial functions in a single governmental body, but until the early 1950s they stood almost alone in their criticism.

In 1959, however, a scholar of administrative law could declare with reason, "The present crisis in the commissions, to put it bluntly, arises from the fact that these agencies have, for years, been disproving the basic assumptions which led to their creation. Set up to regulate the public interest, they have . . . tended to equate that concept with the private interests of those being regulated. . . . Intended to promote competition, they have fostered monopoly."[2] This radical shift in attitude seems not so much the result of any flaw in the design of commissions as a refusal to set any reasonable limits upon the weight of regulatory responsibility which might be shifted to these bodies. Until the effects of the Depression provided the federal government with a new economic mission, most agencies, reflecting a heritage of state regulation which had developed during the nineteenth century, simply supervised the rates and services of industries of a public utility nature to insure that they were reasonable and equitable.

Such modest aims, however, would not suffice during an era when irrational pessimism about the strength of the nation's economy was giving way to unreasoned faith in the wisdom of its government. Neither Congress nor the president could offer immediate solutions to the host of problems posed by the tremors of industrial collapse, but each could provide hope of ultimate resolution through the creation of agencies specifically designed to remedy such situations. Thus, establishing a new commission or agency became almost an instinctive response to each societal crisis, with the result a proliferation of institutions without coordination, guidance, or the capacity to perform the miracles promised. Agencies had been successful as bodies carrying out rather specific legislative policies, but they could not parallel that success during an era in which delegation was simply a means of avoiding responsibility for failure, for in that case, as David Truman points out, "The administrator is called upon to resolve difficulties that were too thorny for the legislature to solve, and he must do so in the face of the very forces that were acting in the legislature."[3]

Yet despite the impossibility of achieving an immediate solution to societal problems so broad as to be beyond legislative definition, the almost uniform failure of Congress to furnish specific regulatory objectives when establishing these agencies has been matched by its unwillingness or inability to prescribe clearer goals since the crises which prompted their creation have passed. Since no organization can operate indefinitely without basic standards to simplify its decision-making process, this void has typically been filled by the agency itself. A commission might in time develop a series of long-range policies if given adequate research facilities and relative autonomy within its sphere of control. Denied either empirical information or administrative independence, these commissions have had no alternative but to base regulatory judgments upon an accretion of internal procedures and industry practices. Thus, past behavior is codified without the ability to amend these customs periodically to reflect social or technological change. A recent study of the FCC points out that, because of this administrative weakness, the commission seems unable to distinguish between fundamental principles and incidental practices when formulating policy and therefore has "elevated guidelines and specific criteria . . . to the status of policy objectives. It also seems that the FCC, even when it may have recognized the derivative nature of guidelines and specific criteria, either did not clearly trace these derivative elements from what should have been its basic policy objectives—or imperfectly traced them on *a priori* grounds rather than on analytical and statistical grounds."[4]

Instinctive reliance upon traditional rules and precedent must inevitably place any challenger to the established industry in the untenable position of threatening a system too rigid to accommodate change and yet too firmly entrenched to be defied. The outside competitor compels action and flexibility. While "tendencies towards inertia and inflexibility are the natural and inevitable attributes of all bureaus, creativity is not."[5]

As Louis Jaffe has observed, the hostility of the typical agency toward competitive challenge is not so much a reflection of partisanship in favor of the clientele industry as a reflection of basic antipathy toward change itself: "The charge against the ICC and CAB is that they are 'industry minded.' I would say that they are 'regulation minded.' . . . Competition became the equivalent of 'chaos,' of 'waste,' of 'destruction'; regulation [would] assure neat, explicable, rational ordering."[6]

Predisposition against change, a characteristic inherent in human institutions, is intensified by the fear that its force may wash away a body of rules formed by years of deliberations, causing severe internal disruptions as an agency must seek once again, without guidance or direction, to establish equilibrium within its structure. There is thus strong motivation for preserving the existing system at all costs, for "an agency working with a stable program over a long period of time develops a definite philosophy and point of view. It develops strong tendencies to harmonize its present and past decisions. . . . By providing a rule of *stare decisis* it fills in most of the gaps of discretion left by formal controls, giving it a safe way of exercising discretion and making decisions."[7]

While change is a painful process for a large agency, with "patterns of extended drift, followed by intermittent catch ups occurring at each depth of a bureau's structure," an even more pervasive element in the bureaucratic reaction against competitive innovation may be fear at the middle, or control, level of regulatory behavior. Max Weber has written that "knowledge is the basic source of power" in an administrative agency, and a threat to existing industry practices thus poses the same threat of obsolescence to a bureau expert as it does to the industry he regulates. Even if his job is secured by civil service rules, his prestige and the status of his particular section of the agency are endangered by advances which challenge the relevance of his area of experience.

The attitude of these career agency officers is, of course, a crucial factor in determining general agency policy since, "what an administrator proposes to do . . . making his choice from among policy alternatives is largely dependent upon his subordinates."[8] Information reaching the commissioners must be condensed, simplified, and reshaped at each agency level. This dependence of FCC commissioners upon the guidance of their staff is clearly illustrated by an analysis of two alternative organizational plans being considered in 1950: "They can organize the staff [and suffer delays] to have the assurance that the Commission will get a full disclosure of important considerations which they ought to take into account . . . *or organize [for faster informational flow] and take a chance that these men will not consciously prejudice the decision of the Commission by failure to make available the information . . . which they ought to consider*" (emphasis added).[9] In selecting the second alternative the agency was simply following the traditional administrative pattern of according a higher priority to speed and brevity than to depth or breadth in staff reports, but the effect of this decision was to delegate a substantial degree of influence to those generally least likely to be sympathetic to change. Several studies indicate that "the middle level of a bureau hierarchy normally contains a higher proportion of 'conservers' than either the lowest or highest levels. At the lowest levels . . . recruits are still imbued with ambition and enthusiasm; the highest level contains many successful climbers and advocates."[10]

Yet even if these middle-level officials could approach technological challenge impartially, there is no effective information-gathering process within the FCC capable of providing the material necessary to evaluate the potential for public service of new communications techniques. During the 1930s this defect led to a policy discouraging the development of television in the United States because "television was regulated by a body that had little time to devote to it . . . and possessed only a very limited resource of expertise for coping with problems arising from its peculiar technical nature."[11] Lacking the resources to obtain such information, the commission had to place its reliance upon research supplied by an industry "whose presentation might not be altogether free from self-serving coloration."[12] If this was a problem in intraindustry disputes, it became an almost insurmountable barrier when the broadcast industry became the primary source of information about an outside competitor. While the agency might attempt to equalize the bias inherent in such procedures by allowing the competitor to file data in its own behalf, it would be difficult to avoid according greater weight to evidence presented by a regulated industry subject to sanctions for improper representations and able, because of its established position, to compile much more elaborate and extensive studies than the competitor.

It might therefore be fair to conclude that factors of custom, innate conservatism, and limited analytical ability all operate to create an initial bias against any group seeking to change the established procedures of a regulated industry, with the degree of hostility probably related to the magnitude of the change. If this instinctive bias is to be avoided, and innovation judged on the basis of its own distinct qualities, it seems essential that evaluative standards emerge from a broader base than past agency practices or precedents. Since there is little reason to believe that Congress will now assume the role, and thus the responsibility it avoided by creating the FCC, the only other hope for intelligent guidance in neutralizing instinctive staff reaction appears to lie in the seven commissioners who lead the agency.

Is there any justification for this hope? The history of the FCC now encompasses almost four decades of complex communications issues faced by more than fifty different commissioners with widely divergent backgrounds and regulatory philosophies. Therefore, perhaps the most accurate basis for determining the probability that future commissioners will formulate long-range communications policies circumventing internal bias is the performance of their predecessors, who operated within the same agency structure. Policy making has been described as "the ultimate test of administration," and thus evaluation of the capacity of past combinations and coalitions of commissioners to perform this vital function would seem to provide a valid basis for predicting the probable value of future regulatory guidance in this field.[13]

Innovation: The Need for Communications Policy

If there is one thread linking a series of various governmental studies of the FCC, extending from the inception of the agency through the beginning of this decade, it has been the nearly universal condemnation of its efficacy in formulating communications policy. Robert Cushman, a scholar of administrative law who advised the President's Committee on Administrative Management during the 1930s, declared when concluding his analysis of broadcast regulation, "*Neither the Radio Commission nor its successor, the Federal Communications Commission, has come to grips with the major policy problems which are involved in the regulation of the radio industry.* The two commissions have followed the line of least resistance and have assumed that what is best for the radio industry as a business enterprise must also be best for the country" (emphasis added).[14]

Almost a decade later the first Hoover Commission, created to enhance the efficiency of the administrative process, singled out the FCC for particularly stringent criticism. Although acknowledging that an unusually rapid turnover in the agency's staff made consistent interpretation of rules difficult to achieve, the Hoover Commission's staff report maintained that the FCC had "been far from successful in achieving continuity of policies in areas where it was possible to do so. Even during periods when the composition of the commission was fairly continuous, *stated policies were either transgressed or neglected*" (emphasis added).[15]

In 1951 President Truman's Communication Policy Board reiterated criticisms of the earlier investigative groups, pointing out that the FCC had been unable to "deal effectively with the workload before it *because it has not formulated the broad policies to guide its decisions*, and thereby expedite handling of cases. . . . The Hoover experts also reported that the *FCC has characteristically faced its tasks by dealing with them as they arise, rather than by conscious policy-making*, planning and programming for the broad future of communications regulation and development" (emphasis added).[16]

In a December 1960 report on administrative agencies to President-elect Kennedy, Dean James Landis stated, "The Federal Communications Commission presents a somewhat extraordinary spectacle. Despite considerable technical skill on the part of its staff, the Commission has drifted, vacillated and stalled in almost every major area. *It seems incapable of policy planning*, of disposing within a reasonable period of time the business before it, of fashioning procedures that are effective to deal with its problems" (emphasis added).[17]

In 1962, Booz-Allen and Hamilton, a management survey team retained to modernize the FCC, reported to the Bureau of the Budget that the agency did not have the capacity to "anticipate emerging issues" and therefore was continually reacting to crisis rather than anticipating it, because "*it lacks the time and organizational support to develop national communications policy* and carry out long-range planning in a fully effective manner" (emphasis added).[18]

Two years later the Federal Communications Bar Association, an organization formed by attorneys practicing before the commission, released a report which declared, "In the AM field the Commission has floundered interminably. The Clear Channel proceeding took over a decade to be decided and since it was decided, no final steps have as yet been taken to effectuate it. . . . the new freeze is an attempt to repair conditions which have been permitted to grow *because of the inability of the Commission to decide upon standards and policies before the evils were created* or became difficult to remedy" (emphasis added).[19]

In December 1968 President Johnson's Task Force on Telecommunications Policy declared that the commission, despite internal reorganization, computer data facilities, and other techniques of the modern business world, still lacked the "resources to develop sufficient in-house capacity for the analysis of major issues having technical, economic and regulatory policy dimensions, even when these issues are central to its regulatory responsibilities."[20]

Recommendations flowing from these studies and reports have urged a wide variety of remedies to strengthen the policy-making capacity of the commission. They have generally centered on either increasing the competency of its staff or broadening the effectiveness of its process of empirical evaluation. Yet despite the virtual unanimity of these findings, there is every reason to believe that Congress will not voluntarily enact any of the recommendations advanced, even though the end result may be continued restriction upon communications growth. Unfortunately, while a tradition-bound staff and dependent commissioners are not efficient communications regulators, they are far more useful than forceful administrators would be in carrying out the directives of individual congressmen.

The FCC as an "Arm of Congress"

Each agency exercising power delegated by Congress must respond continually to a wide variety of orders and requests emanating from that body. Some reflect the highest level of guidance from the legislative committee overseeing a particular agency's operation. Others, occurring outside the formal channels of congressional review, involve, in some instances, overt pressure applied by members of Congress seeking special consideration on matters to be decided by regulatory bodies.

While Congress possesses formidable legal powers over governmental agencies—including those of dissolution; reduction of authority, staff, or funds; public castigation before a hearing committee; and a host of less drastic sanctions—there is every reason to believe that "off-the-record" contacts by individual congressmen may equal or even exceed the influence exerted formally. The chairman of the FCC, for instance, testified that in 1958 he alone had received more than nine hundred letters and countless telephone calls from congressmen interested in matters then pending before the commission.[21]

When legislation was introduced in 1959 to prohibit such ex parte congressional contact, Senator Dirksen objected, declaring with characteristic honesty, "Ever since 1933, since I came here as a freshman congressman, I've been calling every agency in government in the interest of my constituents and I expect I am going to continue to do it whether this becomes law or not, and I am afraid this is not going to become law with my sanction."[22] After a distinguished attorney advocating this law admitted that he, too, had consulted agencies to determine the status of a pending matter but said he would never consult the hearing examiner actually conducting the inquiry, Dirksen brushed this legal nicety aside: "I went way beyond the trial examiner. I didn't even bother with him, he is just an intermediary. I went where the decision is to be made. The commissioner I talked to would have a vote. If it is a five-man commission and I get three votes for my constituent, everything is hunkydory."[23] Thus, in essence, what Senator Dirksen was defending, and countless other members of Congress have taken part in without defending, is the transformation of administrative justice into a medieval forum where truth is measured, not by the preponderance of evidence, but by the strength of the champion representing each party before the agency.

Although every agency has experienced particularized congressional pressure, perhaps no agency is subjected to a greater degree of constant individual contact than the FCC. This, one writer maintains, is because the FCC has the authority to grant each congressman the most valuable prize available from any governmental agency, a broadcast license. "Over two dozen members of Congress are known to have personal interests in broadcasting properties, in their own names or in the names of members of their immediate families. No other companies in industries that are regulated by the federal government seem to have offered such attractive investment possibilities to members of Congress, and particularly to those members who sit on the House and Senate Commerce Committees or Appropriations Committees."[24] Yet a motive far more compelling than pecuniary interest appears to be reflected in these continual congressional pressures upon the Commission. Each congressman's constituent broadcast stations represent this primary line of communication to his electorate, with his access to these forums dependent to some extent upon his ability to protect their interests before the FCC. While section 315 of the Communications Act prohibits favoritism in the granting of broadcast time during the campaign period, it is silent regarding the prominence a congressman's "report from Washington" or other similar image-building programs might be given in the much more extensive period between elections, or the number of references local news programs might make to his continuing achievements in Congress even during the election period.

Increasing the independent policy-making function of the FCC would lessen the opportunity for congressmen to gain individualized treatment for their constituent broadcasters. Since Congress is run by politicians rather than philosophers, it is doubtful whether abstract benefits to public communications gained by granting such independence will ever be judged to outweigh the loss of influence this greater autonomy would entail.

The FCC as a Quasi-executive Agency

The executive branch of the government also has an interest in maintaining a malleable communications regulator, although its influence over the commission is somewhat less direct than that of Congress. As one scholar has noted, "The President has never fully accepted the theory of the regulatory commission as a wholly independent agency. Starting with Theodore Roosevelt, all of our Presidents (even the so-called 'weak ones' such as Coolidge and Harding) have sought to exercise some degree of control over one or more of the regulatory commissions."[25]

Since 1950, the president has held the power to designate the chairman of the FCC, with the chairman in turn empowered to select personnel at the highest staff level. In addition, the president's Office of Management and Budget evaluates the commission's annual request for funds, reviewing its performance and on occasion slashing amounts proposed for particular agency functions before submitting the request to Congress for consideration.

While members of the executive branch may not contact the FCC with quite the same regularity as their congressional counterparts, there is little question that presidential arguments conveyed in this fashion are given careful consideration. As a member of the FCC told Robert Cushman in 1936, "The commission has always complied with all orders and requests made of it by the President, and has never raised any question about its obligation to do so."[26]

Since 1970 most of these "orders and requests" have been channeled through a single executive bureau, the Office of Telecommunications Policy (OTP), whose energetic chief, Clay T. Whitehead, is reported to have declared that "the White House has no qualms about seeking to influence the Commission or any other so-called independent agency."[27] This office, formed to coordinate all governmental uses of radio spectrum, has taken an active role in negotiations to establish terms to permit cable carriage of broadcast signals. While the office has been granted no direct authority over private broadcast or cable operations, it has been remarkably successful in exerting its influence in this field because of the vacuum created by prior commission indecisiveness in applying pressure to achieve a compromise agreement.

In view of the broad range of sub rosa powers already available to the executive branch, and the growing influence of the OTP, it appears highly unlikely that the president will have any greater motivation than the Congress to strengthen a regulatory process over which he now exercises such effective control.

The FCC and Its Industry

The commission, like most independent regulatory agencies, has often been termed a captive of the industry it regulates. If this means simply that the FCC is generally sympathetic to the needs of its clientele broadcasters, the term is accurate, for there is a commonality of concern shared by the regulator and regulated in all commissions which tends to make the agency particularly sensitive to problems faced by its own industry. In a federal structure cluttered with organizations, issues peculiar to the broadcast industry are generally obscured by more pressing matters of national interest. As a result the agency and its licensees are isolated from public view and thereby alienated from the broader aspects of the formation of public policy. In these circumstances it is perhaps not surprising that staff administrators lacking other standards begin in time to judge their effectiveness solely in terms of industry prosperity, or that commissioners, denied access to power, gravitate toward the group whose trade press avidly follows their every action and whose leaders treat them with deference.

This affinity, however, does not necessarily limit the ability of the commission to act as a mediator in industry disputes, simply because "the industry" is in no sense a homogeneous group, but rather a vast number of disparate competitive enterprises struggling for a maximum share of similar business. A general commitment on the part of the agency to industry prosperity, therefore, does not prevent the FCC from deliberating impartially when weighing conflicting contentions concerning proper disposition of a particular license application, or enacting rules governing the general operations of broadcast stations. In addition, within the agency itself the seven constantly changing commissioners and their staff members hold widely divergent views which result in the coalescence of a new alliance around almost every issue. Thus, within the fraternity of regulator and regulated, a vigorous and often vicious byplay prevents permanent dominance by any narrow segment of the broadcast industry.

Industry unity is the primary threat to the effectiveness of this type of regulatory control, a unity generally emerging only when the entire group faces serious challenge from the superior technology of an outside competitor. In that instance a commission, with a staff usually diligent in its "commitment to the maintenance of the status quo of the industry," can constitute the most valuable ally a regulated business could desire, by using government sanctions to prevent the expansion of the rival until it can be assimilated within existing industry operations.[28] Considering the state of flux in the development of communications techniques today, there seems little reason to expect that the established industry will have any greater interest than Congress or the executive branch in enhancing the effectiveness of the present regulatory process of the commission.

The FCC as a Dependent Independent Commission

Despite the foregoing comments, it would be inaccurate to contend that the FCC is uniquely limited by the inadequacies of its fact-gathering or policy-making processes, or less capable than similar agencies of carrying out its basic regulatory mandates. Although the commission, like other agencies, must respond to shifting currents of political pressure, it is not therefore simply adrift on a regulatory sea. A skilled administrator, like an experienced sailor, can often use the interaction of forces to tack and yaw against a prevailing wind and thus maintain a degree of control over his ultimate destination.

One administrative expert has observed that, to protect its independence from the demands of any one interest group, an agency must constantly "adapt its program to various interests. To neutralize its enemies it must sometimes sacrifice elements in its programs that attract most effective political opposition. Hence, organizations are in a continual process of adjusting to the political environment that surrounds them—an adjustment that seeks to keep a favorable balance of political support and political opposition."[29]

In this manner the FCC—offsetting the influence of one industry faction by satisfying the demands of another; accepting the directives of one governmental body in order to escape the orders of its rivals—can, by constantly varying the balance in this process of accommodation, retain a degree of autonomy. There are those who argue that this is exactly the way independent commissions should function, since they were designed to introduce flexibility into a regulatory order otherwise too rigid to react to rapid changes within an industry or a society. Some administrative scholars maintain that policy making is never the result of the rational selection of a series of objectives and techniques to achieve these goals, but rather a far more humble step-by-step, or "incremental," response to a limited range of known problems through controls already at hand.[30] In that sense, then, inadequate information, inaccurate transmission of that information, and incessant interjection or extraneous pressures into the process of policy making would not be viewed as serious flaws in the commission's structure, but only as characteristics insuring its continuing responsiveness to pragmatic considerations of economics and politics.

Unfortunately, this process of balancing conflicting influences is completely ineffective in deliberations involving industry innovation, for the outside competitor typically does not yet have the economic power to generate substantial political force, and the public lacks sufficient knowledge concerning the innovation's promise to cause it to unite into a cohesive pressure group. As a result, the commission, structured to respond only to existing influences, not to projected promise, finds itself driven in only one direction when facing the question of innovation: away from any decision according the new challenger access to the public it has the capacity to serve.

This pattern of conduct emerges from past commission reactions to television experimenters and FM pioneers, and parallels responses of similar agencies such as the Civil Aeronautics Board, Interstate Commerce Commission, and Federal Maritime Board to outside challenge.

> The non-scheduled airlines which have sought to compete with the "big twelve" have been harassed and most of them have been forced out of business by the Board.

> The railroads have constantly been permitted to quote competitive rates of a type denied to the truckers. . . . More recently, the Commission has been permitting the railroads to obtain control of competing motor carriers.

> New entry is drastically restricted by the Federal Maritime Board's use of its subsidy powers. . . . The FMB has encouraged so-called shipping conferences to engage in collusive rate-fixing and . . . impose penalty rates upon shippers using non-conference vessels.[31]

As a recent study of independent commissions indicates, the uniform solution to a crisis caused by the introduction of new techniques into a regulated environment has been "to shield all regulated modes often without sufficient assessment of . . . efficiency factors that might intrinsically favor one of several modes."[32]

While the cost in societal benefits lost through ineffectual supervision of industrial innovation seems unfortunate in any area of commerce, it seems uniquely unfortunate in the field of communications. To the extent that commission procedures inhibit the evolution of electronic media services, they impair a basic public "right to knowledge" during an era when, in the terms of a report recently filed with the FCC, "The mushrooming growth in available information and the demand for access to this information is bringing about a revolution in communications which will produce a profound change in the way society is structured and in the way we live."[33]

Yet the prospect for improvement in this process is extremely dim, simply because, despite its ineffectiveness in evaluating the promise inherent in technology, it is far too effective in preserving the interests of those groups with the present capacity to achieve modification of the commission structure. In essence, then, the very restraints inherent in the present commission procedures allowing communications innovators access to the public guarantee their perpetuation in the absence of concerted action on the part of audience groups thus far uninvolved in this aspect of communications control.

This in turn would seem to guarantee that, lacking such aroused public response, the regulatory restrictions imposed upon cable television are destined to be repeated with the advent of each new communications challenger in the future, at an ever increasing cost in services denied the public. No administrator, no matter how perceptive, can formulate an intelligent policy for integrating new techniques into existing communications services without the capacity to project their probable patterns of growth, determine their most valuable functions within these patterns, and design a regulatory program based solely on those considerations before these innovations emerge full-grown and ready for operation. Otherwise, failure of vision and limited autonomy will continually transform long-range promise into immediate peril, and inadequate preparation into overactive restriction. Thus, to the extent that this lack of policy-making capacity has shaped and continues to shape the commission's control of innovation, this study, while written as a case history, may also serve as a bleak prophesy of future communications repression.

II

Cable Regulation as a Derivative History

Cable television represented an unforeseen by-product of a regulatory experiment designed to achieve an entirely different result, the establishment of a nationwide system of community-oriented television stations. As such a by-product its presence could be tolerated only as long as it did not appear to be impeding attainment of the desired reaction.

Thus the gradual hardening of the commission's attitude toward cable evolution can best be understood in the context of the broader and more universal regulatory objectives it challenged. The cable emphasis upon program delivery made it heir to a tradition of enmity previously experienced by network and "clear channel" broadcast operations. Therefore, chapter 3 will explore the underlying historical factors revealed through these earlier conflicts which dictated the objectives by which cable would be judged, while chapter 4 will consider the specific effect of these objectives both in creating initial opportunities for cable growth and in setting the outer perimeters of its permissible expansion.

41

3   The Background of a Regulation Gap: Origins of the "Local Service" Theory, 1927–52

The FCC's basic policy, like that of the Federal Radio Commission before it, has often been described as favoring "local broadcast service." "Policy," however, in this typical regulatory sense, does not imply a system of comprehensive objectives with programs designed to attain them. Instead, it refers more generally to explanations imposed upon a series of similar administrative decisions after the fact, thus justifying but not dictating regulatory conduct.

In this sense both federal broadcast regulators have displayed such a policy, consistently evincing greater concern for creating new opportunities for broadcasters than for broadening the number of alternative program sources available to various audiences. If this constant pattern of regulatory preference were traceable to the position of this "local service" goal within a broader philosophy of regulatory priorities, it might then be properly viewed as a conscious creation of the agency, and its value judged only in relation to that total program. However, since both agencies have lacked such long-range objectives, a consistent course of conduct spanning almost a half-century—remarkable in a realm otherwise noted for its incessant fluctuation and change—appears to reflect an extremely strong influence upon the actions of a long succession of regulatory regimes, propelling each toward the same general destination. Since the function of cable television was to offer varied programming to audiences rather than expanded opportunities for broadcasters, it would operate in direct contravention, not only of this regulatory doctrine, but of the forces which had shaped it.

Long before the first primitive community antenna systems had begun operating in the late 1940s, each broadcast agency had in turn become deeply involved in efforts to weigh the public interest value of community-oriented broadcasting against that of a more varied selection of broadcast programming options. Nationwide demands for network programming, regional demands for clear channel service, and local demands for adequate television coverage have each in turn been disregarded by these agencies in their untiring efforts to cast electronic mass communications in the role of a "local service" facility. Thus, to the extent that cable systems challenged these efforts, they became heirs to a legacy of regulatory hostility extending back to the Radio Act of 1927. It therefore seems essential to begin by tracing this "local service" doctrine to its source to discover both its initial basis at law and its continuing validity as broadcasting evolved.

Source of the Local Service Principle: The Radio Act of 1927

A local broadcast service should be authorized in as many different communities as possible to assure coverages responsive to distinct local needs,

or

The audiences in each area of the United States should have access to as many different broadcast signals as possible to permit the broadest range of program options.[1]

These are the two fundamental, and to a large extent mutually exclusive, objectives of broadcast service which might have been accorded highest regulatory priority by the FRC and the FCC. Neither agency received a clear mandate from Congress indicating the proper choice, since both the Radio Act of 1927 and its successor, the Communications Act of 1934, were rather Delphic in direction. The act of 1934, as an example, urged in one paragraph that the FCC make available the most "rapid, efficient, nationwide" radio service possible, while declaring in another that the agency should distribute broadcast licenses among the various states in a "fair, efficient and equitable" fashion.[2] Yet, despite the lack of explicit instruction, neither agency has ever deviated from its dedication to the "local service" alternative. As the Presidential Task Force on Telecommunications observed in 1968, "The present structure of broadcasting was foreshadowed in the 1920's during the early days of radio. . . . The premises and methods of this regulatory design were carried over to television essentially unchanged. Decisions . . .

were designed to insure that broadcasting stations served particular communities and were allocated only enough power to cover a particular area. *The concept of a nationwide scheme of local stations produced* a relatively large number of individual stations but *relatively few accessible broadcast signals for the individual listener"* (emphasis added).[3]

The regulatory presumption favoring local service over diverse programming grew from administration of the Radio Act of 1927, but it is important to realize that the act when drafted accurately reflected the existing status of the broadcast industry. If the statute could be said to have had a local orientation, it was only because at that stage of its evolution nearly all broadcasting was local in origin.

To support the contention that perpetuation of the local service doctrine has reflected agency interpretation far more than legislative intent, it may be helpful to sketch in a brief outline the patterns of industry growth in the years immediately preceding and following the assertion of federal broadcast controls.

When the FRC was created in March 1927, no radio station had yet earned sufficient advertising revenues to meet its annual expenses.[4] In fact, less than a decade earlier, the commercial value of radio was still being debated. There was little doubt that it would make a poor point-to-point common carrier, since anyone tuned to the proper frequency could intercept its messages. Thus the history of radio broadcasting from 1920 to 1927 was primarily a chronicle of attempts to transform this defect in the system into some type of economic benefit.

No early broadcaster could depend upon the sale of air time for a substantial amount of revenue, since use of the airwaves for commercial messages was generally considered an improper if not illegal appropriation of a public resource.[5] Therefore, broadcasters during this era came from only two general groups: the group that was forced to supply programming in order to sell radio receivers, and the group that operated stations simply to enhance its image or ego. The first class, composed of radio manufacturers, department stores, and electronic shops, was probably the more professional in respect to equipment, but it, like the second class, composed of church groups, newspapers, and hobbyists, was limited by a lack of funds for programming.

In order to capture the public interest, the message of these early stations had to be entertainment. Yet the term "entertainment" during this period seems a rather charitable generic description for the procession of singers, lecturers, and comics whose performances were usually amateurish, at least in the sense that the performers were almost always unpaid. There could be no regularly scheduled professional programming without paid performers; no paid performers without regular revenues; and, since more than half of the broadcast licenses issued by the Commerce Department between 1921 and 1926 were being returned by their disappointed owners, the question of how to survive economically in this new medium had yet to be answered.[6]

In March 1927 the Federal Radio Commission began supervising this profitless industry and ended the chaotic patterns of frequency usage which had restricted station coverages. At that time the local station was predominant in broadcasting. There were as yet no national radio networks, and differences between major and local stations, although marked in respect to equipment and programming, were still unreflected in any business balance sheet.

This predominance of the local station lasted less than a year. The commission, in solving the destructive interference problem which had hindered growth, had also unleashed economic forces it was unable to handle. The flood of advertising revenues into this newly ordered industry vitalized the latent economic and technological advantages of larger stations and network affiliates, opening a gulf in comparative profit margins that would widen with almost every passing year.

In 1926 total revenues from sales of broadcast time were $200,000, or an average of less than $400 for each of the approximately six hundred broadcast stations. By the end of 1927, and only eight months after the FRC had assumed control, revenues skyrocketed to $4.8 million, more than twenty times this amount, and by the end of 1928 soared to more than $14 million, or sixty times the 1926 total. This surge of advertising revenues flowed in narrow channels, however, with less than one-sixth of the nation's broadcasters reporting significant profits in 1928.[7]

This configuration of 80–100 major stations and 500 minor operations had become an immutable reality within a year after the FRC began its supervisory role, but the commission did not seem to recognize or respond to this trend. Advertising was almost the sole force responsible for this cleavage among broadcasters, but both the Radio Act and the FRC were silent as to its control. Two networks had spanned the nation, but the FRC ignored the functions of these wired systems, still viewing broadcast stations as independently programmed entities.

In a classic *Journal of Broadcasting* article, John Spalding designated 1928 as the year in which radio became a medium for mass advertising in the United States; he maintained that improved transmitting and receiving equipment, network connections, an audience of one radio household in three, regular programming, and increased sponsorship made the industry truly economically viable only after that time.[8] Yet the FRC continued to regulate broadcasting as if 1927 had never ended, refusing to recognize changing conditions challenging both the vitality and the independence of myriad local stations charged with the responsibility of providing significant community-oriented service. Broadcast chronicler Erik Barnouw contended that "the Radio Act of 1927 . . . was already obsolete when passed. . . . The law assumed that each station controlled its own programming . . . the field would . . . be governed by a law written for a world that no longer existed."[9]

Yet although the Radio Act would be replaced in time, the outmoded view of broadcasting as a system of locally programmed entities would remain. It might as accurately be said that the agency courted its own obsolescence through its refusal either to request more realistic powers or to use existing authority with greater imagination. Instead of proposing amendments to conform law with fact, the legal fiction of local control over programming was perpetuated in such pronouncements as the following in the FCC licensing report of 1960: "The foundation of the American system of broadcasting was laid in the Radio Act of 1927 when Congress placed the basic responsibility for all matter broadcast . . . at the grass roots level in the hands of the station licensee. That obligation was carried forward into the Communications Act of 1934 and remains unaltered and undivided."[10]

This narrow focus upon broadcasters as the primary object of commission attention distorted the regulatory view of the electronic communications process in its entirety. As a result the agencies have been insensitive to public needs and desires for communications services and unwilling to grant them high priority in their deliberations. But despite regulatory presumptions and priorities, American audiences appear from the beginning to have been more concerned with national programming than with local broadcast coverage.

Local Service vs. Economic Reality:
The Rise of National Programming

The earliest evidence of this desire for distant if not national programming emerged within a year after the first broadcast station was licensed in the United States. By the fall of 1922 listeners in various regions of the nation were demanding that their local radio stations cease transmissions for at least one night each week so that listeners might pick up distant broadcast signals without interference. These "silent night" proposals seem to have had substantial public support. A newspaper poll in Chicago during this period, for instance, revealed that those favoring a silent night outnumbered opponents by a margin of more than ten to one.[11] While much of this early support may have come from DXers (radio hobbyists more interested in the sensitivity of their sets than in the quality of the programming received), this interest coninued long after DXers had dwindled to only a minimal segment of a much larger audience.

In March 1927, as the FRC began its supervision of broadcasting, *Popular Radio*, a respected electronics journal, was urging its readers to listen regularly to their local stations. In one issue Charles Adams declared that community audiences were essential if the industry were to continue to expand. He concluded with the optimistic observation that "the delusion that distant programs are inherently better than home-town offerings may be slowly being dispelled."[12]

Unfortunately for advocates of listening to local stations, this delusion was often dispelled by the station's decision to provide more professional programming through network affiliation. In effect, long-distance network wires were simply being offered as a substitute for long-distance spectrum reception. By 1927, as a recent broadcast history notes, "Network operation was . . . beginning to affect radio. . . . One effect was the death of long distance listening. During 1925 the *Cedar Rapids Gazette* told its readers about special programming on . . . KDKA, Pittsburgh; WLW, Cincinnati; . . . WEAF, New York; . . . KGO, Oakland. In 1927 such information was dropped because the same programs appeared on station after station."[13]

Thus the shift from DXing to the dominance of network programming seems to have been a rapid one in most regions of the nation; if there was an era of local program preeminence anywhere, that era must have been extremely brief. The economic advantages of network affiliation simply outweighed the risk of regulatory displeasure.

Programming was the one item of station overhead which could be reduced by distribution techniques. While broadcasters generally could not share transmitters or sales staffs, they could pool broadcast productions through relatively inexpensive wire linkages to a source of national programming. The cost of a single program could thus be spread out over a nationwide audience, a factor significantly diminishing the network advertiser's cost per exposure. As broadcasters of the early 1920s had turned to nationally distributed phonograph records to avoid the expense of live talent, broadcasters a few years later turned to networks, whose programming not only carried with it a portion of network advertising revenues but also contained the professional polish necessary to increase each station's share of the local audience.

This process of distribution naturally tended to widen the gulf between network-affiliate and independent stations. Networks could attract the best local talent because of the higher salaries their national base of revenues allowed, and better talent in turn enhanced the size of each affiliate's audience, which generated even more revenues for the next cycle of growth. The effects of this process were already apparent as early as 1929, when the less than 20 percent of all stations with network affiliation claimed almost 80 percent of the $27 million spent on broadcast advertising.[14]

The FRC was never active in its opposition to the growth in the use of network programming. Instead, the agency simply ignored the existence of this programming service when formulating regulatory policy. However, in rejecting reality, the commission was also ignoring the needs of at least 20 million people desiring network services but located in areas unable to support the local broadcast facility the FRC insisted be inserted between this service and its audience.

Local Service vs. Demographics: The Clear Channel Possibility

The United States was in the process of transition from a rural to an urban society in 1927. At the turn of the century fewer than 500 American cities could claim a population in excess of 8,000. That number had doubled by 1920, and only a decade later more than half of the nation's citizens lived in one of 1,200 such communities.[15] Parallel movements of urbanization, transportation, and communication were shifting attention from local to regional and even national concerns. Forcing a parochial, community-oriented focus upon broadcast service at this particular moment in history seems to have been a reactionary regulatory tactic, even if such focus were possible to achieve.

In fact, it was impossible, simply because migratory trends had distorted regional variants in population to such an extent that "local service" no longer had any universal meaning; its definition depended upon the area in which it was applied. Two-thirds of the 1,200 communities were clustered in only three sections of the country: New England, Middle Atlantic, and East North Central states. While this concentration had attracted sixty-one broadcasters to New York by April 1927, the huge land masses of Montana, Idaho, and Nevada were at the same time being served by a total of only three broadcast stations.[16]

Local service was thus too narrow a scheme for populous states where a large mass of stations could offer program diversity as well, and too grandiose a plan for sparsely settled regions without sufficient population to support any community broadcaster. Only one technique—"clear channel" broadcasting—was available to provide radio service for homes scattered across western prairie and mountain regions.

The principle was simple, but it demanded a long-term system of frequency reservations to make it operative. During the hours between dusk and dawn signals within the broadcast band of frequencies do not penetrate the outer atmosphere but are reflected back down to Earth. This rebound action results in a sizable extension of the signal's coverage area. If several stations are using the same frequencies simultaneously, however, each will experience a similar extension and cause an overlapping of coverage which makes the reception of any signal impossible. Thus, the only way this nighttime rebound action could be employed to furnish service for vast areas unable to support a local station was to set aside certain frequencies for the exclusive use of a single maximum-power station, a "clear channel" allocation.

In 1928, the FRC assigned forty of the ninety-six radio frequency channels then in use to individual high-power stations for such clear channel transmission. Fewer than half of these grants went to midwestern or western broadcasters, however, since the commission's assignments appeared to be more a recognition of the power potential of existing stations than concern for the coverage needs of underserved areas. Because of this lack of understanding of or interest in the vital function these clear channel coverages could perform in western areas, the FRC was allowing nighttime duplication on ten of the original forty allocations by 1933. The Institute of Radio Engineers warned the commission that "decreasing the number of clear channels by assigning any additional stations [for nighttime operation] to the channels now used by only one station at a time would have the effect of affording additional services to certain localized urban groups but at the expense of decreasing service to rural listeners and those in remote areas."[17]

Despite this warning four additional western clear channel stations—KOA, Denver; KGO, San Francisco; KOMO, Seattle; and KNX, Hollywood—were soon added to the list of broadcasters with duplicated, and thus restricted, coverage. The history of KOA, the only station offering nighttime radio service to rural areas within a 300-mile radius of its transmitter, serves as an excellent case in point. It illustrates both the apparent rationale for clear channel erosion and its impact upon rural audiences.

In 1939 KOA was reclassified from I-A to I-B, a category which would eventually claim all but twelve of the original forty channels. This new category allowed the commission to assign other limited-power stations to the same channel, which encouraged wider use of previously exclusive nighttime frequencies in areas not being served by the clear channel station's signal. The problem with this theory was that those areas not being served were typically in urban sections of the East, so that western service was further reduced without any corresponding return benefit. The flow of frequencies from the West to the East was not counterbalanced by the expansion of western stations using eastern clear channel assignments, because there were far fewer communities in the West able to support such limited-power facilities. In 1939 KOA complained that the Boston station transmitting on its channel was interfering with its nighttime rural coverage. By 1958 nine other stations were using this once-clear channel, only one of which was west of the Mississippi. Others covered such "underserved" areas as Cleveland, Ohio; Gainesville, Florida; Reading, Pennsylvania; Norfolk, Virginia; and Birmingham, Alabama.

The FRC had set the maximum power for clear channels at 50 kw (50,000 w), although international agreements allowed 500 kw. In 1934 the FCC approved a request from WLW, Cincinnati, to operate experimentally at 500 kw. Other clear channel broadcasters applied for similar authorizations, arguing that increased power could achieve a substantial reduction in "white areas," a term describing areas in which 20 million Americans had no nighttime radio service. The FCC denied these applications, although admitting that "the evidence shows conclusively that, from a technical standpoint, the use of power in excess of 50 kilowatts has a distinct advantage because it provides better quality service to the vast population residing in rural areas . . . which neither have broadcasting stations of their own, nor are located within the primary service areas of any station. . . . *It is safe to conclude that . . . greater kilowatt power tends to equalize the quality of service rendered to the population of rural areas compared to the service rendered . . . urban communities equipped with broadcast facilities*" (emphasis added).[18]

Yet, having made this "safe conclusion," the FCC was unwilling to take any action which might equalize these services. Despite the rapid expansion in broadcast facilities after World War II, the "white area" continued to linger at the 20-million mark through the decades. As the FCC itself observed in 1959, "The increment . . .

of nearly 2,000 additional standard broadcast stations appears to
have reduced the nighttime white area to only a minor extent. . . .
*It follows that improvement of service throughout most of the
existing white areas must be provided, if at all, by new or improved
skywave service"* (emphasis added).[19]

"If at all" appears to have been the operational phrase. The FCC
displayed no interest in encouraging additional skywave, or clear
channel, facilities, whatever the broadcast service needs of these
white areas might be. A decade later a presidential task force
pointed out the alternative regulatory course the commission could
have chosen: "If high-powered regional or national stations had
been preferred to the local stations, a larger number of signals, and
accordingly, a wider choice of programs would have been available
to most listeners but at a sacrifice in the number of local stations in
each area."[20]

This, though, was the one sacrifice the commission was totally
unwilling to make. The FCC did not seem to oppose clear channels
any more than the FRC had opposed networks. Both agencies,
rather than retreat from a regulatory position giving complete support to the establishment of local broadcast stations, simply ignored
public interest in programming.

In contrast to its lack of action in areas of program delivery, the
FCC's tactics in launching a truly local radio service in the years following World War II were bold and innovative. When the wartime
freeze on station licensing ended, the commission moved immediately to harness an explosive demand for spectrum access, using
this demand to transform traditional contours designed by the
FRC into new, narrow, community-oriented coverages.

The Actuality of Local Service: The Rise of
Regional Stations

The FRC had created a pattern of concentric circles of service,
centered on numerous low-powered local stations and widened in
turn by regional and clear channel broadcasters. To avoid interference among these various rings of coverage, each of the ninety-six
frequency channels then in use (as well as all the stations assigned
to them) was classified clear channel (class I), regional (class
III), or local (class IV). From 1928 through 1945 the proportionate sizes of these three groups remained relatively constant, but the

postwar boom caused a pronounced distortion in the growth of regional stations (see table1).

Table 1   Growth of Stations by Frequency Classification

YEAR	CLASSIFICATION								TOTAL
	Clear				Regional		Local		
	Dominant No. %		Secondary No. %		No. %		No. %		
1935	38	7	56	10	226	39	260	45	580
1945	44	5	86	9	351	38	434	47	915
1960	52	1	596	17	1,905	57	947	27	3,500
1970	97	2	1,098	25	2,131	49	1,002	23	4,328

SOURCE: *Broadcasting Yearbooks.*
NOTE: The total number of stations is the computed total by frequency as listed in the above source; it thus may vary slightly from the announced total reported by the FCC. There were only 96 channels in 1935, but 107 in 1945 and thereafter. All I-A and I-B stations are classified as "Clear Dominant," while all others assigned to clear channels, both U.S. and foreign, are listed as "Clear Secondary." Percentages are rounded to whole numbers.

This rapid expansion in the number of regional stations after World War II resulted from the FCC's decision to open these channels, which had formerly been the preserve of older, prosperous sectional broadcasters, to hundreds of eager applicants willing to accept extreme limitations upon their contours and hours of operation. By 1960 more than half of all "regional" stations, and thus almost one-third of all stations, were restricted to daytime-only transmission or required to use antennas directing their signals to narrow segments of the audiences they might otherwise have served.

The new class of regional stations achieved two intermediate goals long sought by the FCC. By flooding regional channels with limited-coverage facilities while reducing the number of unduplicated clear channels, the agency was able to convert all but a small portion of the industry into local broadcasters. In addition, the explosive growth of new stations—the number of facilities was doubled within only five years—far outdistanced the affiliation capabilities of the radio networks.

But despite the fact that by 1948 the number of communities served by broadcasting had tripled, as local revenues for the first time in two decades surpassed network payments, the commission's broader purposes had yet to be realized.[21] In 1946 the FCC had issued a report outlining the functions to be performed by community-oriented stations, and thus the success of this regulatory policy can best be measured in terms of those aims.

The commission had envisioned a new era in broadcast service arising from the influx of postwar licensees, with each station to serve as a forum for discussion of community issues, a platform from which local officials could address their electorate, a showcase for community talent, and a medium for local advertisers. As the agency expressed it, such stations would "give the community a means of self-expression, a voice as well as an ear."[22]

Unfortunately, station functions would once again be dictated by economic factors rather than by regulatory hopes. These new "regionals," typically dawn-to-dusk independents serving urban-suburban audiences, had neither the time nor the capacity to provide distinctive coverage for each community within their contours. They reverted instead to the practice of the pre-network era, filling empty schedules with recorded music. In actuality, the coverage of national news and special events was shunted aside to realize only one of the commission's myriad objectives of community service, giving the local advertiser access to the medium.

While FCC licensing procedures were primarily responsible for limited coverage and the lessening importance of national programming after World War II, it was the emergence of television which eventually ended any chance of radio's rallying to regain its former position. This new force, however, while blocking the advance toward one regulatory objective, offered the opportunity of beginning anew in a field uncluttered by past administrative actions.

Two decades of the radio regulatory policy of constantly sacrificing program coverage for local service had resulted in a broadcast system in which one family in six still remained without nighttime entertainment or news while urban dwellers received multiple channels of music, covering areas, not communities, with homogeneous, nationally distributed recorded programming. Now, however, the FCC could reevaluate its public interest priorities for television in the light of consistent audience demands and the conspicuous failure of its recent experiment in community coverage. In 1948 the commission imposed a freeze upon further licensing of television stations in order to work out the most effective methods for shaping the growth and functions of the new medium.

Local Service and Television: The Sixth Report and Order

From 1948 to 1952 the FCC faced conditions in the television industry which paralleled to a remarkable extent those confronting its predecessor, the FRC, in 1927. In 1948, the FCC, like the FRC in 1927, was fashioning a regulatory design for an evolving industry still operating at a loss. Costs were again being absorbed by the licensee's other business interests, in this era most often radio stations, whose owners held 87 of the 108 prefreeze television licenses. Programming was again being influenced by the need for inexpensive talent as stations awaited completion of network linkages and development of more efficient electronic equipment.

Even the initial motivation for government action—the problem of interference—was the same. By July 1948 the commission was aware that its licensing plan distributing the twelve VHF channels which then constituted the entire television band among 340 cities could not be accomplished without creating a serious hazard of interference in various parts of the country. At this point the commission imposed its freeze on television licensing and spent the next three and a half years revamping its procedures. The agency held hearings on three issues basic to the future of television: a new system of channel allocation and assignment, a uniform standard for color transmission, and the possibilities of educational broadcasting. The first color-transmission technique was approved in 1950, but it took two additional years to work out all aspects of the integrated plan for community and educational allocation.

At the commencement of the proceedings the FCC had announced its interest in establishing a truly locally oriented licensing system, rather than in simply perpetuating the first-come, first-served philosophy used in radio. The agency envisioned only a single class of television stations, instead of the clear channel, regional, and local divisions of the earlier medium, with contours or coverages as uniform as power and tower-height adjustments would allow. Each channel would be assigned directly to a specific community and reserved until an applicant appeared who was willing to use the channel to serve that community. Although some broadcasters argued that this scheme would allow valuable spectrum space to lie fallow while many areas without additional allocations were denied the maximum service economically possible, the commission, rather predictably, rejected this argument. Eventually the commission completed its deliberations and assigned television channels to almost thirteen hundred communities it judged large enough to support such grants. To provide spectrum space for the more than two thousand channels authorized, the FCC carved seventy ultra-high frequencies (UHF) from the spectrum and used this space for almost 75 percent of these allocations. In some two hundred fifty communities these UHF stations were intermixed, or placed in direct competition with either existing or proposed VHF stations. Noncommercial, educational television broadcasters received approximately two hundred fifty allocations, most in the new UHF band.

These allocations were based upon a structure of five goals to be achieved by television regulation, listed by the commission in order of priority:

1. To provide at least *one television service* to all parts of the United States.

2. To provide *each community* with at least *one television station*.

3. To provide a choice of at least *two television services* to all parts of the United States.

4. To provide *each community* with at least *two television stations*.

5. To re-assign any channels remaining after accomplishment of the above goals on a basis of community need [emphasis added].[23]

In April 1952 when the FCC issued this long-awaited "Sixth Report and Order" establishing these licensing procedures, similarities between the situations in 1927 and 1952 seemed even more remarkable. The beginning of each administration, a quarter of a century apart from the other, marked the launching of a new, dominant medium of mass communication. In each case coast-to-coast network connections had been completed almost contemporaneously with the enactment of the new regulatory program, and each medium already served one in every three American families. In each era this figure doubled in less than a decade. DXing was less prevalent during television's pioneering period simply because of the limited propagation characteristics of those frequencies to which its broadcasters had been assigned, but the eagerness with which stations sought network affiliation and connection indicated that the demand for national programming had not lessened.

In essence, the only substantial difference between the positions of the two federal regulatory agencies facing similar challenges was the quarter of a century of administrative experience the FCC could draw upon in reaching its decisions. It inherited a tradition accentuating the primacy of local service.

Long-range Implications of the Local Service Theory

Local service as a political concept seems admirably suited to the needs of a democracy, in that it furnishes a medium responsive to its audience, and a valuable forum for full discussion of community issues. And such a system was not impossible to achieve. There might well have been a time during 1927 when the FRC could have created a predominantly local structure, had it been fully prepared with a regulatory program restricting maximum station power; prohibiting interconnections; and providing for some financial base for community programming, either through license fees or production grants. However, once the FRC had ended the chaotic interference inhibiting broadcast growth without immediately imposing this type of regulation, the time had passed. Natural economic forces gained momentum, and the major stations could employ the leverage of superior technology and programming capacity to widen the gaps between classes of broadcasters. Their ability to pool production costs and advertising funds forced the smaller stations into the position of fighting for the privilege of acting simply as outlets for their programming.

Whatever the actual prospects for local service might have been in 1927, however, the crucial weakness in both FRC and FCC regulation thereafter was the failure to recognize that national programming did in fact constitute the primary concern of the public, a concern that could not be altered by inhibiting the efficiency of either network or clear channel service. Ignoring public demand for national service did not result in a system of locally programmed entities; decimating clear channels did not provide community coverages for "white" areas; flooding regional channels did not create a broadcast voice for local issues. And yet, with the advent of television, the FCC, still wedded to objectives rather than public needs, would once again attempt to impose a policy rather than respond to economic reality.

But although the apparent wisdom and rationality of FRC and FCC decisions concerning local service can be judged abstractly, the factors consistently causing this principle to prevail can only be considered subjectively, in terms of political pressures. In this sense, then, while the congressional language establishing regulatory standards in the field of broadcasting did not provide a clear and unambiguous mandate for the preeminence of local service, its status as the primary goal of the FRC and the FCC seems largely to have been the result of continual congressional pressures through the years.

This congressional influence, for the most part, did not emerge from any general philosophy of broadcast service held by a substantial body of legislators. Instead, it was simply the collective reflection of a vast number of individual efforts by congressmen to protect the interests of broadcasters or potential broadcasters in their own districts or states. There was no concerted effort by Congress to deny either network outlets or clear channel service to rural areas of the nation. Yet the cumulative effect of these efforts was to convert the public resource of radio spectrum, held in trust for all citizens, into a base for business opportunities primarily in urban areas. The only technique which might have been effective in preventing this gradual erosion of rural broadcast coverages would have been a preexisting commission standard of broadcast service uniformly enforced to prevent any diminishing of signals available in sparsely settled regions of the nation. Perhaps in any case the commission could not have withstood congressional pressure. Yet, since the FCC, not the Congress, has the primary responsibility of insuring an equitable distribution of broadcast services on a nationwide basis, it seems that the agency has had at least an obligation to point out to Congress the ultimate result of basing coverage patterns upon the needs of constituent broadcasters rather than upon the desires of national audiences.

The fact that the FCC has never advanced such an argument, however, appears to reflect a lack of perspective far more than a lack of dedication. Even if the terms "local service" and "local broadcaster" had not been so closely synonymous in 1927, it seems reasonable to believe that regulatory practice would eventually have blurred any distinctions between them, simply because of the tendency of administrators to seek clear and tangible goals. The commission did not have the capacity to determine whether somewhat nebulous public interests were being served by broadcasters in various regions of the nation, but it could have easily discovered whether broadcasters were content with the opportunities afforded them by existing licensing procedures. The commission, therefore, was no more sensitive than Congress to the needs of the public, because it was unable to weigh the interests it was created to protect.

Community antenna systems would thus emerge in a regulatory process conditioned by political pressure and administrative custom to consider public interest in programming primarily in terms of the opportunities this public demand created for additional broadcast stations. Since these community systems, like clear channel and network services before them, would perform a function of program delivery not directly related to that objective, they would be viewed at best as an extraneous element in the broadcast structure. Classified in this way, cable could not expand without experiencing regulatory opposition, for the process assessing its value could measure only the peril it presented, not its promise.

4   Community Antenna: Filling the Coverage Vacuum, 1952–56

As the FCC lifted its freeze on the granting of new licenses to television broadcasters in April 1952, the market seemed ready for an explosive expansion in television stations across the nation. During the forty-three months of commission deliberation the industry had been artificially restricted to 108 stations while the number of television homes swelled from less than a million in 1949 to more than fifteen million in 1952. Only eight cities were being served by three or more television broadcasters in April 1952, while sixteen had two and cities such at St. Louis, Pittsburgh, Milwaukee, Seattle, and Kansas City, among others, had only one station. Yet, despite the apparent promise of general prosperity, revenues during the years following 1952 were channeled as they had been a quarter of a century before, once again continuously widening the gulf between major- and small-market broadcasters.

UHF Stations and the Breakdown of National Television Distribution

Although the FCC had set aside nearly fifteen hundred channel allocations for UHF broadcasting in its "Sixth Report and Order" of 1952, only about one in ten of these channels had been claimed by 1956 in an industry whose overall revenues had tripled during the three intervening years.[1] Even stations operating on these selected UHF channels had difficulty surviving (see table 2). The combined deficits of all UHF stations ranged from a high of $10 million in 1954 to a low of $2 million in 1956, but this "improvement" may well reflect only in the increase in the number of unprofitable stations which had gone dark. Start-up expenses customarily cause a period of unprofitable operation, but the plight of UHF stations is revealed by the fact that in 1959, when their

60

number had been reduced even further to seventy-six, UHF stations as a group were still operating at a loss.[2]

Table 2   UHF Stations in Operation, 1952–56

	1952	1953	1954	1955	1956	Total
Going ON	6	117	25	9	6	163
Going OFF	0	2	29	27	14	72
Total ON	6	121	117	99	91	91

SOURCE: U.S., Congress, Senate, Committee on Interstate and Foreign Commerce, *Television Inquiry, Television Allocations*, 86th Cong., 2d sess., 1960, pt. 8, p. 4572.

By 1958 the commission was willing to acknowledge that the UHF experiment, which was to have created three-fourths of all television service, had been a bitter disappointment. The failure, according to the FCC, was attributable to inferior UHF technology: "The head start of the VHF systems, the present disparity in performance between UHF and VHF transmitting and receiving equipment, and the small number of sets . . . capable of receiving . . . UHF signals are the principal reasons for the difficulties. Other factors [advertiser and network preference for VHF stations] have flowed from the principal reasons and have aggravated UHF difficulties."[3]

Early UHF stations were hampered by the lack of efficient transmission equipment resulting from military demands during the Korean War, but there was no marked expansion in UHF facilities after such equipment became available in 1956. Manufacturers were reluctant to produce all-channel receivers; yet this appears less a symptom of industrial failure than of lack of public interest.[4]

The UHF problem appears to have been more deeply rooted in broadcast economics than in electronics, with technology significant only to the extent that it limited the ability of these stations to compete in larger VHF-served markets. The primacy of market size, rather than frequency, as the determinant of station revenues is illustrated by the plight of smaller-market VHF stations. In 1955, for example, at least twenty-five VHF network affiliates broadcasting in the lowest range of national markets were losing money for the third consecutive year.[5] As late as 1960, despite the intense demand for VHF allocations, more than seventy of these channels remained unclaimed, almost exclusively those assigned to smaller communities in western and North Central states.

The most damaging aspect of a UHF assignment, then, was simply that the need for receiver-conversion units made it difficult to gain access to larger markets already served by VHF stations. The commission itself admitted in 1959 that "UHF stations tend to persist mainly in those areas where only negligible VHF service is available to the community. . . . Outside of the top 103 markets, UHF is in operation in 43 communities; all but five of these are UHF only. . . . *The fact that the UHF-only market is typically small leads in most cases to unprofitable operation for UHF*" (emphasis added).[6] In essence, what no station, whether VHF or UHF, could do was operate profitably in a vast majority of the 1,200 communities outside top-100 markets to which channels had been allocated. The significant difference between the two classes was that UHF, because of its inability to compete at parity with VHF, was forced to play the role assigned it by the commission.

Thus the failure of UHF appears to reflect an underlying failure of analysis on the part of the FCC, an unwillingness once again to reconcile political policy with economic reality. No matter how meritorious the concept of television oriented to local service, no small or even moderate-sized community could logically have been expected to generate the half-million dollars in annual broadcast revenues necessary to support such a facility.[7]

The visual demands of television transmission required five to ten times the funds needed to construct and operate a typical local radio station, and programming inflexibility imposed by this overhead made survival marginal even at that point. As communications expert Sydney Head noted, "No parallel in television exists for the . . . 'coffeepot' radio station which can be operated successfully in a small community by an efficient owner-manager. Market size is the dominant variable in television operation."[8] Market size was the dominant variable because community television stations had neither the production capabilities nor the base of local advertising support necessary to operate independently of the national marketing system. A study commissioned by the broadcast industry observed that experiences in producing shows for local entertainment were generally unsatisfactory, because of both high cost and

lack of public enthusiasm. As in the radio era, mass-produced professional programming made local efforts uneconomical. By 1954 it
was estimated that in the average locality an hour of live production cost three times as much as the rental of a syndicated film of
similar length.[9] Even more important, perhaps, was the fact that
professional productions had again lessened public tolerance for
amateur community efforts. In 1956, Sydney Head predicted the
limited future of such programming: "The only economic incentive
countering the trend towards virtual disappearance of local live
programs is the value of such programs in enhancing a station's
prestige. . . . The hard fact is that few local advertisers can afford
to be program sponsors."[10]

An equally hard fact was the inability of smaller stations to
enhance their prestige by the expensive luxury of local programming. By the end of 1956 even stations without network connections were scheduling local live programs during less than 25 percent of each broadcast day, and this percentage has not been
exceeded since then.[11]

Denied the possibility of effective local production, the community television broadcaster had basically only one remaining source
from which to create a unique station image—his selection and
scheduling of syndicated programming. Here again he was hampered by lack of funds, despite the fact that syndication prices were
generally lower in smaller markets. The problem in this case was
not expense, but lack of revenues, for less than 10 percent of all
expenditures for national spot advertising escaped top-100 markets
to support this type of programming in outlying communities.[12]

The vicious circle restraining the upward mobility of small-market television was thus complete. Community stations had no alternative but to rely upon national advertising revenues for support,
with network and national spot payments based almost exclusively
upon the size of potential audience. Because of small audiences,
their revenues were limited; because of limited revenues, their ability either to improve coverage with more advanced equipment or to
increase audience through better programming or a longer broadcast day was equally limited.

In actuality, then, the commission's effort to create local television service had resulted only in marginal community stations with-

out the capacity to provide such service. Even more damaging to the public interest, this regulatory policy restricted the flow of information and entertainment to sparsely settled or isolated regions unable to support the half-million-dollar disseminators the FCC made prerequisite to reception of each network signal.

Although the commission remained adamant in its commitment to the coverage concepts of its "Sixth Report and Order," refusing to measure television service in terms of network coverages, both the industry and the public had adopted this national programming standard. By 1956, 80 percent of all television revenues was earned at the national level. The average affiliate's network outlet role grew from thirty-nine hours a week in 1954 to sixty-eight hours a week by the end of the decade.[13] In these circumstances it is not surprising that a Senate report of a network investigation declared that the most important task performed by a station manager was negotiation of a contract for network affiliation, since it "determines in substantial measure the programming which the station offers the public. It also determines the economic well-being of the station. Consequently, most stations consider network affiliation contracts their most important single asset, next to their Commission license."[14]

By the same token, an audience dependent upon its local station's network for 60 percent of its service and almost all of its prime-time viewing was far less concerned with the competency of its own licensee than with the quality of the network he chose. Station managers reported that no single aspect of broadcast operation stimulated the same degree of public response as schedule changes which affected such network programming.[15]

In its efforts to impose the principle of local service upon television coverages, the commission challenged not only traditional economic factors, but technological and demographic problems far more complex than those faced during the radio era. Because of the wide band of frequencies necessary to carry each of television's sophisticated electronic messages, local service had to be exiled to wave lengths with less favorable propagation characteristics in order to minimize the drain upon spectrum space. This limited range, coupled with the need for high signal strength to compensate for the poor sensitivity of the average receiver, restricted television coverage to a usual radius of fifty to sixty miles. In effect, then, any household not located within sixty miles of at least three television stations, each affiliated with a different network, was being denied a significant portion of the television news and entertainment intended for the American public.

Demographic trends magnified to an even greater extent the disparity in coverages imposed by these rigid contours lacking the regional and clear channel augmentation of their radio counterparts. To avoid "white areas" in the West, the FCC was forced to spread its allocations over an extremely thin base of population. Although network studies had indicated that no affiliate station could operate successfully with an unduplicated audience of less than 50,000, and other research had placed the absolute minimum at 25,000, the commission required twenty-six allocations to cover the state of Wyoming with one television signal; the average applicant was offered an audience of 3,600. In Nevada, the base was 5,000 citizens per license allocation; in Montana, 5,100; in North Dakota, 5,600. Such assignments were obviously only empty gestures, offering service on paper which could never be provided.[16]

At the other end of the demographic scale were urban areas so closely contiguous as to make individual local services impossible. While the problem in Wyoming was insufficient coverage, in New Jersey it was "overabundance." This state of more than seven million people had no local station because its eight allocations were completely overshadowed by coverage contours of surrounding major-market broadcasters. A report commissioned by the FCC in the 1960s viewed this situation with concern ("The broad coverage permitted broadcasters in politically differentiated but contiguous urban areas has prevented . . . the search for an inner identification and spirit of local civic pride for which large cities are constantly striving"[17]), but the commission was flooded, not with complaints from New Jersey residents denied local service, but with angry demands from western citizens for more network programming.

The FCC, without question, faced an almost impossible situation in its attempt to apportion television service on a fairly uniform basis over such a vast and heterogeneous nation, but to at least some extent the ordeal seems to have been self-imposed. Instead of asking whether "local" had the same meaning to a Wyoming rancher, whose "community" might be scattered homes linked by dirt roads, and to an urban dweller, whose "community" could be encompassed within a single housing development, the commission simply attempted to impose rigid patterns on a diverse population. Since the patterns could not yield to human needs, they shattered, leaving certain areas without local or national service.

The commission had ignored economic, technological, and demographic factors to insert an artificial element of spectrum dissemination into programming which flowed smoothly along cable and microwave connections from each of the three networks to local communities throughout America. Between 1952 and 1960, UHF stations abandoned more than half of the 117 markets they had entered during the decade, including 70 percent of those in which they would have provided a second or third network service in competition with existing VHF stations.[18] VHF broadcasters, claiming less than one-fourth of all allocations, could not carry the coverage burden alone. As a result, approximately half of the 34 million television homes, or 70 percent of the population in 1956, could not receive three network signals from the spectrum, and a sizable percentage, perhaps 20, could receive no signal at all without some system of reception augmentation.[19] As in 1927, it was not the basic structure of the broadcast industry which seemed to dictate these restricted patterns of coverage, but rather the philosophy of its regulator. By 1952, however, an auxiliary method of program delivery which did not parallel that of the earlier period had begun to emerge in a handful of communities just beyond the contours of existing stations. This method, the operation of master antennas, at first appeared innocuous, but it held a potential to threaten the authority of the commission, for it offered the public the option, for the first time, of defining its own interest in terms of program diversity rather than in terms of local service.

The Master Antenna: Cable History as a
Reflection of Broadcast Patterns

The commission's television allocation structure seemed perfectly designed for the insertion of a community antenna component. Although open spaces in the system had been planned and reserved for local stations, their failure to materialize left a coverage vacuum that cable television could expand to fill. Polished and heavily promoted national programming lacked only a local distributor.

Since the gap was local in nature, community businessmen without capital or experience sufficient to operate national or even regional services could set up CATV systems in their own areas with minimal investment and little knowledge of broadcast procedures. This local basis not only stimulated immediate growth but also helped to allay citizens' concern about this alien device, "pay-TV," in their communities. Owners of cable television systems generally had closer ties with the areas they served than the nearest local television station and thus were able to win a degree of public acceptance no national or even statewide organization could have achieved.

A second appeal, far more compelling than civic pride in stimulating subscriber support, was that of the network programming the system carried. Each family had already committed at least $300 for a receiver to obtain this programming, and in view of the additional $125 to $175 necessary to erect an antenna tower in fringe areas, a typical CATV installation charge of $100, plus $5 a month for service, did not appear exorbitant, especially since it meant clearer reception and perhaps an additional channel not otherwise available.

Even the number of network services seemed to have been planned with cable capabilities in mind. Most community antenna systems constructed before 1960 could carry only three signals, but with the demise of the Du Mont network in 1955 and the lack of strong regional or independent programming, this limited capacity was sufficient to offer subscribers full television coverage.

As radio broadcasting had been pioneered in the 1920s by the radio sales industry, which offered programming to sell its receivers, so a community antenna was used by television dealers in outlying communities to perform a similar function some thirty years later. In each case program delivery was initially considered only an evil necessary to achieve another end. Viewed historically, these early efforts reveal a discernible pattern of evolving functions. Yet in the context of the times, pioneers during both eras were much more likely to measure success in terms of sales than to measure it in terms of services or audience.

The point at which a particular master antenna hookup became the nation's first community antenna television system is shrouded in the same definitional haze which has obscured the origins of most "firsts" in broadcast innovation. A single channel linked

receivers in Seattle as early as 1946; a group of hotel rooms in
New York City was served by a single antenna in 1947; a more
elaborate system with an amplified single signal was operating non-
commercially in Astoria, Oregon, in 1949; but Lansford, Pennsylvania, seems the most likely candidate for the location of the
nation's first true community antenna system.[20] According to the
description given in the initial judicial decision involving a community antenna ("a system which receives programs broadcast by
licensed television stations and distributes them by wire to individual customers at a flat rate"[21]), this multichanneled business operation planned in October 1949 appears to have been the earliest to
function as more than an elaborate master antenna. This system,
constructed by Milton Shapp's Jerrold Electronics early in 1950,
offered three amplified television signals to subscribers paying
installation and monthly service charges. Although the system was
far more advanced electronically than any master antenna operation, the main distinction between it and previous systems was its
design as a profit-making venture, rather than simply as a cooperative effort to enhance reception or as an inducement to prospective
purchasers of television sets. Thirteen other commercial systems
began operation by the end of 1950, and only two years later there
were seventy of these systems, serving some fourteen thousand subscriber homes.[22]

One system typical of this early era was begun by Martin Malarkey in Pottsville, Pennsylvania, only twenty miles west of the Lansford system. Malarkey's family owned a department store that was
backlogged with television sets because of its location in an Appa-
lachian valley whose encircling mountains shut off all television
reception. After studying the Lansford operation Malarkey gained
permission from the Pottsville Common Council to furnish television to town residents. He then negotiated a contract with the local
telephone company, leasing the right to string his cable from its
poles. Within a year Malarkey was able to sign up 1,000 subscribers, using their installation charges to repay more than a third of
the half-million dollars he had borrowed to start the system. By the
end of the decade the two-channel service had been expanded to
five signals, including an independent and an educational station.

The success of these operations in the Pennsylvania mountain
valleys brought in delegations of businessmen and investors from

other regions who returned home to lay the groundwork for systems in their own areas based upon the same techniques. In 1952 Malarkey founded and became the first president of the National Community Antenna Television Association (NCTA), an organization boasting nineteen members as it moved from Pottsville to Washington, D.C., the following year.

Cable television in 1953, with its 65,000 subscriber homes and annual revenues of perhaps a half-million dollars, was still clearly an extremely minor operation, viewed with no particular concern by most broadcasters.[23] What did trouble the few television station owners with CATV systems on the fringes of their contours was the fact that these community antennas seemed to be expanding rather than, as had been expected, curtailing operations. During the freeze on the licensing of television stations, cable had been tolerated because it was believed to be a temporary reaction to a lack of signals. The appearance of these "freeze-era" systems ("small groups of homes connected to a single master antenna by one or two amplifiers and a few hundred feet of open line wire, usually strung from tree to tree, rooftop to rooftop"[24]) justified this belief, but newer operations had foresaken wire for shielded cable connected with a rather disconcerting look of permanence to homes in many smaller communities.

The older "canyon" systems threading through mountainous valleys of the East and West remained, for a time, unreported in any survey, unheralded in any history; but, having launched the concept and fulfilled the original needs of their audiences, they would eventually be either converted to modern techniques or abandoned, victims of the technology they founded.

Officials of both the government and the broadcast industry had believed that cable television would not evolve beyond these canyon operations. In 1959 a Senate Commerce subcommittee report suggesting legislation to license CATV's provided a succinct expression of the expected and actual growth of these systems during the decade: "When the TV freeze was lifted in 1952, it was widely felt that the community antenna system, having provided a valuable interim service, would disappear when faced with the competition of many new stations which were expected shortly to blanket the country with local service. However . . . many communities did not get local stations. . . . After a temporary pause, the rate of CATV systems again picked up."[25] In fact, there was a close parallel between the growth of television and the growth of cable facilities, both in the era of expansion and during the plateau period of development extending from 1956 to 1959 (see table 3).

Table 3   Television and CATV Growth, 1952–59

Year (1 January)	Number of TV Stations	TV Audience (In Millions)	Number of CATVs[a]	CATV Subscribers[a] (In Thousands)
1952	108	15	70	14
1953	120	20	150	30
1954	356	26	300	65
1955	411	30	400	150
1956	461	34	450	300
1959	510	43	560	550

SOURCE: *Television Factbook*, service vol. 39 (Washington, D.C.: Television Digest, 1970), pp. 72a, 79a.
NOTE: For an annual comparison of TV-CATV growth, see Appendix A.
a. Estimated.

Perhaps the most interesting aspect of this comparison is the yearly totals of each group. Television stations surpassed community antenna systems in the surge of construction activity following the lifting of the freeze, but by 1956 cable had regained the lead and did not relinquish it again during this era. On the most elemental level this growth in both broadcasting and cable systems can be explained in terms of potential audience: the percentage of American homes with television rose from 34 in 1952 to 78 by the end of 1956. However, this increase may reflect an effect as well as a cause of diffusion, with the purchase of sets stimulated by the availability of more television signals.

Although broadcasters had been confident that their growth would end the need for cable, cable's share of audience had grown from less than one-tenth of 1 percent of all television homes in 1952 to almost 1 percent in 1956, an actual increase of 1,000 percent. In fact, as long as the number of television stations expanded without saturating all markets with coverage, this growth actually stimulated community antenna development, because of the symbiotic relationship between station contours and cable services. The ideal location for a community antenna system was in a community just beyond the effective coverages of two or three television stations. This location allowed an antenna to receive and distribute signals without the expense of long-distance wire relays or complex amplification equipment. Cable could not reach into rural areas because construction costs of $3,500–$4,000 a mile demanded a clustering of homes to defray this expense.[26] Thus, cable soon saturated all communities on the peripheries of existing contours and could only expand again when new stations created additional communities of this type.

This was the reason, then, that cable expanded with the lifting of the television freeze in 1952 and paused as the television industry paused in 1956. During this period broadcasters began to understand cable's potential to grow with the industry rather than wither away under its challenge. With this realization, the first substantial broadcast opposition to CATV arose, together with the earliest significant pressure upon the FCC to end its threat.

The Regulatory Dilemma: CATV as a Broadcaster or Common Carrier

The commission had been aware of the existence of community antenna operations at least since 1949, when an engineer from its staff inspected the L. E. Parsons system in Astoria, Oregon, but the first attempt to determine their legal status did not occur until March 1952. At that time the commission's general counsel and the chiefs of the Common Carrier and Broadcast bureaus joined in a memorandum suggesting rule-making procedures to determine if cable systems operated as common carriers subject to FCC jurisdiction. The memorandum observed, "During the past 2 years the Commission has received a substantial number of inquiries from the public concerning the status of so-called community antenna television . . . particularly with respect to the nature of the authority, if any, which would have to be obtained from the Commission to construct and operate such systems. . . . The nature of the CATV operations suggests two lines of inquiry: (1) Do such operations constitute broadcasting within the meaning . . . of the Act . . . or (2) do such operations constitute interstate common carrier operations within the meaning . . . of the Act."[27]

Since the FCC had been granted two separate and distinct types of regulatory authority under the terms of the Communications Act of 1934, it could avoid responsibility for supervising community antenna systems only through a determination that these systems were neither common carriers as defined by title 2 of the act, or broadcasters under the jurisdictional definition of title 3. Law, a philosophical system whose effects are dictated by categorization, thus made this classification process crucial.

As early as October 1951 a television station, WMCT, Memphis, Tennessee, had demanded that the FCC classify cable signal carriage as "broadcasting" so that a competing CATV system would be barred, under section 325(a) of the act from carrying "the program or any part thereof of another broadcasting station without the express authority of the originating station." While "retransmission consent" offered the advantage of giving television stations control of antenna systems without imposing a supervisory burden upon the commission, the agency rejected this approach for both legal and administrative reasons.

"Broadcasting" under title 3 was described as disseminating messages to the public at large by means of electromagnetic radiation. CATV, by contrast, was engaged in "narrowcasting," that is, using cable to restrict its messages to only those members of the public willing to pay for its services. Even if the FCC had been willing to ignore this clear distinction between functions, no federal court would have been likely to sustain its right to expand juristictional authority by such questionable definition.

From an administrative standpoint, too, definition had far broader ramifications than solution of a particular problem. If cable operation could properly have been classified as broadcasting, not only section 325(a), but the entire regulatory structure of title 3 would have been involved. The commission had been directed by Congress to allow broadcasting only by licensed facilities: so the small, overburdened agency staff would have been forced under this mandate to assume a new obligation—licensing and supervising an additional industry.

It was this administrative burden, coupled with the limited advantages derived from its assumption, which also caused the commission to reject the classification "common carrier" for cable television. Although the staff memorandum of March 1952 had concluded that CATV systems might properly be defined as interstate common carriers, and thus within FCC jurisdiction, because they operated for hire and carried the interstate product of television programming to individual homes, the commission made no effort to assert such authority. Perhaps a reason for this reluctance to act is reflected in the list of statutory procedures the staff indicated would be necessary once cable came within its control: "Significant provisions of the title . . . include section 201(b) which provides that all charges, rates, practices, classifications and regulations . . . be just and reasonable; section 203(b) which requires that all such charges and related practices . . . be filed with the Commission; section 205(a) which authorizes the Commission to prescribe just and reasonable charges for such services, and section 202(a) prohibiting unjust or unreasonable discrimination in charges, practices . . . facilities or services."[28]

In the first public, though unofficial, explanation of the commission's refusal to claim either broadcast or common carrier jurisdiction over CATV, Commissioner John C. Doerfer stressed the pragmatic view that such control, whether or not legally possible, would be of little benefit to complaining broadcasters. Speaking before a state association for the regulation of public utilities in 1955, Doerfer, who was soon to become FCC chairman, declared that federal incursion would simply threaten the authority of state and local bodies offering the broadcaster his only effective protection from unfair competition.[29]

If the FCC declared cable television to be broadcasting, he pointed out, this declaration would end all state or local supervision, since the courts had held broadcasting to be an exclusive concern of the federal regulator. Yet, in doing so, the commission would gain no authority over CATV rates and services, a primary source of broadcaster complaints, because this type of control could only be exercised over common carriers, and the Communications Act had specified that broadcasters could not be considered common carriers. If the FCC were instead to assume the burden of common carrier jurisdiction over cable, it still could not use its power over rates and services to shield broadcasters from competition, because in this field, the sole standard dictating administrative actions was maximum service to the public, not private protection from competing services. Doerfer maintained that in view of these barriers the only necessary step the FCC had not yet taken in the field was to insure that cable operation did not cause electrical interference with broadcast reception, a power it could exercise without asserting jurisdiction over CATV.

In 1956 the commission did enact rules setting permissible limits for cable electronic emissions. These rules constituted the sole federal regulation of any aspect of cable systems during the decade.[30] The commission's refusal to become more deeply involved in these early clashes between broadcasters and cable operators seems completely reasonable. Its failure to consider the long-range implications of these clashes, however, cannot be so easily justified. Neither the FCC's apparent lack of authority nor the necessity for immediate action appears to excuse the absence of a comprehensive analysis of the potential of cable television. Lacking such an analysis, the FCC could not possibly have foreseen the ultimate impact of its deliberations on private cable microwaves, not only upon CATV, but upon small-market television stations as well.

The Decision on Microwave Relay

The FCC memorandum of March 1952 which had raised the issue of cable television's legal status had been prompted, ironically enough, not by an inquiry involving a CATV system, but the microwave relay network which was to serve it. J. E. Belknap and Associates, a partnership of Poplar Bluff, Missouri, businessmen, had applied to the commission in July 1951 for an interstate common carrier license authorizing construction of a chain of microwave stations to relay the signal of a Memphis, Tennessee, television station to a local community antenna system owned by the group.[31]

Spectrum space for the use of common carriers had been reserved with the intent that each licensee would construct facilities for the use of the general public in transmitting individual point-to-point messages. The Belknap proposal contained an elaborate projection of future users of its microwave link, but the FCC staff challenged its validity. It rejected the Belknap application in June 1953, indicating its belief that the claim of public use was simply a subterfuge by which a private closed-circuit group sought access to a public resource.

During the period the Belknap application was under consideration the commission accepted a tariff filed by certain Bell systems setting rates and charges for proposed carriage of television signals to CATV systems and, in November 1953, approved the first formal common carrier application to provide such service. Approval of common carrier service for a cable system, however, was far less advantageous for the CATV operator than granting him the right to construct his own carrier facilities. In negotiations with a common carrier the cable owner was only one of many possible carrier customers and was dealing with a business tending to view CATV as an operation of high risk and limited volume. As long as common carriers held a monopoly in microwave relay, they could simply wait—as Bell did for several months after filing its tariff—unconcerned by the lack of customers, realizing that cable systems could not import television signals without eventually contracting for use of their facilities. Thus, in order to obtain more competitive rates, cable television systems needed authorization from the FCC to operate their own microwave relays, whether or not classified as "public" common carriers.

This authorization came in May 1954 from a rehearing of the Belknap common carrier application. Although the only immediate service contemplated was the relaying of television signals to the Poplar Bluff cable system, Belknap's application had been carefully amended, in the light of FCC objections, to show that ownership ties between the two facilities had been officially severed, that a public need for such common carriage existed, and that reasonable rates had been established for public use.

Within a year electronic firms had developed moderately priced relay equipment specially designed for cable use, and the precedent established by the issuance of the Belknap common carrier license began to have profound effects upon cable growth. By the end of 1955 the CATV owner planning to import television signals had the option of either constructing his own system or simply filing a license application; he could be confident that the latter act in itself would make the neighboring common carrier more amenable during negotiations concerning rates and services.

The commission could properly authorize an essentially private use of spectrum space and had done so in licensing industrial, land transportation, and marine services, among others, in the past. The issue in this case—the right of cable relays to use particular frequencies allocated for public common carrier operations—was much narrower, and the end result was not as significant as the opportunity for analysis the commission had rejected. By accepting a legal fiction rather than convening rule-making proceedings to determine the actual legal status of CATV signal importation, the FCC lost both the time and the knowledge it needed to govern its growth. Thus the commission was unprepared as the cable industry used its immediate microwave access to transform its systems from community antennas to program distributors, changing in the process from marginal competitors to major challengers of many small-market broadcasters.

The Implications of a Failure in
Regulatory Definition

Congress seems clearly to have been vested with sufficient constitutional authority to govern the interstate commerce activities of cable television. Thus, although congressional authority expressly delegated to the FCC by the Communications Act of 1934 may not have been considered broad enough in itself to support cable regulation, the commission could, at any time, have requested additional powers to expand its jurisdiction in conformance with expanding communications technology. A request for legislation, however, would have demanded an analysis of the distinctive elements defining the legal status of CATV so that those functions endangering spectrum broadcasting could be brought under control. Having failed to make this request or even to have performed the underlying study, the commission's explanation for its lack of action, in terms of either restricted jurisdiction or ineffectual remedies, appears more like legal sophistry than legal reasoning.

The factor which apparently convinced the FCC that no immediate regulatory action was required was the relatively insignificant threat cable systems posed for television broadcasters as late as 1955. In its administrative judgment, therefore, the limited nature of the problem did not justify the magnitude of the supervisory task necessary to control it. To the extent that this explanation is correct, the FCC's reluctance to formulate a policy on cable television and obtain legislation designed to carry it out was thus the result of incomplete economic research as well as inadequate legal analysis.

As long as cable systems functioned basically as master antennas dependent upon spectrum signals to fill their channels, they remained equally dependent upon the growth of television stations for the expansion of their industry. Community antenna operations soon saturated most communities on the edges of existing contours, but they were unable either to reach out into rural areas or to penetrate the more densely settled localities within broadcast markets. When the FCC began granting CATV the privilege of microwave relay without imposing restrictions upon its use, cable was suddenly freed from its dependent position and given the capacity to invade the broadcast markets' communities. To justify its service charges, it offered additional microwave-imported channels.

Although most major markets served by three or more stations still provided little opportunity for cable growth, smaller markets with one and two stations were far more vulnerable. CATV systems could not only offer subscribers the programming of the networks without a local affiliate but could also import a more complete schedule of network shows than any affiliate might wish to carry. Thus a television station which had entered a marginal market of perhaps thirty thousand television homes with the expectation of serving an exclusive audience now faced competition which, by eroding its narrow base of support, threatened its continued existence.

From a short-range viewpoint, the commission's inability to foresee the implications of its decision to authorize CATV microwave relay seemed to benefit both the cable industry and the small-market audiences. Long-term effects, however, were far less beneficial, for both cable and the general public. As the commission's goal of local service had created a coverage vacuum for cable to fill, so its failure to guide cable expansion created a policy vacuum for political forces to exploit.

When it became apparent that the FCC was unwilling or unable to end the CATV menace to smaller television stations, a group of western senators representing most of the beleaguered broadcasters began demanding congressional intervention to restrain cable functions. Despite their concern, it was not the cable growth in itself which endangered broadcasters, but, like cellular tissue, the cancerous nature of a growth lacking constructive control.

Because the commission had shown itself incapable of defining, analyzing, and thus formulating policy which would allow eventual CATV integration into a nationwide system of electronic mass communication, the regulatory initiative was reclaimed for a time by Congress, whose political process was geared to immediate solution of specific grievances rather than to ultimate attainment of broader goals. The time for basic research had ended and the era of interindustry debate had begun. Such debate might eventually resolve the question of which industry had the stronger political support or the superior legal right, but it could not answer another, more salient question: which had the greater potential to satisfy the public need for communication?

III

The Cable Case History

Cable television became a distinct communications medium in the United States only after microwave relays offered operators of community antennas the opportunity of ending their dependence upon available spectrum television signals. This capacity to select programming from various regions transformed the earliest cable systems from passive antenna installations into active importation and distribution mechanisms, capable for the first time of invading the markets of television stations in search of audiences.

This change in the nature of cable's communications function was not immediately apparent to broadcasters, the commission, or even the cable industry itself. Community antenna systems would continue to be built, three-station markets would remain impervious to challenge, and the occasional clash between a station and its cable competitor would be seen, not as part of a larger evolutionary pattern, but simply as another illustration of the difficulties involved in the operation of television in marginal markets.

Yet at this juncture all that was lacking was a realization of the import of cable's new role in the broadcast structure, a realization that would soon spread from western markets to the halls of Congress. Thus, while there is no way of drawing an accurate line to separate eras in history, it seems that regulatory reaction to cable as a true communications challenger can be dated from the earliest impact of CATV systems upon television stations in 1957 and 1958.

5   Master Antenna to Program Distributor: The Small-Market Challenges, 1957–60

The commission's regulatory design for the television industry, as outlined in its "Sixth Report and Order," specified that when all areas of the United States were able to receive at least one television signal, priority would be given to its second objective—establishing local stations in each of the almost thirteen hundred communities assigned television channels. By the end of 1956 the FCC claimed that 90 percent of all regions of the nation were within range of television service, but techniques aiding the achievement of this percentage were blocking attainment of its second goal. The contours of 475 commercial broadcasters were being extended into at least one thousand additional communities by unlicensed auxiliary delivery systems, either community antennas or repeater devices. Although the FCC was willing to acknowledge the significant public benefit these supplemental services provided, their functions threatened the economic foundations of local broadcasters. Once again, and despite recently declared commission priorities, the objective of local service would prevail over public demands for coverage.

Western Markets: Clear Channel Revisited

The repeater, or on-channel booster, was the western equivalent of the community antenna and was actually much more a "community" institution than the cable system. Its function is aptly described by its designations: it "repeats" a television signal, and it "boosts" its coverage by retransmitting the channel at a power higher than that received. Television stations had been authorized on occasion to use such facilities to fill in gaps in their coverage contours, but the commission had been adamant in its refusal to allow community groups the right to import television coverages by this mechanism of spectrum relay.

Yet, despite the illegality of these unlicensed transmitters, they were being erected in countless settlements of 500–2,000 people scattered across western mountain states from Colorado to Idaho during the mid-1950s. There was no other way of receiving television service in a region containing only 2 percent of the nation's population, where the nearest "local" station might be 200 miles away and no village was large enough to attract a CATV system. Groups of enterprising television dealers, repairmen, and electricians, backed by local service clubs, built facilities sufficient to deliver discernible if not studio-quality pictures (their efforts were limited by the voluntary nature of their support). Since there was no way of restricting spectrum transmission to deny service to those who refused to pay for it, most boosters were constantly in the red, lacking funds for modernization or even for maintenance of existing equipment. Some of the flavor of these primitive installations was captured in a report on booster operations in Montana and North Dakota submitted to the FCC in 1957 by Archer Taylor, a consulting electrical engineer.[1]

> [Sidney and Fairview, Montana.] Cost is estimated by the installation man to be $3,000, though the sum has not yet been raised. . . . Equipment is installed in an old bus parked on a hill. . . . Coaxial transmission lines . . . are free to swing in the wind.
> [Saltese, Montana.] Installation was planned . . . by radio parts wholesaler. Actual installation was done by nontechnical personnel in accordance with directions of the wholesale house salesman. There is no . . . serviceman in the area.
> [Fort Peck, Montana.] There has been considerable experimentation on this and several antennas are in place. . . . The Channel 8 quad was supported on a wood pole about 15′ or less above the ground. . . . The installer seemed to be rather discouraged about prospects of making it work.

Generally, Taylor found that

> electronic equipment was . . . laid out on a bench, presenting an appearance of experimentation and disorder. . . . Some systems had flimsy antenna installations, and coaxial cables were . . . quite subject to damage in the wind. . . .

However homemade these installations might have been, however, they inspired a strong sense of viewer loyalty.

> The farmer who lives across the road keeps close guard on the facilities. I was told that when an airplane circled the site, the farmer had the registration number checked . . . because he wondered if he should "open up on it with a shotgun."

From 1954 until 1957 booster representatives had been asking the FCC for a licensing system authorizing the operation of facilities for VHF community relays until adequate spectrum service was available in each area. Instead the commission offered translator licenses approving the use of a device which converted VHF channels to the highest television frequencies and relayed them as UHF transmissions.[2] This offer meant little to the smaller communities, for as Archer Taylor had informed the commission, "Universally, operators complained that the UHF Translators were prohibitively costly in the very small communities of 1,500 or less . . . particularly in view of the need for conversion at most receiving sets. . . . I encountered an estimate of $30,000 to install a technically sound, FCC approved UHF translator facility. . . . A similar VHF on channel booster in operation cost less than $2,000.[3]

The commission had maintained, in extending its prohibition against booster operation, that these VHF transmissions posed a serious threat of interference, not only for licensed television stations, but for land mobile and aircraft communications as well. Yet Commissioner Craven, the only engineer among the seven commissioners, challenged this argument sharply: "Apparently the Commission did not realize that these low-power boosters are the only practical way in which people residing in these isolated areas can secure any television service whatsoever. . . . It is true that low-power television boosters have interference capabilities of a few miles. However, properly installed and operated, the low-power booster should not cause harmful interference to interstate radio communications."[4]

The commission's attempt to enforce its ban upon booster operations met with bitter opposition. Colorado Governor Edwin C. Johnson, former chairman of the Senate Commerce Committee, declared the threatened prosecution of a Steamboat Springs, Colorado, operator to be "contrary to the public interest . . . and an abuse of Federal authority" as he signed a decree appointing this operator and eleven others as staff members of his newly created "Governor's Committee to Improve Television Reception in Colorado."[5]

Two years later Montana reacted even more violently; its legislature enacted a bill granting the Montana Public Service Commission complete and absolute authority to supervise and license some one hundred VHF boosters in the state serving more than 20 percent of its population. On 17 February 1959, Governor J. Hugo Aronson signed this bill into law and vetoed a companion bill which would also have vested the state commission with the same authority over cable television.[6]

Yet despite widespread protests from these regions the FCC continued its efforts to enforce its prohibition order. Since each booster was transmitting in violation of federal criminal law, the logical course of action would have been to file criminal charges against such operators. This, however, would have allowed the defendant to be tried in his own state, and, as FCC General Counsel Warren Baker explained commission tactics, "The judges . . . might well have shown considerable sympathy for the equitable position of the local people. We decided, therefore, to choose a longer but surer course of action. . . . The Commission issued an order directing the operator of a Bridgeport, Washington, booster to cease and desist from operating a booster station without a license. . . . The appeal had to be taken before the U.S. Court of Appeals for the District of Columbia Circuit."[7]

Thus, the FCC managed not only to avoid granting an operator a hearing in his own judicial district but also to select the defendant who would have to travel the maximum distance to pursue his appeal. The tactic was successful in that the circuit court upheld the commission's authority: "We are satisfied . . . that Congress intended to assert control by the federal government over 'all the channels of interstate . . . radio transmission' and that the sweep of the Commission's authority includes the booster stations here involved." But, in doing so, this court, generally considered sympathetic to administrative agencies, criticized the FCC severely for its laxity in this area of regulation: "despite the Commission's clear duty to 'provide for the use of such channels,' throughout the past 22 years of the Commission's life it has failed to adopt rules under which signals . . . useless in Bridgeport without a booster, might be picked up . . . and made available to residents of the town. We suggest, therefore, that the Commission may well get on with its rule-making proceedings . . . examining . . . means of filling in the service area of television stations."[8]

The victory, either by intent or necessity, was only a symbolic one. The commission did not use this case as a basis for further enforcement proceedings. Instead the agency was content simply to employ this power as a threat, while extending the time during which booster operators could apply for translator licenses without being forever barred, by their illegal actions, from such privilege.

It is difficult to see what the commission gained by this pressure; what was lost is far more apparent. The relative positions, by 1959, of the various delivery devices are shown in table 4. If this table were adjusted to reflect only those television markets ranked below the top 100, the dimensions of the penetration of auxiliary systems would increase considerably. In these markets, 185 television stations serving seven million homes were being challenged by a coalition of cable and repeater devices claiming an audience almost one-fifth the size of the broadcasters'. With an additional modification to isolate smaller western markets, the booster function would

Table 4   Television Distribution Techniques, January 1959

Auxiliary System	Number of Facilities[a]	Communities Served[a]	Homes Served[a]	Percentage of Homes[a]
CATV	600	600	750,000	1.6
Satellite[b]	25	25	25,000	0.05
Translator	200	120	125,000	0.25
Booster	1,000	800	300,000	0.70
Auxiliary total	1,825	1,545	1,200,000	2.7
TV station	509	325	44,000,000	97.3

NOTE: This table is a composite of estimates made by the FCC in Docket 12443, and of NBC research data reported in the *TV Factbook*. The problem in assembling accurate information is that neither CATV systems nor boosters were required to report to any agency, so that all figures during this era can only be approximations.
a. All figures except those for TV stations are estimated.
b. TV station exempted from local programming requirement.

loom even larger, reaching 15–20 percent of all homes while cable served an audience of less than 10 percent.

Yet despite its size, the booster threat was far more apparent than real. Although boosters may have caused short-term problems for local television stations in isolated areas, they posed no long-range threat because they had no economic motive for continuing operation after adequate broadcast service was available. In fact, these devices often fought an effective holding action against cable invasion, by providing television programming in market areas until a station could be established.

Thus the FCC, to the extent that it intended to protect areas for the future expansion of television broadcasters by the banning of the temporary booster facilities, was actually undercutting its own efforts by encouraging instead the growth of permanent cable systems. This, in turn, resulted from the commission's inability to perceive the differing economic factors dictating the spread of each; it classified them both as "auxiliary" to broadcasting rather than analyzing each as a unique entity. Lacking economic data, the commission could only administer by blind adherence to statute, prohibiting boosters simply because, through the FCC's own actions, they were unlicensed and therefore operating in violation of the law. The primary reason the commission's policy was not of great benefit to CATV operators was simply that it was so universally ignored.

This insensitivity to the needs of western audiences—clearly reminiscent of the FCC's attitude during the "clear channel" controversy—had another unfortunate side effect. By forcing the West once again to be the victim of its policy of local service, the commission stimulated a resentment among the western congressmen which made later attempts at compromise extremely difficult.

Cable subscribers in the states of Wyoming, Montana, Colorado, Idaho, Nevada, and Utah accounted for less than 10 percent of the nation's subscribers in 1959, but a substantial number of them lived in the larger western towns, the most vital locations for the operation of local television. Isolated rural communities were of little interest to advertisers, and thus to broadcasters. Cable forces were also willing to cede these small settlements to boosters, declaring before the commission in 1957, "There is a need for VHF repeater service . . . in rural communities where terrain or distance

precludes direct TV reception, and low population density makes
. . . cable TV uneconomical."[9]

Battles between cable and booster operators occurred in moderate-sized communities such as Shelby or Whitefish, Montana, with populations ranging from 4,000 to 7,000. In these cases, the broadcaster and the booster operators formed a natural alliance. An editorial from a Montana newspaper during this era explained that affinity: "Why are the people of Montana fighting so hard for their free TV and booster installations? The answer is simple. Montana is a large State with mountainous terrain. . . . Very few cities are large enough to support a . . . television station. . . . Signals can be picked up economically via TV boosters, thus transmitting the signal to towns, rural communities, and farms and ranches which otherwise would never have this . . . modern entertainment."[10]

CATV, the editorial continued, was tied by the cost of its cable construction to larger communities and thus, in challenging the broadcasters in those cities, threatened the only source of continuing rural television coverage. However bitter these feuds might have been, though, they were basically local in nature, showdowns between the VFW or the Lions Club, perhaps, and an ambitious appliance dealer.

The clashes of national significance occurred in the larger cities —Cheyenne, Wyoming; Helena, Montana; Twin Falls, Idaho— with audiences of from 20,000 to 40,000, which were too rare in the West to be surrendered without full-scale conflict. These areas, then, were the staging grounds for the first congressional assault upon the cable challenge.

Congressional Reaction: The Revolt of the Western Senators

The Senate Interstate and Foreign Commerce Committee, charged with the responsibility of supervising the FCC and its management of broadcasting, began in 1954 what ultimately became an eight-part series of hearings collectively titled the "Television Inquiry." Between 1954 and 1960 the committee on four separate occasions took testimony concerning small-market television problems and, in other phases of its investigations, conducted a study of television network practices, quiz scandals, and rating services.

In 1958, as a part of this inquiry, Chairman Warren Magnuson convened a special session of the committee to examine the problems of western small-market television stations. Magnuson had often indicated his deep concern over the plight of his fellow westerners, and by appointing as special council for the hearings his own former assistant, attorney, and later FCC commissioner Kenneth Cox, he made his purpose apparent: these sessions would provide complaining station owners with a sympathetic forum from which to launch an attack on rival cable systems and on an FCC indifferent to their difficulties.

Although western Congressional leaders had been receiving sporadic complaints during the previous year from smaller communities whose booster services were being threatened, the one FCC action which seemed to trigger the call for a hearing was the commission's decision in *Frontier Broadcasting* v. *Collier*.[11] William Grove, station manager of Frontier's KFBC-TV, Cheyenne, Wyoming, perhaps the first active opponent of CATV in the West, had threatened as early as 1954 to enjoin a neighboring cable system from carrying his station's programming. In April 1956, Grove, together with twelve other western broadcasters, petitioned the FCC to declare 268 CATV systems listed by the group to be interstate common carriers, subject to commission jurisdiction and regulation.

The commission spent two years on a study of the case, which included a careful reexamination of the factors weighed in the Belknap deliberations, before issuing a decision similar to that in the Belknap case. Although the final memorandum concluded, as had that of two years earlier, "It is the opinion of the staff, that, under the provisions of the Act, and upon certain reasonable assumptions, CATV might be deemed to be common carriers for hire in interstate commerce,"[12] it also pointed out that "assertion of jurisdiction would require the regulation of rates and services of several hundred CATV systems. It would entail an administrative burden which the Commission is not equipped to handle."

This contention seemed compelling, especially in view of the fact that it was extremely questionable whether the FCC, armed with controls over common carriers, could actually "restrict or control entry of CATV systems in the interests of protecting or fostering television broadcast service in the communities involved, which is the real objective of those urging the assertion of common carrier jurisdiction."

In essence, once again the degree of benefit obtainable did not justify the additional burden of administration. Perhaps even more significant, assuming jurisdiction would have made the FCC, without sufficient authority to be successful in the task, responsible for ending the damage that cable systems were alleged to be causing broadcasters. It was a position any agency would seek to avoid, and the FCC did so, in April 1958, by declaring that CATV systems were not interstate common carriers because their customers did not select the particular messages they could receive. Broadcasters, denied relief in this forum, turned to Congress for aid.

On 27 May 1958, one month after issuing the *Frontier* decision, the FCC commissioners were summoned to appear before Senator Magnuson's committee. The following two days of the hearing were devoted to the western broadcasters' testimony, and on 25 June 1958, the cable industry gave its rebuttal.

Commission Chairman Doerfer was the first witness called, and his responses to the pointed questions of Staff Counsel Cox set the acrimonious tone which would be typical of the sessions. Before an audience packed with western broadcasters waiting to testify, Doerfer declared that he saw no way the FCC could encourage the establishment of additional television stations in smaller markts: "Remember that the motivation for operating a television station is profit. . . . There is no motivation to take care of fringe areas because there is no profit compared to the additional expenditures. . . . *The only way that I can see is perhaps by community antenna systems, boosters or translators*" (emphasis added).[13]

He rejected Cox's suggestion that the commission might have an obligation to protect local broadcasters from cable competition: "I felt I could no more protect a television station from a community antenna service than I could protect it from a local drive-in movie house or whatever other form of attraction might develop within the service area of a television station."[14]

When the acting committee chairman, Senator Lausche, asked what legislation might help the FCC carry out its responsibility in this area, Doerfer urged that Congress take no action until the commission had completed its own investigation of small-market problems. Surprisingly, Vincent T. Wasilewski, then government-relations director of the National Association of Broadcasters (NAB) and later its president, was no more certain than Commissioner Doerfer of the position Congress should take. He recommended no specific legislation to aid these western members of his organization, suggesting only that the FCC might use its microwave relay powers to control cable growth: "Quite frankly, at the moment we are in somewhat of a quandry ourselves as to the ultimate solution of what, before too long, will become a problem so large it cannot be coped with. . . . The Commission does . . . have the jurisdiction to grant or withhold microwave relay authorizations. . . . In considering such grants we believe the Commission should take into consideration the effect . . . on its nationwide allocation system and public interest."[15]

The station owners themselves were far less hesitant in recommending regulatory remedies. Frontier's William Grove urged a statute similar to section 325(a) for cable, making the carriage of CATV programs subject to broadcaster approval. This was the oldest proposal made by station owners, and possibly the most popular. However, this technique would have been protective only to the extent that large-market operators refused to sell permission; so the small-market stations of Idaho, Montana, and Wyoming, through their spokesman Edward Craney of KXLF-TV, Butte, Montana, asked instead for immediate suspension of all microwave service to cable systems, coupled with only minimal restrictions upon broadcaster use of microwaves. Other suggestions ranged in complexity from a simple freeze upon future cable microwave services to comprehensive common carrier regulation of cable, but witnesses who had appeared at similar hearings in the past seemed less interested in making proposals for research than in obtaining immediate results. William Putnam, a Massachusetts UHF station manager and perennial Television Inquiry witness, chided the commission and Congress for talking of research as a means of avoiding regulation: "I believe that to a political problem you need a political answer and I think we have enough politicians in this room to tell us that no matter what technical problems there may be for or against a particular plan, if it requires a political answer that's what it ought to get—and that's what it will get, sooner or later."[16]

Putnam's "political" answer to the CATV problem simply required that cable systems carry all local television signals, a pragmatic approach perhaps in keeping with his limited expectation of legislative relief. Marshall Pengra, another veteran CATV opponent whose station, KLTV, Tyler, Texas, had faced cable competition since beginning operation in 1954, spoke in similar fashion: "We don't need a new law to remedy the situation. . . . Under existing statute the Commission has the jurisdiction to . . . refuse microwave facilities . . . to CATV systems which resort to unfair or illegal methods of competition."[17]

The limited requests of these experienced witnesses may have reflected their realization that the 1958 hearings were not designed to produce prompt congressional relief. Broadcasters might submit drafts of statutes, but what Senator Magnuson's committee seemed to want was, not a set of proposals, but a series of personal case histories which would document the need for future congressional intervention. Frank Reardon, KGEZ-TV, Kalispell, Montana, was thus the star witness, for his was the only station which claimed to have been forced out of business by a cable system. Reardon's plea for the countless rural viewers destined to be deprived of television service without community stations would emerge in some form in nearly every future government report advocating cable control: "After the FCC approved the application of the microwave company, the community antenna in Kalispell was able to offer . . . a choice of three Spokane signals. . . . Stop for a moment and think what that means—three signals from Spokane—the Missoula signal and the local signal. . . . With a split audience in Kalispell, advertiser interest in my station was inevitably reduced. . . . The community antenna system serves only Kalispell proper. . . . Dealers estimate they have sold over a quarter of a million dollars of sets to people residing beyond the reach of cable. . . . To those isolated ranchers and farmers television service is the greatest possible joy and they are . . . to be without it if local stations cannot compete with CATV."[18]

Mrs. Milred Ernst, owner of KWRB-TV, Riverton, Wyoming, made a similar argument on behalf of the audience in her area: "If conditions become so bad that we have to give up our operation, 50,000 to 60,000 persons now enjoying television would be without any television. The towns in the area, yes, they would still have paid television via cable but two blocks from the concentrated area, no."[19]

Other witnesses echoed the same sentiments, mainaining that cable was a threat, not just to their industry, but to the public as well. Yet hidden in this record were some naïve and touching tributes to the value of cable in isolated areas. Unfortunately, because this evidence was submitted for another purpose, it sank into the bulky transcript of the proceedings without being noticed by any of the trade papers or journals.

Earlier in 1958 certain western broadcasters had launched a campaign against cable television as a form of pay-TV. They were not particularly concerned that their viewers might confuse the two terms. Senator Morse received more than one hundred letters from cable subscribers who, unaware that it was their cable service that the broadcasters were referring to, protested that pay-TV would threaten their service. At the committee's request Morse furnished twenty-five of these letters, which mentioned cable rates or installation charges, but, far more important, revealed small pockets of people as desperately committed to cable as the broadcasters' "ranchers" to spectrum transmission:[20]

> Here in Baker we got three TV stations all from Spokane. We have to pay $3.60 a month, we got TV on the cable . . . and the only pleasure we get from life is our television set. We can choose the programs we want from the three stations. We like our television just the way it is.
>
> Those of us who get our TV by cable must pay $135 to have it installed and $3.65 service charge per month. But we are so glad we can have the pleasure of bringing in all the latest happenings of the world right into our home that we consider it a great privilege and blessing to have TV brought to us by cable.
>
> You just about have to be on cable down here to get any kind of picture. TV is just about all we have left—please don't let them end our cable service with this pay-TV.

The actual hearings were extremely disappointing for witnesses traveling more than two thousand miles to present testimony about a situation they considered to be vitally significant. Committee attendance was poor, even judged by usual Senate standards. During the second day the proceedings were forced into adjournment when the only senator present left the hearing room, and *Broadcasting* subsequently lashed out with a scathing editorial "Who Does the Senate Think It Is?"[21]

Perhaps the reason for this poor attendance was simply the press of other legislative business, as Senator Magnuson said in excuse as the hearings convened. Then, too, there might have been limited general interest in this predominently regional problem, since aside from the chairman only one member, Senator Yarborough of Texas, represented a western state. A third reason seems even more likely. Senator Magnuson had decided in advance that the FCC would be pressured into exercising controls over CATV growth, and these hearings were for informational purposes only. Whether this supposition was accurate or not, the Senate Commerce Committee report, written by the committee counsel Kenneth Cox, did advocate every position taken by the western broadcast witnesses.

The Cox report, officially titled "The Problems of Television Service for Smaller Communities," was released in December 1958.[22] Based upon testimony presented at the hearing, the report recommended that the commission establish a system of priorities to use as a guide when considering the merits of various competing systems of television program delivery in an area. The highest priority, according to the report, should be given to local television stations. Then would come "semi-satellites"—or limited local service facilities—pure satellites, booster-translators, and community-antenna systems, in that descending scale of public interest values. The study chided the commission for the fact that less than 25 percent of all communities allocated television channels had stations on the air and declared that "unless the Commission develops and pursues sound basic policies in discharging its obligation . . . the desired degree of local service may never be attained. *The Commission should always keep the goal of the greatest possible degree of local service in the forefront of all its deliberations and actions*" (emphasis added).[23]

To achieve this goal of local service the committee was now pressing on the commission, the report urged the licensing of all auxiliary services, including VHF boosters and CATV systems. In addition, it advocated prohibiting the importation of local stations' network programming from other sources, and a constant surveillance over the growth of auxiliary systems. The service with the lesser priority in each instance would be required to show absence of economic threat to the higher-ranked service before being allowed to begin or expand its service. The report was thus a complete victory for the small-market broadcasters, too complete to be effective politically. Because there were no aspects favorable to cable television, the document could not serve as a starting point for legislative negotiations, but it could and did serve as a rallying point for the western campaign directed at the FCC.

If the underlying purpose of the 1958 hearings had been, not to create statutes, but to stimulate a strong sentiment of support for western broadcasters among other members of the industry and Congress, the sessions were at least moderately successful. They allowed Chairman Magnuson to enlist the support of western senators who had previously stood aloof from the controversy. These men could now present a unified demand for a new commission policy in the West, confident that the economic hardships experienced by its stations could no longer be buried in interoffice memos. Perhaps most important of all, the personal case histories presented by the various broadcasters would form a significant portion of the report supporting CATV regulation in 1959, and the human element for all subsequent arguments against cable growth.

The First Federal Deliberations

In April 1959 the commission finally completed the difficult task of drafting a statement evaluating the dangers of competition among the auxiliary services in small markets. This evaluation, viewed in the light of the broadcasters' testimony at the 1958 hearings, was not likely to please the newly unified western group.

The commission had spent eleven months analyzing comments submitted by some forty broadcasters, twenty-five cable groups, and several booster associations. On the basis of this information and its own independent research, the agency found that "of the 96 stations which have gone off the air since 1952 [89 UHF and 7 VHF] in only three cases has the existence of an auxiliary service . . . been mentioned as a factor in the demise. We have no reason to believe that there are any other cases in which the presence of an auxiliary service has been a substantial factor."[24]

The report also observed that, while 19 broadcasters had filed complaints about CATV operation, approximately 250 broadcasters with CATV systems within fifty miles of their stations, including at least 50 with cable in the same community, had not felt sufficiently threatened to ask the commission's help. The study then analyzed in detail the three cases in which cable television was alleged to have been the cause of a television station's ceasing operation. The first involved the Kalispell, Montana, facility of witness Frank Reardon.

The station had been licensed to serve a community of 9,737, with only one other town, Whitefish (population 2,500), within its coverage area. CATV systems serving more than 6,000 people with three-network coverage imported by microwave from Seattle, Washington, were already operating in both communities when Reardon applied for his license. KGEZ-TV began broadcasting in July 1957 as a satellite of a Spokane, Washington, station, carrying only a half-hour of its own programming from October 1957 until it ended operation in April 1958. During 1957 a crisis in the lumber industry, the main industry in the area, made Kalispell the region with the highest unemployment rate in the state of Montana. The FCC admitted that, in a market this marginal, the refusal of the Kalispell cable system to carry the local station's channel to its subscribers could have been the one last unfavorable factor causing the station to go dark.

The second case, involving KXLJ-TV, Helena, Montana, was similar in many respects to the Kalispell case. KXLJ-TV began operation in January 1958 as a satellite of its sister station, KXLF-TV, Butte. The station not only faced competition from an existing cable system serving 6,000 of the estimated 30,000 people in its coverage area, but it had the additional problem of broadcast competition from stations in Great Falls and Butte. CATV spokesmen claimed that both stations had been badly planned and operated, and that KXLJ-TV's suspension of broadcasting in January 1959 resulted, not from competition, but from simple mismanagement.

The final case in which the FCC found some evidence of CATV impact involved an Eastern UHF station, WJPB-TV, Fairmont, West Virginia. Here again the cable system, serving almost one-third of the 15,000 homes within the station's projected coverage area, was in operation when the television allocation was claimed. The station began broadcasting in March 1954 and continued intermittently until closing down completely in December 1955. As in the Kalispell situation, the basic complaint of the broadcaster was that the CATV system refused to carry his signal. There was evidence that the cable owner, limited by the three-channel capacity of his system, had polled his subscribers, who chose not to substitute the new station for any of the three VHF's being carried. Whatever the justification, noncarriage effectively denied WJPB-TV one-third of its potential audience, and it eventually went dark.

Although the Commission's "First Report and Order on Docket 12443" challenged the claim that CATV constituted a clear and present danger to small-market television, it could not rebut the contention that cable operations might be such a menace in the future. Nor could it maintain that failure of broadcasters to show a distinct cause-and-effect relationship between such competition and the demise of a station meant that CATV had played no part in that result.

No one questioned cable's potential to fragment a market by introducing new signals and thereby reduce the local broadcaster's share of audience. There was also no question that those markets most likely to be fragmented were the less populated areas in which each station needed a virtual monopoly to survive. As the commission itself admitted, "There is a likelihood, or even a probability, of adverse economic impact from auxiliary services upon regular television stations. But in what situations this impact becomes serious enough to threaten a station's continued existence . . . we cannot tell from the data before us."[25] Yet the agency seemed little concerned by its inability to analyze and project economic tendencies, as the conclusion of the paragraph indicates: "as we have stated many times in considering economic injury, broadcasting is a dynamic industry. If one station goes under, another station, or here another form of service fulfilling many or all of the same functions, may well soon replace it."

The FCC's unwillingness to become involved in purely economic issues seemed well justified, both because of its limited congressional mandate in this area and because of an interpretation of that mandate by the Supreme Court in 1940. The court declared, in the *Sanders Brothers* case, "The [Communications] Act does not essay to regulate the business of the licensee. The Commission is given no supervisory control . . . of business management or of

policy. . . . Resulting economic injury of a rival is not of itself . . .
an element which the FCC must weigh in passing on an application
for a broadcast license. If such loss were a valid reason for refusing
a license, this would mean that the Commission's function is to
grant a monopoly in the field of broadcasting, a result which the
Act clearly negates."[26]

Yet, in refusing even to evaluate evidence of the economic
effects of intermedia competition, the commission gained no
insights into the manner in which the industry was evolving. Thus,
in relying upon *Sanders*, the FCC had only recently rejected the
offer of economic evidence in a series of contests among translator,
CATV, and television operators which might have added to its
understanding of the developing areas of competition.

In March 1957 a cable owner in Palm Springs, California, had
filed an objection to the licensing of a translator to serve that same
city. As one of several factors supporting his objection, the cable
operator alleged that the translator would cause a significant reduction in the number of people who would subscribe to the cable
service. The commission responded, "We would not be warranted
in withholding authorization of translators, designed to provide television service to isolated communities, simply because they would
compete with CATV. . . . Investments in community antennas are
not made with any assurance that the areas served by them would
remain without any direct television reception. The public interest
would not be served by depriving a community of the privilege of
obtaining direct television reception to protect these investments."[27]

When positions were reversed the following year and a translator
organization, Hill County Television Club of Havre, Montana,
protested FCC approval of additional microwave channels to serve
a competing CATV system, the FCC reacted in similar fashion.
According to the FCC, the fact that the translator group had
invested $17,000 in equipment and buildings gave it no right to
demand freedom from competition, even if, as it alleged, these
additional cable channels appeared almost certain to force the
translator to cease operation by eroding its base of voluntary con-
tributors.

In that same month, January 1958, the commission also rejected
the plea of television station KLEW-TV, Lewiston, Idaho, to
revoke two construction permits granted a translator group in that

city. The station manager claimed to have sixty-five local advertisers in a market of only 12,000 homes and expressed a willingness to continue to compete with existing CATV and booster operations in the area, but he maintained that the proposed translator importation of two Spokane, Washington, stations would fragment his market to such an extent that it could no longer support a local broadcaster. Again the commission disputed, not the accuracy of the contention, but simply its relevance, for as Chairman Doerfer explained, "The prime objective of the FCC in the field of television broadcasting is to create the opportunity for each person in this country to have at least one television service. It is not to guarantee the success of business enterprise."

In July 1958, however, the U.S. Court of Appeals for the District of Columbia attempted to force the commission at least to the edge of such business disputes, directing the *Carroll* case that the agency consider evidence of economic injury if such injury might eventually impair or end existing broadcast service to a particular audience: "Whether a station makes $5,000, $10,000 or $50,000 is a matter in which the public has no interest as long as service is not adversely affected. But if the situation in a given area is such that available revenue will not support good service in more than one station, the public interest may well be in the licensing of one rather than two stations."[28]

Despite the admonition of this federal court, the commission during this era was not interested even in gathering such evidence of injury as might aid it in projecting future tendencies in the industry. In its request for legislation based upon the findings of its "First Report and Order on Docket 12443," the commission did not request additional research facilities to obtain and evaluate such information but simply asked for a statute to make retransmission consent applicable to cable, and for a provision making carriage of all local television stations mandatory upon broadcaster request.

These legislative proposals were expedient from an administrative standpoint but had little chance of success. Of all possible solutions, the FCC in championing retransmission consent had selected the only one guaranteed to unify cable opposition, since it seemed an open invitation to destroy CATV. One veteran cable opponent was already alleged to have demanded $20,000 a year for the privilege of carrying his station's signal, and rumors abounded that western broadcasters were working out an elaborate schedule of charges designed to end cable services in their areas.

The FCC choice was obviously influenced by the fact that these controls would be self-administered, so that broadcasters rather than the commission would regulate their competitors. Yet in avoiding the role of mediator in this dispute, the commission also rejected the opportunity of harnessing the unique attributes of each competing technique in a single electronic delivery system of maximum benefit to the public. Perhaps such a goal was impossible to achieve, but, lacking a basic understanding of the competitive elements of either group, the commission was unable even to make the attempt.

In this same report the FCC reiterated its refusal to use its common carrier powers to restrict the growth of microwave-served CATV systems: "We are of the opinion, that, in relation to the authorization of a common carrier facility . . . it is neither proper, pertinent or necessary for us to consider the specific lawful use which the common carrier subscriber may make of the facilities of the carrier."[29]

Two months later, Carter Mountain, a private microwave common carrier serving CATV systems in Wyoming, filed with the FCC Common Carrier Bureau a rather routine request to expand the number of signals offered a subscriber cable system operating within the service area of KWRB-TV, Riverton, Wyoming. The television station, owned by Mrs. Mildred Ernst, prime witness at the 1958 hearings, filed an opposing petition alleging that increased cable service in this region would jeopardize the economic base of the station. The commission's Broadcast Bureau interceded, and, in an unprecedented move, the request was refused pending a full investigation of the possible adverse economic impact alleged by the station.[30] The action was not only surprising, in the light of the FCC's previous custom of simply rubber-stamping such applications; it was amazing, in the light of the FCC's traditional avoidance of economic questions, which was restated with specific reference to cable common carriers in its "First Report." Two factors may have been significant in this revolution at staff level. The first was the identity of the complaining station, and the second was the date of the staff decision, 29 June 1959, one day before the Senate

Subcommittee on Communications began its hearings on the commission's CATV and booster practices in small markets.

Ironically, after the congressional battles had ended in 1960, only this single beachhead of federal cable jurisdiction would remain. Its rationale of economic impact, however, would never be developed beyond the stage necessary to justify authority.

Despite this tightening in procedure at staff level, Senator Magnuson and his supporters seemed no more pleased with the commission's general position, as outlined in its "First Report," than they had been with the *Frontier* decision the previous year. The group wanted action, not justification for inaction, and there seemed little hope of relief without congressional intervention. The chances for successful intervention had improved considerably during this period, however, as the Senate Subcommittee on Communications, at the request of the parent Commerce Committee, began deliberations to draft a workable bill on auxiliary television services. Chairman John O. Pastore declared as the sessions opened in the early summer of 1959 that the purpose of the hearings was not simply to gather additional information, but to draw up an equitable regulatory proposal which would protect all interests, including those of the public.

There were basically three types of bills submitted to the committee: the narrow, specifically designed proposals of the FCC concerning boosters and retransmission consent; the broad and comprehensive cable regulations proposed by Senators Moss and Murray of Utah; and the extremely limited set of cable controls submitted by Senator Monroney of Oklahoma on behalf of NCTA, the cable trade organization. From these divergent approaches, Senator Pastore managed during only eight sessions to find a common thread of agreement which seemed to assure passage of the committee's own compromise bill; it was reported out favorably by the Commerce Committee in September 1959.

Senator Pastore's success seemed attributable to his ability to pressure rival factions toward a central ground of agreement through use of equal parts of ruthless logic, charm, and pure tenacity. The FCC had proposed three bills for consideration: S. 1739 and S. 1741, which dealt solely with boosters; and S. 1801, codifying the two legislative proposals, retransmission consent and mandatory local carriage, advanced by its docket 12443 report. The chairman soon separated S. 1739 and S. 1741 from the cable bill to avoid jeopardizing passage of the more popular booster legislation. As a result of this maneuver Congress in 1960 enacted the booster proposals authorizing FCC licensing of these facilities, subject to their compliance with certain minimum engineering standards.

A week before the sessions began Senator Moss amended S. 1886, a simple omnibus bill incorporating the two FCC proposals in a single document, to transform it into a comprehensive set of cable controls. The amended S. 1886 required FCC licensing of all cable systems, with the proviso that the commission must refuse a license in any case where CATV operation would adversely affect the establishment or maintenance of a regular television station. Senator Monroney then submitted the NCTA bill, S. 2303, which, at the other extreme, granted the commission jurisdiction but only limited authority over CATV. While the Moss-Murray proposal virtually excluded cable from all broadcast markets, the Monroney bill virtually exempted cable from control; it preempted state and local regulation to grant the FCC a single power—to deny future systems certificates if their proposed operations did not appear to be in the public interest. All systems in operation or under construction were "grandfathered," or exempted from the law, and the certificates, once issued, were to be perpetual.

During the first four sessions the broadcast position was presented through most of the same witnesses who had testified at the 1958 hearings. Near the end of the third session Pastore began to isolate and challenge the two proposals making a compromise solution impossible: retransmission consent and cable restriction based upon absolute protection of television stations. He interrupted the statement of a western station manager to declare, "Now, if you are asking that the CATV get the consent of the station originating the signal for purposes of regulation, that is one point. But if we are to assume that the doing of this is going to subject them to certain negotiations which will inure to the disadvantage of the people who are the subscribers, then we have . . . a horse of a different color."[31] The next day his comments were even more pointed. After an exchange with a witness revealed that networks rather than local stations were the proper parties to be paid for retransmission consent, since they held title to most popular programming, Pastore stated that "insofar as the network . . . is concerned, he is losing nothing by way of property rights as long as that signal is being enjoyed by the most people in the widest audience. Now your argument here is: who is going to pay the cost of this signal if the other people are going to pick it up and carry it away? Now, the fact is nothing is being taken away from him. . . . He isn't reaching that market to begin with. So we say here that CATV is only servicing beyond the capacity of the broadcaster."[32]

As he indicated his lack of enthusiasm for retransmission controls, the chairman was also applying his persuasive powers privately to achieve his second goal, the reduction of the extreme economic safeguards accorded television stations by the amended S. 1886. Pastore argued that the section requiring that the CATV operator prove lack of economic impact upon any actual or potential television station before being allowed to provide service seemed not only unfair, but impossible to administer. Senator Moss acknowledged these objections in his letter to the committee of 9 July 1959 and replaced these stringent restrictions with more generalized language allowing the FCC greater discretion: "The question raised by you [Senator Pastore] . . . was whether it was wise to introduce a new and undefined standard into the Act which will invite differing interpretations. . . . I have concluded that your point was well taken . . . [amended S. 1886] will read as follows . . . 'No such application will be granted unless . . . the Commission shall first find that such authorization will serve the public interest . . . such finding to be with due regard for the desirability of encouraging and maintaining local television service.' "[33]

As cable representatives opened their testimony the following session, Chairman Pastore began to exert pressure on the other side to move this group toward a compromise position. He bore down hard on E. Stratford Smith, NCTA general counsel, who had drafted the cable industry's regulatory proposal, S. 2303.

Pastore: I understand your position to be clearly that you have no objection to the spirit of the so-called Moss bill [amended S. 1886] with the exception of being required to obtain consent.

Smith: If we define the spirit of the Moss bill to put community antenna systems under the same general type of regulation, with the same public interest standards . . . as in broadcasting, yes.

Pastore: You are perfectly willing to carry, upon orders of the FCC, a local channel? You are perfectly willing to come under

the supervision of the FCC? You are perfectly willing to subscribe to the rules of convenience and necessity? But you do
object to the requirements that you shall get the permission of
the broadcasting facility that originates the signal before you can
take it on your antenna?
Smith: Yes sir, that is correct—
Pastore: In other words, *the crux of your presentation lies in the
fact that you object to the obtaining of consent?* [emphasis
added].
Smith: Yes sir. We think—
Pastore: That is the obstacle as far as you are concerned?
Smith: Yes sir. It could destroy the industry or at least some community systems.[34]

At this point in the hearing it must have appeared that the seven-
year legislative stalemate was ending. Senator McGee, one of the
western group not in particular sympathy with cable, seemed
impressed by the reasonable attitude of the NCTA representative.
He commented, possibly with more candor than discretion,

McGee: I have been quite impressed with the retreats made in the
testimony today, on both sides.
Pastore: Would you amend the word "retreat" to "willingness to
compromise"?
McGee: Yes. [To E. Stratford Smith]: You are willing to subject
yourself to responsible regulation, to give up your free decision
making, which is just as serious as the protests of the broadcasters. I think that gives us a ground of understanding that will
enable us to draw up a fair law. I want to commend you on this
not "yielding of ground" but this effort of cooperation.[35]

But the chairman's skill in welding an agreement during the heat
generated by a hearing was no measure of its ability to withstand
the lengthy cooling-off period between the drafting and enacting of
compromise legislation. Only a month later the NCTA issued a
"clarification" of its position, reiterating its objection not only to
retransmission consent but to mandatory local carriage as well,
while renewing its demand for preemption of state and local regulation, for grandfathering of existing systems, and for licenses not
subject to periodic renewal.[36] Although these specifications were
received by the Senate committee on 19 August 1959, the group
apparently decided to rely instead upon the more expansive agree-

ments Chairman Pastore had gained from NCTA counsel Smith as it completed work on its own bill, S. 2653.

The committee bill seemed to steer a carefully charted course between the demands of the western broadcasters and the concerns of the NCTA. The proposed regulations, covering less than two printed pages, provided for the licensing of all but the smallest cable systems and the grandfathering of existing CATV operations if the owners applied for commission licenses within 120 days after the bill's enactment.

Although S. 2653 contained no language expressly preempting state or local jurisdiction, placing the provision under title 3, the broadcast section of the Communications Act, might well have been construed by the courts as achieving that result. At the same time the bill specifically exempted CATV from one requirement of title 3, the retransmission-consent provision of section 325(a): "It should be noted, however, that this section would not apply section 325(a) . . . to community antenna systems which would require such systems to obtain the consent of the originating television stations before the community antenna systems could redistribute the originating station's signals."[37]

In the nature of political compromises, however, these grants of grandfathering, probable preemption of state and local control, and exclusion from retransmission consent could only be won at the expense of other losses. All systems were to be subject to periodic renewal and, to some undefined extent, also subject to FCC control upon petition from a competing television station.

The statute restricted the right to petition for a hearing to challenge a CATV application for construction or expansion of service solely to a broadcaster who was the "licensee of a television station assigned to a community in which . . . it is providing the only available broadcast program service." If "community" were synonymous with "municipality," this problem would involve no more than sixty cable systems. However, the implication of the committee report accompanying the bill was that "community" could mean "market" and thus could encompass nearly all CATV operations: "Your committee is keenly aware that a television station serves an area outside the principal community in which it is located and . . . Commission policy requires a television station to consider the needs of its entire service area."[38]

This ambiguity, perfectly understandable, both from the stand-point of granting some range for administrative discretion and from the standpoint of achieving a compromise expression including without deciding all disputed points, raised serious doubts in the minds of some members of the cable industry about the sincerity of the committee and its proposal. These doubts would continue to grow during the eight months between the drafting of S. 2653 and final debate on the floor of the Senate.

The First Federal Failure

In October and December of 1959, Chairman Pastore and mem-bers of his subcommittee toured the western states of Montana, Idaho, Utah, Colorado, and Wyoming, seeking the viewpoint of its citizens concerning the provisions of the bill. One witness, Ray Horner, owner of a small, 250-subscriber cable system in Soda Springs, Idaho, typified the plight of concerned operators unable to decipher its language.

Horner: In other words, the community is strictly up to the FCC, the definition of "community" is strictly up to the FCC?
Pastore: That is right. The FCC has the final judgment on that. If they don't have, they don't regulate . . .
Horner: If we knew where we stood, then we would know what to say. I don't know, for instance, whether it applies to me . . .
Pastore: I think in a small way it does. I don't want to delude you about that. If there is a clear picture coming into your area from a local broadcasting station, and they feel you infringed upon their service, they have a right to petition. It doesn't mean because they petition they are going to succeed, but they have a right to try.[39]

Mr. Horner may have been uttering the thoughts of other bewil-dered owners of small systems when he concluded by saying, "You can see our point, I believe . . . inasmuch as even by reading the bill we can't tell what the final outcome is going to be. . . . So we are on the fence. We don't know whether to support the bill or not support the bill."

Few other questioners seemed as interested or open-minded as Mr. Horner. Most used the opportunity simply to present their per-sonal grievances against a particular cable or broadcast facility, apparently either unaware or unconcerned about the broader purpose of these unusual Senate investigative proceedings. Senator Pastore's disappointment at this response was evident in his closing remarks at one hearing: "I leave this as a recommendation, not an admonition. . . . The people interested in both sides of this problem should read the legislation carefully. Every time I interrogate anyone they say, 'I have only read it in a cursory manner.' Study it thoroughly. If there is anything wrong with the bill . . . if you feel there is an economic disadvantage that will lead to extinction, an extinction no one proposes . . . then you should come to Congress and we will study these suggestions."[40]

Instead of turning to Congress, the cable industry returned to the FCC in hopes of negotiating some private settlement with the western broadcasters. On 16 November 1959, Chairman Doerfer received a letter from A. J. Malin, president of the NCTA, proposing that an ad hoc committee of station and cable owners consider, under FCC guidance, possible solution of basic broadcaster complaints against CATV. Efforts of the NCTA to reinvolve the commission might have resulted from the agency's vigorous defense of the value of auxiliary services in comments filed on S. 1886: "In many cases television stations in the smaller communities, although they are able to provide a local TV outlet, have not been in a position to furnish programming comparable with that made available . . . by repeaters and CATV's. For this reason the question of where the public interest lies in any given community as between a station . . . serving as a local outlet and another . . . service capable of providing a wider range of program choice should not be determined by sole reference to the advantages of service through a local . . . television station."[41]

On a more mundane level, of course, just as the unusually strong FCC argument may simply have been an excuse for avoiding economic mediation, so the NCTA request may only have been a device to halt congressional deliberations. Whatever the underlying motivations, Chairman Doerfer ultimately rejected the NCTA request. Congress was now grappling with this complex issue, and he was understandably reluctant to move the FCC back into the fray.

After it became apparent that the FCC would not act as an intermediary between cable and broadcast representatives in the negotiation of a private agreement, the NCTA made its position on

S. 2653 clear. Bill Daniels, a director and past president of the group, was acting as its spokesman as he declared in one of the final western Senate hearings, "If competition will destroy the small town stations, to what degree short of outright federal subsidies should these stations be protected? . . . We submit . . . that it is not necessary or practical for your committee or Congress to resolve these issues. *Is a bill necessary to resolve the alleged controversy between coexisting stations and community antenna systems? I submit that the bill is not necessary.* The real problem exists . . . in only a few communities. . . . We do not minimize the seriousness of the problem. . . . We merely say that the differences . . . are not so vast in scope as to require the regulatory power of the FCC" (emphasis added).[42]

From this point on, then, only one issue remained with respect to S. 2653: Which faction could line up the larger number of votes before the impending consideration of the bill by the Senate?

When S. 2653 came to the floor of the Senate on 17 May 1960, a flurry of last-minute amendments had clarified words such as "facilitate" and "signal" in the bill, but differences now went far beyond phraseology. Supporters simply hoped to push the bill through the Senate, while opponents sought to refer it back to the Commerce Committee and almost certain oblivion. Senator Pastore began by addressing a gallery apparently packed with CATV representatives: "I am saying that unless something is done promptly, many of the interested people in the galleries today will be surprised. These people have barraged the Senate with telegrams. They have been coming into town in large numbers . . . they have been saying the bill is aimed at the little fellow."[43]

Senator McGee interrupted to ask that the record indicate that, "we are not only being watched, we are being surrounded and I think that fact ought to be brought to the attention of this body."[44]

Pastore regained the floor from his colleague to continue his challenge to the gallery: "How many people who now say they oppose the bill and are here appeared before the committee? I daresay, not many. But now, at the 11th hour, when the bill has come up for action, we are subjected to a blitz in the form of telegrams and personal appearances in an attempt to make the Senate believe that the bill will destroy—yes, destroy—the business. That is not true."[45]

Perhaps because of the emotional tension present, Senator Pastore made no real effort to urge the merits of his bill upon the group or upon the Senate itself. Instead, he spoke on a more personal level, observing that he had no reason to favor either faction, since his own state of Rhode Island had only two television stations and no cable systems. After a bitter exchange between Senators Kerr and Pastore, during which the Oklahoma senator chided the chairman for being unable to draft a bill protecting cable as well as broadcast interests, the session adjourned, only to reopen the following morning at the same level of discussion. Senator Monroney, the chief CATV spokesman, attempted to explain the cable industry's opposition to S. 2653 by declaring, "I think it is very important to realize that these men represent a very small industry, portions of which are operating in widely divergent areas. They felt they were being led astray by following the advice of some Washington lawyer who does not think regulation and licensing every 3 years is such a very bad idea."[46]

This "Washington lawyer," E. Stratford Smith, former executive secretary of NCTA and its general counsel, had drafted S. 2303, the bill Monroney had introduced before the Communications Subcommittee less than a year before. But times had changed, positions had shifted, and in a few minutes the reason for the tension on the Senate floor would become apparent. On a roll-call vote S. 2653 was defeated by the narrowest of margins, 38 to 37, and returned to committee where it eventually died.

Senators voting to recommit and thus kill the bill were:
Aiken, Bridges, Bush, Byrd (Va.), Byrd (W. Va.), Carlson, Clark, Cooper, Cotton, Dirksen, Dworshak, Eastland, Ellender, Fong, Gore, Hickenlooper, Hill, Holland, Javits, Kerr, Long, Lusk, McClellan, Martin, Monroney, Morton, Mundt, Muskie, Prouty, Robertson, Russell, Saltonstall, Scott, Smith, Sparkman, Stennis, and Wiley

Senators voting against recommitment, and thus supporting the bill were:
Allott, Bartlett, Beall, Bible, Butler, Cannon, Carroll, Case (N.J.), Case (S.D.), Chavez, Church, Curtis, Dodd, Douglas, Engle, Goldwater, Gruening, Hart, Hartley, Hayden, Hruska, Humphrey, Jackson, Kuechel, Lausche, Long, Magnuson, Mansfield, McGee, Moss, Murray, Pastore, Proxmire, Schoeppel, Thurmond, Williams, Young (N.D.), and Young (Ohio).

Four senators on the Commerce Committee voted to kill the

bill: Cotton, Monroney, Morton, and Scott; two failed to vote: Yarbourgh and Smathers; and eleven voted to support it: Bartlett, Butler, Case, Engle, Hartke, Lausche, Magnuson, McGee, Pastore, Schoeppel, and Thurmond. To some extent, at least, regional interests seemed more influential than regulatory philosophy. Thus Senators Goldwater, Hruska, and Curtis, among others usually antagonistic toward a increasing administrative power, voted for FCC control of cable, while Senators Javits, Muskie, and Gore, usually considered more sympathetic toward government controls, voted against the bill. But whatever motivated the seventy-five senators who voted and the twenty-one senators, including two from the Commerce Committee, who did not vote, the result was conclusive.

In 1961, at the suggestion of Commissioner Ford, the FCC again sponsored a CATV regulatory bill. It did not provide for licensing of cable but simply authorized the FCC to intervene in cases where economic hardship arose from station and system operation in the same community.[47] No action was taken on this proposal by either the Senate or House Commerce Committees during that session of Congress, and the legislation was not reintroduced during the following session. In fact, no further legislation involving cable television would be introduced in Congress until 1965.

The most obvious question which arises from the Senate vote recommiting S. 2653 is how the NCTA was able to muster sufficient political support to defeat the far more powerful National Association of Broadcasters. The answer seems to be that the NAB did not lose, nor did the NCTA win. At no time did the broadcast association actively campaign for comprehensive regulation of cable television. As *Broadcasting*, the industry's trade organ, observed in an editorial of 16 March 1959, the NAB was not in any sense a unified body, but simply a "federation" of narrow-interest groups.[48] The divergence in economic outlook of major stations and community operators, which constantly widened during the four decades intervening between the Radio Act and the cable challenge, left western broadcasters with little influence in the association at a time when united action was essential. Marginal small-market stations were, after all, the creation of political rather than industry forces; and major-market stations, unmolested by cable, might well have favored the CATV's short-circuiting the uneconomical community station and thus ending this drain upon industry profits.

By the same token, the defeat of S. 2653 was not a victory for the leadership of NCTA. The cable association's board of directors, by unanimous vote in 1958, had declared a willingness to support federal regulation of CATV.[49] Its motive was simple: by centralizing all authority at the federal level, cable operators could avoid the vexing maze of state and local regulatory provisions that was expanding with each passing year. The concept was visionary, but it was a vision not shared by the majority of the association's 300 members or by the almost equal number of nonmember cable operators. The cable owners, who were acting as directors of the group primarily because of their extensive holdings, were attempting to project nationwide objectives for an industry basically local in nature. Most owners, having reached a degree of accommodation with governmental bodies in their own localities or states, had no interest at this point in looking to Washington for control. Thus, their initial level of tolerance for federal supervision was extremely low, and when the Pastore committee pushed beyond that limit, they rebelled. NCTA leaders, claiming tenuous support at best, then had no choice but to follow its membership.

In essence, then, the two groups initially advocating federal intervention could not move their own organizations to support their positions, in both cases because they represented only small, if vocal, portions of their industries. Western senators were a similar minority in the Senate. However powerful they might be on a particular committee, they could not sway their colleagues without the support of at least one of the two nationally based trade groups. Lacking such support, they failed to effect passage of the cable bill, not so much because of opposition as because of simple absence of interest among senators whose constitutents had not advocated any particular stand on it. Thus the rejection of S. 2653 seems to have been neither a victory nor a defeat; it was more the collapse of a compromise no sizable group cared enough to preserve.

Implications of the Lack of a CATV Policy

The first concerted effort to establish federal regulation of cable television had failed, a victim of apathy caused by the limited nature of its challenge. Once again the extent of the threat had not justified the magnitude of the effort necessary to control it. An accurate projection of CATV growth patterns during the next decade might have galvanized NAB support behind western broadcasters; a long-range policy promising eventual parity between CATV and broadcast operators might have strengthened the position of NCTA leaders. Denied either projection or policy, Congress could only respond to broadcaster complaints by attempting to alleviate a symptom of cable growth, although they were still ignorant of its cause.

Senator Pastore and his subcommittee displayed consummate skill in the art of political maneuvering as they strove to forge a legislative solution to complex economic and technological questions. Yet to have entrusted congressional engineering with the creation of such delicate regulatory machinery seems about as wise as employing a blacksmith to design a computer. No legislative committee possesses either the specialized knowledge or the time necessary to design procedures maintaining a proper competitive balance between two industries, especially in a field where the ultimate objective is, not simply preservation of the industries, but maximum satisfaction of the public need for communication.

This legislative problem was compounded by the unwillingness of either trade organization to advance or even support a particular technique of federal control. Thus the committee could only use the tactic of continual compromise to induce rival factions to form a coalition backing its bill, a move which, while lessening opposition, did not create enthusiasm for its passage. Even more significantly, from the standpoint of effective legislation, Congress, trapped in the role of mediator between two partisan groups, had no means of determining the equity of either position, much less of measuring each one's separate or their joint potential to serve the public interest.

The essential element missing from this political equation was the objective and comprehensive guidance only an administrative agency could provide. The commission had had at least seven years' time in which to accomplish what Senator Pastore's group was forced to attempt after two weeks of hearings, and yet the agency was unable to furnish the committee with constructive legislative requests establishing integrated electronic media goals, or even accurate research which might form the foundation for such legislation. If all parties had been advised, for instance, of the probable consequences of continued unregulated cable growth, controls might successfully have been imposed at this stage without the extensive and prolonged repression of its delivery functions later necessary to contain its threat.

All the regulatory procedures which would eventually be employed in the regulation of cable television were considered during this era. With the disintegration of the compromise settlement in 1960, these proposals were discarded as Congress abandoned this apparently insignificant regional squabble to face more pressing problems. The federal government had been the center of action for broadcast-cable controversies between 1958 and 1960, but the center did not hold, and the failure of the federal attempt would be followed by a feudal era of private law suits and political battles before various state legislatures.

Another cycle of abrogation and repression had begun. The FCC, after standing aloof from a political process it might have guided, would now remain a passive bystander as cable expanded; it would wait to act until deliberation was no longer possible. Then those cable operators who had celebrated a "victory" with the rejection of the Pastore bill in 1960 may have seen in retrospect that the vote actually represented a rather serious defeat.

6

The Feudal Era: Indirect Rule and Private Conflicts, 1961—64

The history of cable television unfolded in medieval fashion from 1961 through 1964, with the gradual transformation of its systems obscured by clashes ranging across a broad terrain of issues. State and local governmental bodies were attempting to assert jurisdiction over CATV, while broadcasters were attacking its functions in various courts. As in the Middle Ages, these widespread conflicts were the result of the collapse of central authority; also as in that earlier period, the diverse nature of these skirmishes meant that no pattern emerged until the era had ended.

Thus the commission remained unaware of the evolving nature of the CATV challenge until systems began launching concerted campaigns to enter major markets late in 1964. Unprepared for this onslaught, the FCC could only react to its threat by clamping an embargo upon cable operations in metropolitan areas until policy could be applied after the fact.

The Second Transformation of Cable

The television broadcast industry had reached the outer edges of communities large enough to support television stations by 1959, and thereafter growth was measured primarily in terms of expanding advertising revenues rather than in terms of increased spectrum coverages. While fewer than 50 new commercial stations were joining the 521 in operation in 1959, CATV systems almost doubled in the period between 1961 and 1965 alone (see table 5). Yet cable industry earnings even at the end of this era equaled less than 5 percent of television industry revenues, divided among more than twice as many operators. As in the past, CATV owners had little flexibility in choosing locations for their systems; their opportuni-

115   *The Feudal Era*

Table 5   Television Stations and Markets-Cable Systems, 1961–65

Year (1 January)	TV Stations	TV Markets	CATV Systems[a]
1961	527	273	700
1962	541	274	800
1963	557	276	1,000
1964	564	273	1,200
1965	569	274	1,325

SOURCE: *Television Factbook*, service vol. 39, no. 2 (Washington, D.C.: Television Digest, 1970), p. 58a (TV Stations and Markets), p. 79a (CATV Systems). NOTE: For a complete table of comparative growth figures, see Appendix A. a. Estimated.

ties were determined almost exclusively by the number of communities of at least moderate size lacking full television network coverage. An FCC-sponsored survey of 377 cable franchises granted between January 1960 and August 1964 revealed that 91 percent of these systems would be operating in communities located at least forty miles from any three-station market, and 77 percent more than forty miles distant from even a single two-station market.[1] In actuality, then, CATV seemed to be expanding outside the borders of major broadcast activity, claiming little more than 2 percent of the total television audience.

The number of television homes swelled from 44 to almost 53 million between 1959 and 1965 (see table 6). A substantial share of

Table 6   Television-Cable Audiences and Revenues, 1961–65 (In Millions)

Year (1 January)	TV Homes	CATV Homes[a]	TV Revenues	CATV Revenues[a]
1961	47.2	0.7	$1,429	$35
1962	48.8	0.8	$1,612	$51
1963	50.3	0.9	$1,739	$71
1964	51.6	1.0	$1,958	$100
1965	52.7	1.2	$2,143	$125

SOURCES: *Television Factbook*, service vol. 39, no. 2, p. 72a (TV Homes), p. 79a (CATV Homes), p. 70a (TV Revenues [gross time sales]); CATV Revenues from Albert R. Kroeger, "CATV Revisited," *Television*, September 1962. a. Estimated.

this increase occurred in sparsely settled, less prosperous regions of the nation finally approaching levels of saturation previously achieved in urban areas. Thus, while the proportion of television homes in Northeastern states rose only from 89 to 94 percent during this era, it surged from 55 to 85 percent in East South Central states, from 60 to 85 percent in Mountain states, and from 60 to almost 90 percent in the West South Central region.[2] This expansion in less urbanized television households, coupled with a minimal increase in television broadcast outlets, resulted at the end of this period in the inability of approximately 16 million American families, or more than one-fourth of the population, to receive all three major networks' signals off-the-air.[3]

But such underserved regions could offer only limited opportunities for cable diffusion, since homes in many of these areas were too widely dispersed to support the costs of a linking CATV system. In general, then, this swelling of potential audiences in less densely settled sections of the country simply enhanced the ability of scattered marginal communities within these areas to provide sufficient subscribers to make cable service feasible. Once the bulk of these localities had been claimed—and the relatively uniform nationwide figure of 90 percent saturation of television homes in 1965 indicated that few additional communities would emerge in this fashion—the cable industry was faced by a second barrier. Again, as in 1955, CATV would have to evolve if it were not to stagnate.

The typical industry in such a position might have considered consolidating its ownership, thus reducing overhead and increasing its profits and power. Because CATV systems had been established with no overall design, as a response to the needs of various scattered communities, ownership patterns were diffuse, and the scale of most operations was extremely small. In 1964, for example, the average cable system served only 850 subscribers and earned annual revenues of less than $100,000.[4] While each operator was only a small businessman, a single corporate entity purchasing fifty such systems would have had an audience base larger than a substantial number of small-market television stations, with a far higher rate of return on investment.

No clear movement toward consolidation was apparent before 1965, however, in part as a result of past evolutionary patterns within the industry and, perhaps more significantly, because of the limited economic value of such concentration of control. Historically, cable had not emerged from a parent industry, and thus it began without influence from preexisting monopolistic or cross-media ownership structures. Thus, no segment of the industry launched its operations with a predominant advantage in capital or management which would facilitate its eventual takeover of its less favored rivals.

This initial individualism and independence was reinforced by economic factors which offered little incentive for multiple-system ownership. Expanding the number of subscribers by combining systems would not result in an appreciable increase in profits, because, as an FCC-commissioned survey reported in 1965, "CATV systems of any size can achieve approximately the same rate of profit; there is neither an optimum size nor an established economic limit to the size of a CATV system."[5] This was true because costs were basically a function of only one fixed factor, the cost per mile of cable construction; and profits the product of one variable, the number of subscribers per cable mile. As a result, a small, 500-subscriber system with 50 subscribers per mile would be far more valuable than a 5,000-subscriber system with only 10 per mile. Combining the two would not change the profit ratio of either. Although consolidation might have allowed a reduction in management personnel, this expense generally accounted for less than 20 percent of a system's overhead.[6] In addition, since all governmental negotiations were conducted on the state or the municipal level, a centralized legal or administrative staff, no matter how skilled, was seldom as effective as hometown officials sensitive to local concerns.

Finally, there was no advantage in connecting the audiences of commonly owned systems, since CATV was only a program-delivery, not a program-production, facility. Because of this, cable, serving individual subscribers rather than national advertisers, had no reason to pool subscribers to reduce the cost per exposure of production expenses.

These factors, then, discouraged group ownership to the extent that, as late as 1964, less than 25 percent of all systems were operated by entities owning more than three systems.[7] But while there was little economic incentive to combine systems operationally, there was great incentive to purchase them individually. Cable systems, because of their monthly subscriber payments, had an unusually large amount of revenue continuously available in relation to capital invested.[8] This favorable "cash flow" characteristic began to interest large investment concerns, which began purchasing systems in 1964, not to expand their operations, but simply to acquire ready funds with which to finance other business activities.

The magnitude of this movement was reflected in a trade journal report in September 1964: "Chase Manhattan Bank . . . has some $20 million backing such large CATV entities as TelePrompter, TV Communications Corp., Telesystems Corp. . . . Morgan Guaranty, New York, is working with J. Kent Cooke to the tune of some $9 million including $4.6 million Cooke spent for a group of systems. . . . First insurance company in the field is Mutual of New York, which has loaned Reeves $1 million, promised $3 million more."[9]

These massive corporations were the first cable owners capable of taking full advantage of the relationship between population density and CATV profit. Urban areas clearly offered the largest number of potential subscribers per mile of cable laid, but penetration of these major markets required a system offering prospective cable viewers a choice of channels sufficiently broad to justify a service charge. The equipment for twelve-channel CATV systems developed during the early 1960s allowed urban operators to augment the three network signals most audiences of top-100 markets already received with UHF channels from other areas, carrying motion pictures and other syndicated programs otherwise not available.

This movement was still in the potential stage as the era ended. Franchise applications were being filed in most major-market areas, but few had yet been granted. However, the shift in emphasis in cable growth was already apparent. As "canyon systems" had once marked a terminal phase of development, so CATV operations in smaller communities would now in time recede to a similar position, with their revenues simply providing a financial base for the more promising major-market systems. Thus cable owners, unable to increase profits by consolidating systems, turned instead to technology which transformed their individual operations into major-market competitors capable of reaching the 90 percent of the nation's television homes previously beyond their reach.

This ambitious new role, however, also brought the cable industry into conflict with a much more powerful coalition of opponents than it had faced previously: powerful broadcasters, group owners, program syndicators, networks, and others concerned with controlling the flow of television programming into urban markets. In addition, the importation of signals also seemed to threaten the audience base of the urban market's own independent UHF stations, endangering a class of broadcasters strongly supported by the FCC. In essence, then, if cable appeared to be coming of age in 1964, it was also emerging from the obscurity which had protected it in the past from the full force of the broadcast industry's challenge.

FCC Indirect Control of Microwave: Carter Mountain and Beyond

In January 1962 the NCTA's board of directors appointed a special committee to work with the commission in an attempt to formulate legislation for the regulation of cable television. After a series of conferences, the participants drew up a bill authorizing the FCC to require cable systems to carry all local television programming and to refrain from duplicating that programming from other sources. Two years later, as the proposed legislation was being presented to the commissioners for consideration, the NAB intervened, asking for the opportunity to participate in the proceedings and to submit its own recommendations. The FCC granted this request and suggested that the two associations cooperate in drafting legislation acceptable to both and report back to the agency.

For a time it semed that such a compromise solution might be possible. By December 1964 members of the NCTA legislative committee and a subcommittee of the NAB's Future of Television committee had agreed upon a statement of basic provisions to be embodied in legislation, and simultaneous meetings of the parent organizations were scheduled to approve the language of the proposed bill. The terms would have resulted in only a slight expansion in the powers the commission could have asserted under the statute previously submitted by the NCTA. Cable systems would have been required to "distribute to subscribers . . . all signals of stations assigned to . . . the same community in which the CATV is located . . . all stations within whose predicted grade A contour the

CATV is located . . . all stations within whose predicted B contour the CATV is located," and CATV operators would have been allowed one year in which to comply with these mandates. At the same time, cable systems would have been denied the right to "duplicate the programming of any colocated station . . . and the Commission [may] after hearings on a case by case basis provide additional protection to the station as the Commission may find to be . . . in the public interest."[10]

Other sections would have prohibited program origination by cable systems, but allowed systems with fewer than six channels in operation on the date of enactment to be grandfathered with respect to those channels. These provisions seemed in accord with the initial specifications drawn up by the NAB Television Board, which directed the Future of Television group to seek legislation "giving the FCC powers to regulate cable companies through the imposition of bans on duplication and origination and by establishing technical standards."[11]

Yet, as *Broadcasting* reported on 21 December 1964, "The Future of Television in America Committee of the NAB last week rejected a report by its subcommittee that would have put before the FCC a joint NAB-NCTA compromise proposal on moderate regulation for CATV. . . . Certain influential members of the FTVA felt that the proposal neglected at least one important point, "leapfrogging"—the importation of signals from distant markets. . . . An influential broadcaster-CATV operator who was not present at the Washington meeting said . . . the 'leapfrogging' issue was a 'subterfuge' meant to delay any compromise agreement."[12]

The charge may have had some validity: rejection of the pact was apparently a foregone conclusion prior to the meeting. Only four members of the seven-man board were present for the crucial vote: William Grove, organizer of the *Frontier* cable challenge almost a decade before; Clair McCollough, whose Steinman stations were fighting CATV penetration of its Pennsylvania markets; Willard Walbridge, whose opposition to cable was on record as early as 1962; and the chairman, Dwight Martin. The absence of at least two members whose organizations had significant CATV interests—John T. Murphy of Crosley and G. Richard Shafto of the Broadcasting Company of the South—seemed an indication that the chairman had already made his intentions known.

The NAB might have overridden the action of its committee had the commission declared its support for the proposed legislation. Instead, the FCC by 1964 seemed as little interested in a moderate solution as the most vehement of cable opponents. Soon after the rejection *Broadcasting* reported, "Some Commissioners say they are not particularly disturbed by the impasse that has been reached in the efforts to reach agreement on a bill. They point out that the Commission can continue to condition microwave grants on the CATV's agreement to protect local TV stations."[13]

In fact, a gradual hardening of the commission's attitude toward CATV, as evidenced by the continual expansion of cable microwave controls, encouraged broadcasters to avoid private compromise in hopes of obtaining more stringent restrictions through FCC action. Between 1962 and 1964, the former commission chairman John Doerfer and two other commissioners of similar philosophy, John S. Cross and T. A. M. Craven, were replaced by three administrative activists—the chairman Newton Minow; the commissioner and later chairman E. William Henry; and Kenneth Cox, author of the report urging broad cable restrictions in 1958. As Commissioner Lee Loevinger observed, "In 1962, the Commission experienced a change of view [toward CATV] which was induced not by any new investigations or . . . review of facts, but simply by a change in personnel."[14]

This new viewpoint first became apparent during deliberations in the *Carter Mountain* case.[15] In June 1959 the Common Carrier Bureau of the FCC had denied a request by Carter Mountain, a microwave common carrier, to expand service to a CATV system in the Riverton, Wyoming, area until the commission could determine whether the increased service would seriously threaten the continued operation of Riverton television station KWRB-TV, owned by senate witness Mildred Ernst. In May 1961, the FCC's hearing examiner Walter Guenther set aside the television station's objection as irrelevant, declaring that "whatever impact the operations of the CATV may have . . . are matters of no significance to the ultimate determination made that a grant to . . . Carter, a bona fide communications common carrier, will serve the public interest."[16]

On 16 February 1962, the commissioners reversed the hearing examiner. They stated that the television station's complaint did raise a legitimate and relevant issue of economic impact, and, further, that "when the impact of economic injury is such as to adversely affect the public interest . . . it is our duty to determine the ultimate effect . . . and act in a manner most advantageous to the public."[17]

The FCC decision simply declared, without attempting to prove, that expanded microwave service to the Riverton cable operator would damage the local television station. Having made this determination, the commission then claimed the power to restrict a common carrier in order to avoid this result. Carter Mountain appealed only the second contention; it challenged the authority of the FCC to look beyond a legitimate function of common carriers to judge its long-range effects. A federal circuit court of appeals sustained the commission on this single point: "In determining whether the authorization requested by the appellant would be in the public interest the Commission was entitled—if indeed it was not obliged—to consider the use to which the facilities and frequencies requested were to be put, and to weigh that use as against other legally relevant factors, including the effect on existing local stations."[18]

Thus the court in *Carter Mountain* did not consider either the accuracy of the commission's determination that adverse economic consequences would result from expanded cable services in a television station's market, or the FCC's authority to regulate CATV systems directly. The decision simply affirmed the commission's power to employ controls over common carriers to protect broadcast interests.

The commission greeted this federal decision of December 1963 with renewed activity in its rulemaking proceedings concerning CATV microwaves. As early as 1959 the Common Carrier Bureau had begun challenging the status of common carriers serving primarily as CATV relays. Unless a facility could show that more than half of its total business arose from non-CATV functions, it faced reassignment to the newly created Business Radio Service frequencies.[19] Forcing a shift from 6,000 MHz to 12,700 MHz meant, not only a reduction in propagation, but a far more serious problem of delay because of the lack of equipment available for the new wave bands.

Since most cable microwaves were located in thinly populated areas of the West with few potential customers, satisfaction of the test of 50 percent non-CATV usage was almost impossible. The FCC maintained in promulgating its rules that no private industry should have the privilege of using a public common carrier channel. Western cable carriers argued in response that demands for such frequencies in their region were so limited that the public was deprived of nothing by this usage. The merits of this contention were never determined, because the commission, by classifying the rules as procedural rather than substantive policy making, avoided the statutory requirement of hearings to determine the need for regulation prior to enactment.

By December 1962 cable microwave applications for Business Radio Service frequencies had become more numerous, both because equipment was now available and because lengthy delays in processing were discouraging further common carrier requests. At this point the FCC imposed a freeze upon further Business Radio Service authorizations for CATV relays except for those whose subscriber cable systems bound themselves, by written agreement, to carry all local television signals without duplication from other markets.[20]

After the *Carter Mountain* decision the commission expanded this requirement to include Common Carrier Bureau as well as Business Radio Service licensees.[21] Six months later it instituted rulemaking proceedings to compel yet another frequency change for cable microwaves, which would force them into a narrow Community Antenna Relay Station (CARS) band providing only a separation of 12.5 MHz between users. Carriers who "requested" assignment to the new, less favorable frequencies were granted the right to continue using their presently assigned bands until 1 February 1971, while those who refused to make such a request were to be reassigned to the CARS band immediately after the expirations of their existing three-year licenses.[22]

Approximately 260 of the 1,325 cable systems operating at the end of this era were supplementing spectrum signals with microwave-relayed programming. The constantly proliferating rulemaking proceedings caused delays which hampered the operation of all microwave-served facilities, including those willing to cooperate with the commission. By 1965 the FCC had a backlog of 80 microwave applications, including 25 which had been pending for at least three years. Another 108 applications had been processed only because operators were able to avoid hearings by voluntarily filing agreements restricting the carriage rights of cable systems subscribing to their service.[23]

The commission's indirect control of cable television through manipulation of its microwave carriers does not appear to have emerged from any positive, goal-oriented policy, but rather from attempts to solve particular problems in the most expeditious fashion. Thus, as a result of again sacrificing vision for expediency, the FCC would soon face challenges it had not had the perspective to anticipate.

The State as a Regulatory Ally

Various FCC reports on cable activities during this era expressed the hope that the states would eventually take a more active role in supervising the functions of their local CATV operators. Yet the commission failed to furnish a comprehensive policy these state bodies might augment, or to provide a regulatory domain they could administer without fear of preemption.

Several states had already made attempts to determine the legal status of their own community antenna systems before the FCC issued its first ruling on cable television in 1956. Most of these attempts simply involved efforts by state agencies to claim jurisdiction over cable operations on the basis of existing statutes governing public utilities or common carriers. In 1951 the Wisconsin Public Service Commission became the first governmental agency to issue a CATV decision; it refused to exercise jurisdiction over a community antenna because it held that federal authority in the field of television was supreme.[24]

Other states refused to assert control on narrower grounds, as precedent began to build for the position that the laws governing public utilities or carriers were not broad enough in scope to include CATV functions.[25]

This viewpoint received strong support from a California Supreme Court decision in October 1956.[26] The court, in voiding efforts by the California Public Utilities Commission to compel CATV operators to abide by telephone common carrier rules, declared that differences between two-way telephone communication and one-way cable programming were so basic that no authority could be claimed over CATV simply because the agency regulated telephone carriers.

Two years later a federal district court ended the cable regulatory activities of the Wyoming Public Service Commission, the only state body still supervising CATV functions. The court maintained that federal jurisdiction in the field of television preempted state sovereignty.[27] This finding did not seem to be based as much upon clear constitutional mandate as upon judicial hesitancy to allow fragmentation of authority in an area where the federal government had not yet indicated its future plans for apportionment of controls. There appears little question that the FCC could have requested that Congress expressly delegate to the states power to deal with purely local matters such as subscriber rates and minimum service standards. Thus the responsibility for the failure of state agencies to assume an active role in CATV supervision during the 1950s appears to have rested far more with the commission than with the states themselves.

State regulatory bodies were understandably reluctant to apply existing public utility controls to cable systems, because these regulations were much too cumbersome for this type of operation. If, for example, the Wisconsin Public Service Commission had asserted jurisdiction over cable as a public utility, each small-town community antenna operator would have been subjected to the same vast maze of procedures designed to protect the public from giant corporations holding monopolies over the distribution of necessities.[28] Therefore the cable owner, along with all major telephone and power companies, would have been compelled to comply with more than eighty paragraphs of administrative requirements, which would have necessitated a staff of attorneys and accountants far beyond the means of any local businessman. In effect, then, asserting jurisdiction would simply have been a method of ending all CATV operations in the state.

Yet state legislatures were almost equally reluctant to begin the demanding task of drafting statutes specifically controlling CATV systems without some assurance that the FCC would not eventually assert complete and preemptive authority over these systems. Pennsylvania had considered this type of legislation as early as 1954, and by 1957, West Virginia, Arizona, and Washington had debated similar measures, but Montana was the only state whose legislature was able to pass a regulatory bill.[29] This statute was vetoed by the governor, however, on the advice of his attorney general, who believed federal authority in the television field to be supreme.

After defeats in Wyoming and Montana, state forces favoring CATV controls remained relatively dormant from 1958 through 1960, awaiting the results of deliberations at the federal level. Once the possibility of immediate federal preemption had ended with the defeat of the Senate CATV bill in May 1960, bills were introduced in Maryland, Mississippi, New Hampshire, Oregon, and Vermont; followed by bills in Arkansas, California, and Utah in 1963.[30] Yet despite this flurry of activity, no state actually assumed direct control over cable television on the basis of a specific CATV code until the Connecticut Assembly granted its Public Utilities Commission the power to award all cable franchises late in 1963.[31]

Connecticut seemed uniquely suited for this regulatory role, both because of its traditional centralization of power in state rather than in local bodies and because of a peculiar dispute over a CATV telephone carrier which persuaded the cable industry to actively support state intervention. The Southern New England Bell Telephone Company, the major telephone common carrier in Connecticut, had consistently refused to allow cable systems to lease its poles for system construction, insisting instead that systems use wires strung by the telephone company at a far higher yearly charge. As a result of the carrier's policy, only two of the forty-two franchises granted by Connecticut communities prior to assumption of control by the state agency were actually in operation, and both of these systems had been forced to install their own poles.[32]

However, cable forces were soon convinced that they had made a tactical error. The state agency refused to grant any franchise until it had had the opportunity to hold hearings to set uniform rate and service standards for the state's 169 towns.[33] Twenty-five entities filed for franchises to serve 70 of these 169 towns. The filing procedure required each to furnish expert testimony to establish the technical and financial feasibility for its system on a town-by-town basis, to submit detailed construction schedules and cost projections, and to provide an outline of expected revenues and expenses for a ten-year period. While this was customary Public Utility Commission practice, these CATV applicants were not the usual clientele industries, but rather generally undercapitalized ventures whose financial backing would be eroded by extensive and leisurely paced hearings. It took the state agency two years to complete its procedures. It collected nearly twenty thousand pages of testimony and exhibits during more than ninety public hearings, and it was not until March 1967 that it was finally able to begin granting certificates to successful applicants.

At least in part because of the Connecticut experience the NCTA became increasingly active in its opposition to the establishment of similar cable controls in other states. This attitude persisted despite the fact that the need for impartial arbitration of disagreements between CATV and telephone carriers over system leasing and pole rental increased greatly after 1964.[34] Unfortunately, few cable leaders were aware of the factors which tended to make this case unique: a particularly intransigent and influential opponent of telephone carriers, limited initial cable interest because of relatively good television broadcast coverage in more densely populated areas of the state, and a regulator without any previous regulatory precedents to guide it in its deliberations. However, whatever the justification. "Connecticut" became the rallying cry for those opposing a state role in cable supervision. It was an emotional appeal, bolstered by the philosophical argument that divergent state regulatory requirements would "balkanize" control of a nationwide industry.

Localities and Franchises: A Jumble of Patterns

Devoid of supervision at either the federal or the state level, the only functioning cable controls during this era continued to emerge from individual negotiations between CATV franchise applicants and municipal bodies. Prior to 1960 most communities were either so eager to obtain broader television service or so unsophisticated in the mechanics of franchise granting that arrangements with cable operators tended to be extremely informal. However, when municipal government associations began circulating information about revenues that would be collected for the privilege of using city easements necessary for cable installation, procedures became not only more formal, but more costly for the cable operator. By 1964 it had become customary in all but the smallest communities for a franchise to be granted only for a specified period of time and in return for an annual payment to the city based upon a percentage of the system's subscriber revenues, with other benefits specified either in the franchise ordinance or in the bid submitted by the applicant.[35]

State regulation could have introduced some degree of uniformity into the process, either through the adoption of a single franchise ordinance to be used by every municipal body within each state or through the exercise of the franchise power at the state level. Although cable leaders expressed concern that "balkanization" might occur if other states followed the Connecticut example, the failure of any other state to act during this era meant that hundreds of franchises were being granted that could not easily be revoked, with requirements varying, not only from state to state, but from county to county, or even from township to township.

By 1965 the more than thirteen hundred separate community contracts in existence had created a crazy-quilt pattern of rules which had to be evaluated as a part of every cable sale, and which made unified operation of several systems impossible. While community regulation had posed few obstacles for individual, locally owned and managed systems, it represented a serious problem for corporate owners and dealers entering the industry during this period.[36]

In addition, both growing sophistication among community negotiators and increased competition among CATV groups were continually increasing the price of franchise grants. Early in 1965, as cable operators sought franchises in more than sixty cities with populations in excess of one hundred thousand, model ordinances were being circulated which specified a minimum yearly franchise fee of 5 percent of gross revenues, as well as free educational, governmental, and informational services.

There seems little doubt that rising franchise costs and fear of state intervention unified the more influential members of the CATV industry behind efforts to obtain preemptive federal regulation of cable activities during negotiations with the commission between 1962 and 1965. The FCC, however, displayed little enthusiasm for such NCTA proposals prior to 1965, for while cable leaders saw FCC intervention as the answer to their difficulties with state and local officials, the commission viewed television litigation then pending against CATV systems as a more promising solution

to the entire cable controversy. It was only after the U.S. Supreme
Court late in 1964 finally ended any hope of immediate cable control through judicial enforcement of broadcaster program rights
that the FCC moved to assert jurisdiction over certain CATV functions.

Broadcaster Lawsuits: The Attempts at Private Controls

The commission had consistently supported the principle that television stations should dictate the terms under which cable systems
might carry their programming. This technique of control was
extremely appealing to the commission because it protected broadcasters from economic injury while relieving the agency of any
administrative responsibility for its operation.

The FCC had advocated this approach in its initial legislative
proposal to Congress in 1959, which suggested that the provisions
of section 325(a) concerning retransmission consent be broadened
to include cable as well as broadcast transmissions.[37] When Senator Pastore indicated his unwillingness to grant one industry such
sweeping power over another without proper safeguards, the FCC
revealed a stronger commitment to the proposal's self-administering
feature than to its overall merit. Although Senator Pastore declared
he could not support the commission's bill unless the agency would
supervise the negotiation of these consent agreements, the commission, claiming there was no need for concern, refused to accept this
responsibility: "In the Commission's judgment, there would not
appear to be sound grounds for anticipating that the exercise of
business judgments . . . would be likely to result in excessive burdens being thrust upon the . . . CATV systems as a result of the
station's requirement that the CATV system obtain permission."[38]

Within two years it seemed quite possible that the commission's
faith in the integrity and the business judgment of broadcasters
might be tested, for legal actions had been commenced which, if
successful, would have established the legal authority of television
stations to control their programming in the manner challenged by
the Pastore committee. If broadcast litigants were found to have
the power to restrict usage of their television signals, cable would
truly have become an auxiliary delivery system, with its functions,
profits, and even continued existence dependent upon television

industry decisions. In that event the regulatory design envisioned as ideal by the FCC in 1959 would have become a reality simply through judicial decree.

The two cases crucial to the broadcasters' cause during this era, *Intermountain Broadcasting v. Idaho Microwave* and *Cable Vision vs. KUTV*,[39] advanced three distinct but interrelated legal theories to justify the denial of cable access to television stations' programming: "exclusive contract," "nonexclusive contract," and"unfair competion." Any one of these contentions, if sustained by the courts, would have supported immediate injunctions by television station to bar further unauthorized CATV use of their transmissions.

On the other hand, in seeking judicial clarification of their rights in programming, the television stations were risking decisions which might end any possibility of restraining CATV carriage at the local level. If all three contentions were rejected by the courts, the threat of litigation would no longer inhibit cable operators, for all parties would realize that the only enforceable rights were those of the copyright owner, since the national networks or program syndicators were generally unwilling to become involved in the controversies of the smaller markets.

Both cases emerged from a single dispute, a clash which began in 1959 when Cable Vision, a Twin Falls, Idaho, CATV system, and its microwave common carrier, Intermountain, charged several television stations, including three Salt Lake City broadcasters, with conspiring to destroy the cable television industry through actions in violation of federal antitrust laws. The charges involved the activities of the Hometown Free Television Association, the western broadcasters' political action group, which disbanded during the pendency of the lawsuit. Cable Vision alleged that this group, through its member stations, encouraged the construction of illegal boosters, circulated false and damaging information about CATV, and entered into agreements with advertisers and networks specifically designed to injure cable operators.[40]

Rather than simply await the court's decision, the three defendant Salt Lake City stations took the offensive the following year, asking the Idaho Federal District Court to consider Cable Vision's intended unauthorized use of their television signals as a part of the antitrust proceedings then before it. The petitioners, KUTV, KSL-

TV, and KCPX-TV, local affiliates of NBC, CBS, and ABC, respectively, were somewhat premature in their request for an injunction to bar Intermountain from relaying their network programming to the Idaho CATV, because the FCC had not yet approved the common carrier's application to provide this service. However, Judge William T. Sweigert, after studying the pleadings, agreed to issue a summary judgment, or interim decision based solely on the legal issues involved, because the questions raised were so obviously in need of immediate resolution.

The television stations urged two arguments in support of their demand for injunctive relief. The narrower contention involved contractual rights, while the broader, more universally applicable claim was based upon the theory of unjust enrichment. In this specific case the broadcasters alleged that Cable Vision's proposed importation of their signals would lessen the value of this programming for KLIX-TV, a Twin Falls, Idaho, station which paid each Salt Lake City affiliate for the privilege of rebroadcasting its transmissions in Idaho. Even without such contractual rights, however, the broadcasters contended more generally that no industry should be allowed to appropriate and profit from the property of another, especially if such use and benefit were without its consent.

The decision on the motion for summary judgment in the *Intermountain* controversy was handed down on 27 June 1961, nearly six months after the matter had been argued in open court. During this period the case attracted widespread attention, with other stations preparing to commence actions if the initial opinion were favorable. Judge Sweigert's opinion instead dealt a painful blow to broadcaster hopes. It rejected both theories of control by declaring that stations had no authority to restrict use of their signals after transmission, and, even if they had such right, cable carriage would not be an unfair use of these transmissions. The decision opposed the idea that television stations should attempt to profit from the sale of rights in their signals and pointed out that their broadcast licenses required that transmissions be disseminated to the public freely and without limitation: ". . . stations are in the business of selling their broadcast time and facilities to sponsors to whom they look for profit. They do not and cannot charge the public for their broadcasts which are beamed directly, indiscriminately and without charge through the air to any and all reception sets of the public as may be equipped to receive them. . . . The function of selling rebroadcast rights is not only subordinate to, but inconsistent with the primary purpose of a television station."[41]

Since broadcasters transmitted signals to sell broadcast time, while cable systems carried programming to sell television reception, they "operated in different ways for different purposes."[42] Thus Judge Sweigert distinguished this case from the Associated Press case of 1918 in which the Supreme Court had found the International News Service to be engaging in unfair competition by intercepting Associated Press dispatches and distributing them to subscribers as its own material.[43] The broadcasters maintained that the Associated Press case was controlling, but Judge Sweigert's opinion observed that, while "Associated Press and International News Service were identical businesses engaged in the keenest competition," CATV and television stations served differing societal functions, and cable might well enhance the profitability of a station by "extending the reception of its programs."[44] Because of this lack of direct economic conflict between the two industries, the court refused to extend the doctrine of unfair competition to include unauthorized cable carriage of broadcaster signals. In essence, this was simply an amplification of the court's first conclusion, for if stations should not profit from the sale of rights to their signals, they also should not be able to bar another industry from profiting through broader dissemination of those signals.

While the opinion struck down the assertions of both exclusive and nonexclusive contractual rights, and of unfair competition, on the part of the transmitting station, it did contain a rather broad hint of rights which might be protected against cable infringement. In this case KLIX-TV, the Twin Falls television station, had asserted no claim in its own behalf. Judge Sweigert observed that, although the Salt Lake City stations had no power to prevent the relay of their signals to a distant market, a station located in that market with a contract of network affiliation granting it exclusive rights to program distribution might well challenge the importing cable system's attempt to disseminate those signals in that market.

The *Cable Vision* case thus arose directly from a question of station rights in programming which *Intermountain* could not answer, since KLIX-TV petitioned the court for an injunction to halt the cable system's carriage of network signals that the Twin Falls

broadcaster claimed exclusive right to distribute by virtue of its network contract. In July 1962, some thirteen months after suggesting
this approach, Judge Sweigert found the KLIX-TV standard contract for "first call" affiliation to be sufficiently restrictive, under
Idaho law, to allow the station to prohibit Cable Vision's distribution of the affiliate's network programming in the Twin Falls
market.

The cable system entered an immediate appeal from this lower
court's action, but it is important to note that, for almost two years
during this era, this single federal decision in point held that a network affiliate, and thus, by implication, a station holding an exclusive film or other syndication agreement as well, could prevent
local cable carriage of any programming encompassed within the
terms of its contracts.

This exclusive distribution concept was severely challenged in
July 1964, however, when the Ninth Circuit Court of Appeals
reversed the decision of the lower court, and the last remaining
hope for local station control of programming ended when the
Supreme Court refused certiorari to review the circuit court's decision several months later.[45]

The broadcasters were unfortunate in that the appeal was
decided just after the Supreme Court had declared in the *Sears
Roebuck* and *Compco* cases that federal patent law, and thus by
analogy federal copyright law, was designed to encourage free and
full disclosure and use of ideas; and that no state laws should be
allowed, by protecting these ideas without federal filing, to thwart
this policy.[46] In the *Cable Vision* case this meant that the broadcasters could protect their programming from unauthorized use
only if they were able "to demonstrate a protectable interest by
virtue of the copyright laws or bring themselves within the contem-
plation of some other recognized exception to the policy promoting
free access to all matter in the public domain."[47]

Forcing broadcasters to abandon all means of protecting programming except bringing actions against copyright infringement
was part of a larger objective to guarantee the public the broadest
possible use of creative materials. Federal copyright laws were
based upon a system of reciprocal rights: a monopolistic grant of
usage to the creator in return for public domain status for his concept at the expiration of the copyright period. State laws or judicial

decisions which allowed restraints to be placed upon use without testing copyright title hampered the functioning of this system, and therefore they could not be affirmed.

After July 1964, then, the local stations were compelled to turn to the copyright owners for protection of their programming exclusivity, and, as a law review article of the period pointed out, "since the persons who . . . benefit from copyright protection are those who are threatened least by CATV operations—the networks, authors, producers . . . who own most TV programming—the establishment of a property right in TV programming would be of great aid to small local stations only if . . . the networks used their advantage to drive CATV systems out of business."[48]

Unfortunately for the local television stations, a substantial number of broadcasting groups, including two of the three major networks, were far more interested in obtaining cable franchises than in driving CATV systems out of business. As early as 1965, 13 percent of all cable systems were owned by broadcasters, with others such as Newhouse, Meredith-Avco, and Capital Broadcasting accounting for more than fifty of the franchise applications then being processed.[49]

Instead of presenting a united front against cable penetration, the broadcast industry and its trade organization, the NAB, splintered into various factions that often displayed more bitterness toward each other than toward their CATV rivals. The small-market stations joined one coalition, the major-market operators opposing only the latest cable trend formed another, while a third group crossed over to become owners of the systems their industry challenged.

The divisions among the broadcasters were first apparent during the NAB-NCTA negotiations over cable legislation in 1964, and they became wider as cable pressure increased during the following era. In these circumstances the local television station, denied the power to restrain CATV competition through the courts, could only turn to the FCC for aid. Larger stations, now sensing cable pressure for the first time, joined their demand but specified a different set of remedies tailored to their own needs. Broadcast-cable complexes and cable owners fearing local, telephone, or broadcaster control added other dissonant voices to the chorus imploring some type of federal intervention. There seemed only one point of unanimity in these variant demands: that the problem was assuming the dimensions of a crisis.

Implications of FCC Reliance upon Private Actions

The commission remained relatively aloof from the broadcast-CATV strife during this era, relying upon private negotiations, state action, or litigation to provide some sensible resolution of differences between the two competing industries. In effect, the FCC had gambled that a solution could be achieved without federal guidance, and it had lost.

It is true that Congress had enacted no legislation granting the commission jurisdiction over cable television, but it is equally true that the agency had requested no additional powers after 1961 and was willing to act in 1965 without express statutory authority. The FCC did study several aspects of cable operation in this period; it opened dockets to consider the effects of CATV duplication and nonlocal carriage operations, as well as the implications of joint broadcaster-cable ownership and the proper classification of cable microwave relay services. The problem was not in the information-gathering process, but in analysis, for the commission admitted in 1965 that it still did not possess the ability to abstract from the data any clear measurement of the existing economic impact of cable competition, much less an accurate projection of its future economic effects.

"Economic impact" was obviously a term which could measure only the threat of cable television, not its promise. The FCC had once again omitted the preliminary prerequisites of legal definition and broad economic analysis, ignoring possibly new implications in terms such as "public interest" or "local service" which, through technological advances, might have influenced the traditional viewpoint that the local station was the most effective facility for delivering broadcast news and entertainment. Instead, the commission's deliberations began with the presumption that broadcasters should be protected at all costs. Its objective was simply to discover the degree of peril posed by CATV.

Because the FCC sought only to contain cable television, not to integrate it into a broader communications service, the agency did not object to widespread efforts to restrain CATV growth, from local franchising demands to litigation in the highest federal courts. However, in delegating, or, more accurately, abrogating, its own responsibility for supervising the integration of this more effective delivery technique into the existing electronic media system, the commission had also lost the ability to coordinate overall cable regulatory policy during a time when such coordination seemed most essential.

Such a judgment can certainly be made much more easily in retrospect, when seemingly unrelated events have coalesced into a clearly discernible pattern. No one could properly insist that the FCC should have known that cable, once freed of the threat of broadcast litigation, would so easily find the capital necessary for major-market construction. However, it does seem proper to question the commission's reliance upon microwave rules to restrain cable without attempting to understand it. The agency was left without any options when state controls failed to materialize, and industry negotiations collapsed as this period ended. Since the FCC had not used these four years to enhance its capacity to guide cable growth, it could only act now to retard its expansion.

7 The Federal Era and Major-Market Restrictions, 1965−69

The FCC, when deciding the *Carter Mountain* case in 1962, had simply declared that the expansion of cable television service would cause economic injury to a competing television station.[1] The accuracy of its finding was not immediately challenged in the courts, but it seemed essential that the agency be able to produce more than a vague presumption of broadcaster damage if it intended to use this cable threat as justification for asserting direct control over CATV systems. Neither Congress nor the courts would be likely to support an increase in regulatory authority based primarily upon speculation.

The Search for Economic Impact

The task of establishing the need for cable restrictions through evidence linking station losses to CATV operations appeared to be beyond the limited research capacity of the FCC. For this reason the commission asked the industries involved to collect information and suggest possible techniques for analyzing the data submitted.

In June 1964 the NAB retained Franklin Fisher, a noted economist, to design such an analytical system. Rather than attempt to isolate the specific effects of CATV competition in each broadcast market, Dr. Fisher simply used averages drawn from a cross section of markets and projected economic injury by estimating the monetary value of television homes lost to broadcasters either because their signals were not carried by the local cable system or because they were forced to compete with other programming imported into the market. After fixing the value of each home at $27 per year, a figure reflecting the per household share of annual prime-time station revenues, Dr. Fisher found:

137

1. For every 1,000 TV homes formerly able to view only the local station that subscribe to a CATV not carrying the local station, the station's annual revenue is on the average reduced by $14,000.

2. Where TV homes formerly received a local station and another station, for every 1,000 who subscribe to a CATV not carrying the local station, the station's average loss in revenue is $8,000.

3. Where only a single local station could be viewed previously, and CATV carries the local station with average duplication of the local station's programming, the revenue loss is $9,400 per 1,000 customers.

4. In a formerly two-station market (local and another), where a CATV carries the local outlet with average duplication the annual revenue loss per 1,000 subscribers is $2,900.[2]

What makes these figures, if accurate, so compelling is that the average net earnings of the 172 stations located in one- and two-station markets did not exceed $24,000 annually during this period. Their accuracy was soon challenged, however, by the NCTA's economist, Herbert Arkin, and the commission's own appointee, Martin Seiden. Arkin's challenge went basically to the design of the system, questioning a technique which attributed virtually all loss of broadcaster audience to CATV competition while almost ignoring the effect of competing broadcast signals or other factors which might reduce the size of the actual audience. Seiden's argument, more practical and immediate, was that "advertisers do not buy audience but rather markets. The degree of price rationality on the part of advertisers implied in Fisher's approach is therefore limited. Stations have not been affected by adverse advertiser decisions attributable to CATV penetration if only because the advertisers do not know the facts about CATV penetration."[3]

Expanding upon this point, Seiden illustrated the inaccuracy of a "revenue per television home" measurement to determine the effect of CATV on a station's network or national spot advertising payments:

> *Network advertising.* . . . The advertiser's principal expense is the program whose cost averages $125,000 per hour. A substantial network line up costs . . . $90,000. It would be poor econ-

omy for a network advertiser to prefer a selected group of stations . . . to save on station costs. . . . Thus, even if CATV did reduce the viewing audience of some markets . . . the advertiser would not reject them for it would be to his disadvantage.

Spot advertising. . . . The spot advertiser does not buy audiences, he buys markets. His selection of markets is based on the location of his marketing facilities and his competition, not . . . on the lowest cost-per-thousand of audience. . . . Thus in that component of broadcast revenue . . . it is found that the selection is based upon criteria other than audience per se.[4]

Even at the local level, where advertisers might be assumed to be most aware of the effects of cable operation upon broadcast audiences, the Seiden study found no positive correlation between declining local advertising revenues and CATV competition. Of the eighty-six television stations reporting decreases in such payments between 1961 and 1963, seventy-one had no cable systems within their primary service areas and sixty-one, or almost three-fourths of the broadcasters, had no cable subscribers anywhere within their coverage contours. The same type of results was reported in cases involving stations with declining network or national spot revenues: "In the case of spot revenue, 60 of the 87 stations had no known CATV subscribers in their A contours. . . . Among the 102 stations with declining network revenue, 70 had no known CATV subscribers in their A contour."

In summarizing this portion of the FCC-funded report, Dr. Seiden observed, "On balance, the fewer than 14 stations which can be said to have pronounced CATV penetration are too small a proportion of the group of stations with declining revenues to permit acceptance of CATV penetration as a principal causal factor."[5]

The NCTA challenged the Fisher analysis on even more pragmatic grounds, simply illustrating that the dire consequences predicted for television stations as a result of cable competition had not occurred. In 1958, the association noted, the "Cox" report had declared that "the broadcasters who appeared before the committee have presented a *prima facie* case as to the [damages] likely to flow from . . . invasion of their primary markets." Yet, some six years later, 18 of the 19 television stations listed by the Senate committee as being threatened by CATV competition were still operating, and at least 10 of these broadcasters had increased their advertising rates substantially since that earlier period. In addition, only 3 of the more than 130 stations which had closed down between 1952 and 1964 specified cable television competition as a factor contributing to the decision to cease operations, and no station had made this claim since 1960.[6]

All these studies, however, were necessarily founded upon existing empirical data and thus only described the economic effects of the traditional, smaller community cable system. As the year 1965 began, the commission no longer watched these minor skirmishes as carefully; its concern, instead, was the impending cable invasion of urban markets. Lacking the capacity to project the damage CATV penetration might cause these crucial distribution points, or the particular injury it might inflict upon newly established UHF stations in these markets, the FCC eventually felt impelled to act without clear evidence of economic impact, declaring that, although analysis "did not furnish the tools" necessary to measure damages, "unless we were convinced that the impact of CATV competition upon broadcast service would be negligible, we would favor some restrictions as a partial equalization of the conditions under which CATV and the broadcast service compete. . . . It would be clearly contrary to public interest to defer action until a serious loss of existing and potential service has already occurred."[7]

Even if the commission had been able to produce substantial evidence of adverse economic impact due to CATV operation, however, its justification for imposing cable restrictions might still have been subject to question. The *Carroll* case, the FCC's primary authority for the position that broadcast service could be protected from damage caused by competition, had also stated that "private economic injury is by no means always, or even usually reflected in public detriment. Competitors may severely injure themselves to the great benefit of the public."[8]

According to *Carroll*, economic factors were significant only to the extent that they threatened to impair the overall quantity or quality of broadcast programming available to various audiences. As a law review commentator of the period observed, the commission appeared to have misapplied this doctrine, for the sole premise explaining cable restriction was "the one the FCC gave without examining its validity: that every regular television station must be protected from any economic harm due to CATV. . . . The Commission had chosen to forestall a negligible harm, rather than to use the development of CATV as an entity to modify the harsh limitations upon program choice that adherence to the ideal of local television has produced."[9]

Thus, by focusing attention on just one narrow aspect of cable television, its competitive element, the commission not only blurred important distinctions between "public interest" and "broadcaster interests" when applying its restrictions but also obscured any vision of CATV as an integral part of a larger system of electronic mass media. If the FCC had chosen to supervise cable rather than simply to restrain it, jurisdiction might have been exercised without isolating the elusive variable of CATV impact in each broadcast market. As the Supreme Court would soon point out in the *Southwestern Cable* case, the agency's power to control cable systems was not uniquely dependent upon the CATV threat, but could as properly be based upon the FCC's general authority to encourage, through broadcast and cable functions, the widest possible range of services in spectrum and wire communications.[10]

Whatever the abstract wisdom of the commission's approach, however, the ultimate result of its three-year quest for proof of economic impact would be an action dictated by political pressures rather than by deliberate, impartial policy. In 1965, as in 1959, failure of analysis left the agency without the foreknowledge, and therefore without the capacity, to shape the evolution of the process it regulated.

The First FCC Report and Congressional Reaction

For three years the FCC had been able to avoid full-scale congressional hearings on cable television by assuring both houses that solutions to broadcaster-CATV controversies would be forthcoming, through either industry negotiations or private litigation. With the breakdown in both procedures early in 1965, Congress became restive; *Broadcasting* reported, "Pressure on the FCC to develop policy for regulating community antenna television increased last week. . . . The added pressure was applied by Senator John O. Pastore, chairman of the Senate Communications Subcommittee, who extracted from Chairman E. William Henry an estimate of 'one month' as the time limit within which the Commission will reach fundamental decisions on policy."[11]

Although Senator Pastore had expressed his willingness after this hearing, held late in February 1965, to allow the FCC to issue its own cable rules, his House counterpart, the Commerce Committee chairman Oren Harris, insisted instead that the commission only furnish proposals for legislation to be enacted by Congress. With one house demanding action and the other asking for suggestions, the agency had no way of avoiding conflict; and, more significantly, it was given no congressional guidance in attempting to follow either course of action.

If Congress was reticent in suggesting solutions, however, members of the industry were not. As *Broadcasting* described it, "Ideas for regulating community antenna television systems are sprouting like mushrooms after a spring rain. No fewer than four trade associations and one network have expressed themselves on the subject. . . . Out of the potpourri of ideas and opinions, laced with what the FCC and Congress consider to be the public interest, will come the policy eventually under which the rapidly growing CATV industry will be regulated."[12] This proliferation of proposals reflected the continual splintering of broadcast groups, as dissident factions began filing individual arguments before the commission. Thus, after the Association for Maximum Service Television (AMST), a group dominated by VHF major-market stations, had opposed NAB efforts to unify support behind compromise cable legislation, a substantial number of AMST members broke away from that group to oppose its attempt to rally broadcaster support for restrictive cable controls.

The American Broadcasting Company stood apart from the other two major networks in demanding a ban on unauthorized use of its programming, while various group owners, including Capital Cities, Taft, and Westinghouse, filed their own separate proposals. The most stringent CATV curbs, however, were not advanced by a broadcast organization but by the Television Accessory Manufacturers' Institute (TAME), an association of forty-one suppliers of television antennas and other reception devices. Broadcasters advocated specific rules to protect their own particular interests—restricting program duplication, making local carriage mandatory, prohibiting "leapfrogging," or requiring retransmission consent—but TAME, uniquely challenged by all cable expansion, sought, not to limit this growth, but to end it.

The commission was thus faced with the prospect of selecting a proper regulatory solution to the cable problem, not only lacking a definitive analysis of cable's impact, but even a consensus of broadcaster opinion as to its most damaging functions. This variance in opinion was reflected within the agency itself, as staff members supported a wide variety of approaches, ranging from nonintervention without clear congressional mandate to immediate restriction along the lines of the TAME proposals. There was even disagreement concerning the location of the most crucial CATV challenges. Seiden, for instance, discounted cable as a factor restricting independent UHF station growth in major markets: "The real problem limiting UHF entry into three-station markets and troubling independent broadcasters in general is not CATV but the difficulty of obtaining good programming at reasonable costs. . . . Given a sufficiently large audience base as is found in most three-station markets, there is probably ample room for a CATV system as well as a new UHF broadcaster."[13]

The FCC's staff had prepared a limited set of rules in March 1965 that simply brought all microwave-served cable systems within the terms of carriage restrictions already being imposed on a case-by-case basis. But *Broadcasting* observed that, with Commissioner Loevinger indicating his support for Seiden's arguments and Commissioner Bartley questioning the right of the agency to act without congressional support, "there is no certainty the package will be voted out this week. The principal parts were tentatively approved by a 4 to 2 vote. . . . But it's possible the Commission could deadlock 3 to 3, with the result that a final vote would have to await . . . James J. Wadsworth, who is expected to join the Commission later this month. . . . The line-up on the CATV package now appears to be Chairman E. William Henry and Commissioners Kenneth A. Cox and Robert E. Lee in favor, and Commissioners Robert T. Bartley and Lee Loevinger opposed. The position of Commissioner Rosel H. Hyde, who was in the majority on the preliminary vote, is now considered doubtful."[14]

By 19 April 1965, however, Commissioner Hyde had resolved his doubts and had voted with Robert E. Lee—an active UHF supporter—Chairman Henry, and Commissioner Cox to enact the "First Report and Order" and issue an accompanying "Notice of Inquiry and Notice of Proposed Rulemaking."[15] These two documents, over 120 pages in length, seem best described by Commissioner Loevinger's comment in dissenting in part to the FCC action: "These reports . . . set forth such a mass of detail that the outlines of the problem, as well as the basic issues, are somewhat obscured, if not wholly submerged."[16]

The "First Report and Order" contained only two general regulatory provisions, applicable to all CATV-linked common carriers, whether local or interstate in operation. Every license granted to such a cable relay would thereafter be conditioned upon agreement from each of its subscriber cable owners to carry, upon request, the signal of every television station within approximately sixty miles of his system, and to refrain from carrying, during the period fifteen days prior or subsequent to local broadcast, any programming duplicating that which was being transmitted by any such station.

The rule of mandatory local carriage caused little debate, but the thirty-day nonduplication period, nearly as extensive as that originally demanded by the NAB, brought bitter protests from the cable industry. The NCTA maintained that this type of program protection would injure the very systems the commission claimed to support, the community operators who were augmenting television coverages in isolated areas: "Of the 314 CATV's which would be required to protect one or more stations affiliated with more than one network—196—or 21 percent of the CATV industry . . . are so located that they can receive only network affiliate stations—no independents, no educational stations. These systems . . . would be reduced to . . . making available to their subscribers only two channels at any given time."[17]

In actuality, however, the specific terms of the order were far less significant than the general regulatory attitude they reflected. The controversial thirty-day nonduplication period, for example, was reduced to only one day by the "Second Report and Order" of March 1966, before any carrier had been compelled to restrict program delivery to smaller CATV operators. Yet, both the tone of this decree and the tone of the following decree indicated that the relaxing of the restriction was due, not to any new appreciation of cable services, but simply to the realization that the agency, through lack of knowledge, had initially selected the wrong target. Thereafter, all rules would be aimed at the one class of cable operation most feared by broadcasters, the major-market systems.

Ironically, then, while most debate centered on the nonduplication period contained in the order, the more crucial pronouncements which would govern the course of cable regulation for the remainder of the decade were not in this document, but in the "Notice of Inquiry and Notice of Proposed Rulemaking" which accompanied it. It was in part 1 of this notice that the FCC asserted for the first time its belief that the unfair element of cable competition gave the agency jurisdiction over all CATV systems, and that the only issue to be resolved by further hearings was the need to assert that authority. Part 2 had even greater immediate impact. It imposed with a single paragraph a freeze upon major-market cable expansion which would extend beyond the end of the decade: "Pending the outcome of this proceeding, applications for microwave facilities to . . . relay the signal of any television station to a CATV system in a community with four or more commercial channel assignments . . . must be accompanied by a clear and full showing that in the particular case a grant would not pose a substantial threat to the development of independent UHF service in the area."[18]

Although Senator Pastore expressed his satisfaction with these commission actions, proposals, and interim restraints, the House Commerce Committee chairman Harris was angered by the agency's refusal to consult with his group before enacting regulation. Less than a week after the FCC had issued the report and notice, Harris introduced his own CATV control bill, convened his committee, and summoned the commissioners before him to explain their conduct. Until Congress resolved the matter of commission authority, the validity of the FCC cable rules would remain in doubt.

The bill which Chairman Harris introduced, H.R. 7715, was a direct legislative criticism of existing FCC cable policy. His amendment to the Communications Act of 1934 would have added program diversity as an additional goal to be achieved by commission regulation and would have compelled the commission to follow the regular rather than the "emergency" provisions of the Administrative Procedure Act when enacting cable rules. The regular provisions required the FCC to wait ninety days after issuance before its rules could take effect: "No rule relating to community antenna television shall take effect prior to the expiration of ninety calendar days following the date on which such rule is promulgated. . . . Any interim practice or procedure relating to community antenna television systems which is being followed . . . on the date of enactment of this part . . . after such date shall be void and have no force and effect if . . . it was adopted by the Commission pending promulgation of a rule or rules relating to such systems." This last section would thus have rescinded the major-market importation freeze, at least until ninety days after the commission had completed its inquiry and issued permanent major-market rules. Chairman Henry responded to this challenge by indicating that, "if Congress said we could have no such interim procedure, and . . . the Commission could not find that the grant would serve the public interest, we could not grant it. We would simply have to have . . . a full-scale evidentiary hearing, which just might take longer than the interim policy."[19]

In answering the more basic question of regulatory priorities, Henry indicated that broadcasters had to be protected from serious cable damage because CATV systems had structural weaknesses which prevented them from serving the public interest as well as a local television station: "The Commission, following congressional guidelines, has evolved a basic policy in the specific area of CATV. That policy is to promote CATV as a supplementary service but not to place primary reliance upon it because of its several practical shortcomings, namely, no rural coverage, service only for a fee, and no outlet for local expression."[20]

Congressman Fred Rooney of Pennsylvania asked Chairman Henry whether, in view of the difficulty of financing construction of rural cable systems, the commission would propose and support Rural Electrification Act aid to enhance the possibilities of cable coverage in less densely populated regions of the nation. Henry admitted that the NCTA had already requested such help, but he stated that the FCC had not yet considered the matter and refused to pledge his own personal support for encouraging rural coverage through this technique. NCTA witnesses later pointed out that the absence of locally originated programming, or cablecasting, on CATV systems did not arise from any inherent technical limitations but simply reflected the reluctance of cable owners to develop production facilities until the FCC and the courts resolved the legal implications of such operations. The only justification for cable restraints not challenged during the hearings was the fact that cable subscribers paid a service charge, but as Representative Rooney forced Chairman Henry to admit, this portion of the total viewer investment in reception equipment was often the payment which made viewing possible, or limited service adequate.

The most serious challenge to the commission's cable policy, however, came not from any congressman or NCTA witness but rather from Commissioner Lee Loevinger, who had characterized the policy as "erecting only a gossamer barrier against the evils which it fears. . . . The Commission is doing the wrong things for the wrong reasons in the wrong manner to deal with the wrong problem."[21] The "wrong things," in Loevinger's view, were restrictions on cable program carriage; the "wrong reasons," broadcaster protection; the "wrong manner," the expansion of the agency's jurisdiction; and the "wrong problem," audience fragmentation by CATV (the real question before the commission was the present and future role cable television should play in mass communications to best serve the public interest). In elaborating upon these fundamental objections, Commissioner Loevinger observed, "What I regard as a basic error in the FCC approach is that it is negative and restrictive rather than positive and expansive. It assumes that limitations and restraints upon one mode of transmitting programs will necessarily benefit other modes. . . . I think the objective should be to encourage the expansion of service . . . and this is what Congress has told us to do. Congress hasn't said anything about putting little local stations in every hamlet and crossroads town. . . . The statute does not refer to the multiplicity of small town stations mentioned by Mr. Henry."[22]

Chairman Henry, in responding to this criticism a short time later, declared that local service should not be endangered simply to allow free play to economic or technological forces: "You can say that the thing should simply be allowed to grow like Topsy, . . .

and whichever competitor won out, that would be all right. But . . .
the majority of us are concerned with this concept of a local station,
because . . . the local station can serve as an outlet of expression."

The exchange between the two commissioners had begun to
delineate their divergent philosophies of broadcast regulation. Loevinger, like Chairman Doerfer before him, saw the commission
essentially as an overseer of a relatively independent industry, while
Chairman Henry visualized the FCC as an active participant in
industry affairs. Commissioner Loevinger answered this call for
continued protection of the local television station by commenting,
"Whether you like it or I like it . . . or the Commission likes it . . .
the trend in this country is towards urbanization. . . . The truth is
that in these small communities there are not the economic means to
maintain . . . strong and viable television stations. . . . It is not the
marginal stations that are rendering public service. . . . I think if we
follow what I regard as essentially a repressive policy . . . with
respect to CATV . . . we are going to set up a few little, local marginal stations that might otherwise not exist, but . . . we are going
to have a system which is dependent upon the favor of Government
for its continued existence."

In the final moments of this exchange, Loevinger challenged the
activist position of his colleagues, who construed the term "permit"
as "encourage," or even "require," the establishment of community
television stations in the agency's allocation plan: "I am perfectly
willing to allow the marketplace to decide after the Commission
has made its allocations. The difficulty is that the majority of the
Commission is not so satisfied. It says that we will make the allocations . . . but if the market does not use them, we will institute
measures to see that the market has got to use them one way or
another. We will do this by denying them every other outlet but the
one we favor."

While this debate underscored the irreconcilable approaches
which would produce both the majority and the minority opinions
in cable controversies during the next three years, the contentions
of Commissioner Loevinger which stimulated the most spirited congressional questioning and won the support of Commissioner Bartley dealt with the much more limited issue of FCC cable jurisdiction. As Loevinger pointed out, the FCC had declared after a full
inquiry in 1959 that it did not have authority to regulate CATV.
Yet, after Congress had twice rejected FCC requests to grant it

such power, the agency had now simply declared its right to control
CATV systems unless Congress acted to deprive it of jurisdiction.
Under pressure from the committee, neither Chairman Henry nor
the FCC general counsel Henry Geller could specify any single statutory section among the seven listed by the FCC which furnished
a clear mandate for cable authority, nor could either cite any new
precedent except *Carter Mountain* for reversing the commission's
1959 jurisdictional statement.

Yet, despite the apparent lack of legal reasoning to support the
FCC's shift in position, the agency proved itself more astute than
Chairman Harris in understanding the logic of politics. Harris had
advised the commission, "You mentioned Congress turning these
[cable] problems over to you in broad language and saying, do
anything you want to. Well, . . . I have found out that members of
Congress are simply not that liberal in a matter of this kind. . . .
Most of them like to provide some guidelines."[23] Although the
commission's rejection of Harris's offer to help in formulating cable
policy had caused a surge of outraged statements, especially from
his fellow members of the House Commerce Committee, this wave
soon subsided and the Harris bill eventually died in committee.
From the beginning there must have been some sense of futility
among committee members, for the House could not restrain FCC
cable activities without Senate support. A *Broadcasting* article
reported, "Both Warren G. Magnuson . . . and John O. Pastore . . .
are now on record as feeling that the FCC now has sufficient
authority to regulate all CATV. Senator Pastore said he is not after
headlines . . . and so will wait to see what the House is going to do
before he acts. . . . The key to CATV regulation, he said, is
'whether TV will be hurt.' "[24]

Using this regulatory standard, the only criticism Pastore's committee might have leveled at the commission was that it had not yet
gone far enough in its efforts to protect broadcasters from the cable
threat. That defect, however, would be remedied within a matter of
months.

The Second FCC Report and Congressional Reaction

The commission's "Second Report and Order" was issued in March
1966, less than eleven months after the agency had enacted its first
cable rules and requested industry response to the inquiry which

formed the basis for this set of regulations.[25] The response, which was overwhelming, involved separate filings by twenty-six different broadcast organizations, eight cable groups, and eight other associations, including the National Farmers' Union (NFO), the National Grange, and labor unions affiliated with the AFL-CIO. Most of these responses treated only one or two facets of the broad issues involved, but because of the mass of detailed studies and proposals advanced, a major portion of the report was devoted simply to outlining and discussing this material.

Part 1 of the report, dealing with the commission's right and obligation to assert jurisdiction over all cable systems, appeared to have been decided with little difficulty. By paragraph 8 the FCC was ready to declare, "We are convinced that the case for present jurisdiction is a strong one. Accordingly . . . we conclude that CATV systems are engaged in interstate communication by wire to which the provisions of the Communications Act are applicable. . . . We further conclude that our statutory powers . . . include authority to promulgate necessary and reasonable regulation . . . to prevent frustration of the regulatory scheme by CATV operations, whether or not microwave facilities are used."

After deciding that it possessed sufficient authority to impose direct restraints upon all cable systems without resorting to its microwave common carrier powers, the commission found an immediate need to enact such controls. Paragraphs 22–46 of the report analyzed the various industry studies forming the factual framework for the FCC decision that CATV operation did or soon would pose a substantial threat to continued television broadcast service unless subjected to certain regulatory restrictions. Although the commission's own Seiden report and research submitted by CBS minimizing the cable threat were cited in this summary, primary reliance was placed upon the findings of AMST, one of cable television's most adamant opponents.

Because AMST was basically an association of major television broadcasters, its proof went mainly to the issues involved in part 2 of the inquiry, cable restrictions in top-100 markets. The broadcast group maintained that the question was no longer whether CATV should be allowed to enter urban areas, but how its existing substantial penetration could be halted: "The cities and metropolitan areas with CATV systems operating, pending or applied for account for at least 85,000,000 people. At least 145 communities or standard metropolitan areas with UHF stations operating, authorized or applied for also have CATV activity." After quoting this statement from the AMST report, the commission added, "there is also widespread activity within our major cities. . . . Franchise applications have been filed in San Francisco, Seattle, Pittsburgh, Baltimore, Fresno, Columbus, Tucson, Birmingham, Providence and Sacramento. Two parties to this proceeding are applicants for CATV franchises in Philadelphia . . . CBS refers to applications for CATV in Albany, Syracuse and Galveston, Texas."[26]

However, although the FCC was willing to acknowledge the severity of the CATV challenge, it was not willing to assume the broad regulatory burden proposed to provide stations with full administrative protection. AMST, Midwest, and several other broadcast groups had asked that the FCC prohibit cable use of any broadcast signal carried beyond a station's predicted B contour, or area in which it could generally be received off-the-air. In addition, they proposed that the thirty-day nonduplication rule be continued, that local carriage rules be made more stringent, and that new requirements be imposed upon every cable operation, including a rule making it mandatory that the CATV owner install in each subscriber home a switch allowing the viewer to convert to spectrum reception whenever he wished.

Rather than become involved in this type of detailed supervision, and in order, as the commission expressed it, "to preserve, to the extent practicable, the valuable public contribution of CATV in providing wider access to nationwide programming and a wider selection of programs on any particular day,"[27] the nonduplication protection was reduced to a single day, with mandatory local carriage made applicable to all systems, whether microwave served or not: "Under the new rules, a CATV system will be required, upon request, and within the limits of its channel capacity, to carry without material degradation the signals of all local television stations within whose Grade B contours the CATV system is located. . . . A CATV system will be required, upon request, to avoid duplication of local television stations carried on the system the same day that such programs are broadcast by the local station."[28]

Westinghouse and ABC had proposed that additional restraints upon cable carriage be applied only in the top 100 markets, rather than universally, as AMST had urged. The commission adopted this suggestion, justifying this second layer of restrictions by asserting that a supplemental television service such as CATV should be limited to enhancing existing spectrum reception in markets with a full complement of network stations, rather than allowed to import other signals fragmenting the audience available for independent UHF stations. Thus the FCC denied any cable system the right to extend any television signal beyond its B contour and into a top-100 market, "except upon showing made in an evidentiary hearing that such operations would be consistent with the public interest and particularly the establishment and healthy maintenance of UHF television broadcast service."[29]

Any cable system operating within a top-100 market on 15 February 1966, the date of the original notice of intent to restrict services in such markets, was granted the right to continue existing coverages in communities already being served without effect from the new rules. The commission justified this "grandfather" clause by stating that it wished to avoid disrupting viewing patterns the public had come to rely upon. However, one effect of this provision was to create a privileged class of cable owners; established operators were allowed to prosper, while newer competitors were denied the right to challenge their preeminence in the industry.

These major-market restrictions were made even more severe by a single, almost incidental reference, "footnote 69," which would create a significant barrier limiting even the modest urban growth which appeared possible under the general regulations: "If two major markets each fall within one another's Grade B contour (e.g., Washington and Baltimore) this does not mean there is no question as to the carriage by a Baltimore CATV system of the signals of Washington for . . . in equalizing the quality of the more distant Washington signals, it might be . . . affecting the development of the Baltimore independent UHF station or stations. Such instances rarely arise and can . . . be dealt with by . . . Commission consideration . . . where a problem of this nature might arise."

Contrary to the FCC's assertion, this was not a rare situation, but in fact one which arose in 91 of the top 100 markets. Its effect was to force any cable system operating in any of the 153 cities located in these markets to limit carriage solely to local urban signals or to petition the commission for a waiver of its rule or, failing this, for a full evidentiary hearing. Few operators proceeded beyond the effort to obtain a waiver, for, in addition to the cost and extended duration of such procedures, there seemed little possibility of proving lack of injury to a station not yet in existence.

This hearing procedure was actually the crucial element in the technique of cable control created by the "Second Report and Order." Through an ingenious adaptation of administrative process, the commission was able to achieve both objectives which had eluded it since 1959. On the one hand the agency was able to avoid detailed day-to-day CATV supervision, while on the other it could halt the threat of cable growth without the necessity of relying upon the unpopular freeze device.

The entire regulatory design was founded upon a single mechanism—placing the primary burden in each class of action upon the party in opposition to the commission's overall administrative goal. Thus, in individual controversies concerning carriage or duplication, the FCC delegated the initial responsibility of enforcement to the local station, requiring that it prove it had given proper notice to the cable system, that it establish noncompliance by the system, and that it apply to the commission for a cease-and-desist order before the agency would agree to intervene in federal court on behalf of the complainant. The broadcasters in markets below the top 100 attempting to block CATV signal importation faced a similarly heavy burden, with the FCC under no obligation to convene a hearing except at its own discretion.

In the top 100 markets, however, the burden was reversed, with CATV operators unable to commence service or expand existing service without express commission approval, either by hearing or waiver of hearing. If there were any doubt concerning the intent of the FCC to restrain cable major-market growth in the manner described by Chairman Henry the previous year, this doubt seems to have been dispelled by an NCTA statement quoting figures available to the commissioners during their deliberations: "Under Commission rules, every new CATV system in areas . . . affecting 90 percent of its television homes and every extension of existing service into a new geographical area will require a full evidentiary hearing before the FCC. . . . *There are 406 operating CATV systems in the top 100 television markets; 119 systems under con-*

struction; 500 systems which have been awarded franchises; and approximately 1,200 applications pending. Under the Commission's new rules, every one of these situations must go through the complete hearing process, amounting to . . . 2,000 full evidentiary hearings" (emphasis added).[30]

Yet, even though the time lag in processing a microwave case load less than one-tenth this size had already reached two years, the NCTA observed that "the Commission has announced no staff plans to handle this additional workload. . . . In effect, therefore, the growth of CATV . . . is frozen, except through hearings the Commission is not presently staffed to handle."

No commissioner disputed these statistics presented during the congressional hearings which followed the issuance of the "Second Report and Order." However, the need for justification had lessened by the time the House Subcommittee on Communications convened its sessions on 22 March 1966. Oren Harris, the vigorous critic of the FCC's cable policy, had resigned his chairmanship of the House Commerce Committee to await appointment as a federal judge, and his replacement, Representative Harley Staggers, had already indicated his support for the commission's "Second Report and Order." He described it as a " 'praiseworthy effort' to balance the interests of broadcasters and CATV systems without curtailing programs available to CATV subscribers."[31]

This time congressional opposition was centered at a lower level, in the Communications Subcommittee of the House Commerce Committee, whose chairman, Walter Rogers, felt that the FCC had again bypassed Congress without justification: "In what amounted to a call to arms, Rep. Rogers (D. Tex.) . . . blasted the FCC for posting 'one of the most revolutionary orders in the history of bureaucracy.' Under the guise of rule-making, he asserted, 'the Commission is attempting to make broad policy decisions that should require Congressional legislation.' "[32]

Chairman Rogers introduced a bill which, in effect, would have divested the commission of any cable jurisdiction by adding a sentence to the anticensorship section 326 of the Communications Act of 1934 which read, "Nothing in this Act shall be understood or construed to give the Commission the power to control or regulate the reception of radio communications or signals transmitted by any radio station," but in view of the fate of Chairman Harris's more moderate proposal the previous year, the prospects for passage did not seem encouraging. Despite the fact that these hearings appeared to be only a ritual hazing before the commission was allowed to apply its cable restraints, both the FCC and the NCTA submitted broad legislative proposals for consideration by the committee.

The FCC bill, H.R. 13286, contained three basic provisions: an express affirmation of commission cable authority; a declaration that federal jurisdiction would not preempt state or local rules unless those rules were in direct conflict with federal powers; and a prohibition upon cablecasting, except when specifically approved by the FCC. In addition, the agency asked Congress for guidelines to delineate what programming, if any, might eventually be authorized for cable origination, and to consider, at the same time, "whether community antenna systems should be required to obtain the consent of the originating broadcast station before re-transmitting the station's signal over the system. It has been urged that such a requirement would obviate the need for much, if not all, of the Commission's present regulation in the field."

Chairman Henry, although supporting the "Second Report and Order" as a satisfactory interim solution, revealed rather clearly through his testimony before the committee that he believed the best long-range answer to be legislation governing retransmission consent, combined with state supervision of cable rates and services. Commissioner Cox, displaying even less enthusiasm for the new rules, declared that the commission staff could not possibly handle the greatly expanded cable case load.[33] His solution was much more immediate and drastic—a five-year freeze upon any further importation of cable signals.

Despite its severity, the Cox proposal did at least have the virtue of clarity. No false hopes would have been aroused by the rules he advanced, which would have imposed the extended ban on signal importation upon the continuing restriction of 30-day program nonduplication, widened the requirements of mandatory local station carriage, and prohibited the cross ownership of broadcast and CATV facilities. The somewhat illusory promise of procedural relief had to be created to attract the majority necessary for passage of the order, but the result of this tactic was to obscure the agency's basic cable objectives, and to submerge the staff in a generally meaningless flood of administrative case work.

In a rare moment of agreement the NCTA had also argued that the new rules were impossible to administer. In addition, it claimed that CATV aided rather than inhibited UHF growth, and that, in any case, "local service" as applied to television stations in major markets was a term without meaning. The NCTA-sponsored bill, H.R. 14201, would have granted the FCC authority "to issue orders, make rules and regulations, and prescribe such conditions or restrictions with respect to the construction, technical characteristics and operations of community antenna systems . . . with due regard to both the establishment and maintenance of broadcast services and the provision of multiple services." However, the bill would have accorded carriage and nonduplication protection only to regular television stations, not satellites or translators, located within 30 miles of the CATV system, rather than the 80–100 miles often encompassed by a B contour. The NCTA proposal contained no restrictions upon cable importation into the top 100 markets. The association argued that the UHF growth these restraints were designed to protect would actually be aided by CATV operation because UHF stations, owing to the substantial number of VHF-only receivers still in use, and to the generally limited propagation characteristics of their transmitters, could not claim audience coverages comparable to those of their VHF competitors. A study of the 36 top-100 markets with UHF stations operating in 1966 revealed that "the average audience penetration for all UHF stations in these markets is only 40 percent of the ARB circulation of the largest VHF station in the market. The median is only 37 percent and the range from 9.4 to 60.3 percent."[34] Cable carriage offered a means of equalizing this competitive situation, since it could deliver UHF and VHF signals to each subscriber with the same degree of clarity and resolution.

Seiden had maintained that it was the urban settlements, not the rural regions of the nation, which needed community coverage, because these tightly compacted metropolitan areas lacked a sense of unity, purpose, and citizen identification. Yet, as a cable representative pointed out, the attempt to enhance local service by protecting broadcasters in top-100 markets from cable competition was illogical because "these markets . . . do not represent communities or groups of communities. They are not based on considerations of distance, or of area, or of population. . . . They are merely groupings of stations which . . . one audience survey company . . . has placed together for the purpose of making . . . surveys. . . . For instance, Springfield and Danville, Illinois are in the same market, although they are over 100 miles apart. Springfield is 20 miles closer to St. Louis; Danville is 20 miles closer to Indianapolis."[35]

In effect, the commission seemed to be preserving domains unrelated to local interests, measured by economic standards rather than by municipal needs. Ironically, as the agency was restricting cable activities in major markets and asking congress to ban cablecasting, the city of New York was negotiating with CATV systems offering locally originated and oriented programming for each of the city's boroughs.

The Communications Subcommittee, however, unlike its parent Commerce Committee the year before, was granted little time to delve into apparent contradictions between the FCC's goal of local service and its major-market cable regulations. Chairman Staggers held Representative Rogers in tight check, his primary purpose not to castigate the commission but to achieve legislation. The hearings were closed after only six days of testimony so that the serious business of bill drafting could begin. The *Wall Street Journal* reported, "Only the perseverance of the committee's chairman, Rep. Staggers, has kept the measure from floundering already, by the estimate of his colleagues. His commitment, as they see it, isn't to any particular plan for CATV regulation, but to maintaining at least a semblance of legislative control over regulatory policies. 'By going ahead with CATV regulation on its own . . . the FCC is really the tail that's wagging the Congressional dog, but Staggers thinks we'll be derelict unless we say the Commission was entitled to do it,' remarks one committee Democrat."[36]

In June 1966 the committee, by a vote of 20 to 11, reported out a bill in substantial agreement with the legislative proposals submitted by the FCC. The final draft rejected the commission's request for retransmission-consent legislation but granted the agency the authority to bar cablecasting, except for "news and public affairs programs, weather data and other such presentations if they serve the public interest."

The bill eventually died in the House Rules Committee, and since Senator Pastore had indicated that his group would not enter the cable controversy unless the House took positive action, the commission was free to act without further congressional interference. By the same token, since these two hearings and an abortive session of the House Communications Subcommittee in April 1969 marked the full extent of congressional activity in the field of cable regulation during the decade, the FCC was also forced to act without the policy guidance it had requested.

The Impact of Regulation upon Cable Growth, 1966–68

The enforcement of major-market cable restrictions imposed definite patterns upon CATV expansion during the period from March 1966 through December 1968. The effect was twofold: it diverted investment to medium and smaller markets until cable saturation in these areas often reached 50–60 percent, and it encouraged mergers and consolidations in major-market areas so that the capital necessary for survival under adverse conditions could be accumulated.

By the end of 1966, the cable industry consisted of some 1,750 systems, with more than 92,000 miles of cable, linking 2 million homes to operations earning gross revenues in excess of $150 million. Two years later there were only 500 additional systems, but the industry served 3.5 million homes—more than 6 percent of the entire television audience—and grossed more than $200 million.[37]

The largest proportion of this expansion occurred in communities ranging from 2,500 to 10,000 in population, among systems serving 1,000–5,000 subscribers. In urban areas, where a permit to import signals was almost a prerequisite for operation, the FCC by 1968 was buried under a backlog of more than two hundred applications. Its entire list of top-100 approvals consisted of four systems, one each in Albuquerque and Santa Fe, New Mexico; Lancaster, Pennsylvania; and Kalamazoo, Michigan.

Although there were forty-six systems by December 1968 with 10,000 or more subscribers, growth was relatively sluggish even among "grandfathered" operations because of the commission's insistence upon restricting every aspect of operation to its February 1966 level. *Barron's* reported that the inability of the 35,000-subscriber San Diego system to expand after becoming the largest CATV operation lessened the interest of other systems in penetrating major markets: "Unable to offer more than an improved signal for the reception of local stations, Cox has had little success in signing up additional subscribers . . . and CATV companies generally are not attempting to invade other large cities."[38]

Broadcasters owned more than 30 percent of all systems by the end of the era, and almost 46 percent of the new facilities were constructed in 1967 and 1968. Other major enterprises were active in the field as well: "Some of the large, publicly held CATV companies are growing faster than the industry because of mergers and acquisitions. Thus, American Television & Communications Corp. of Denver merged 44 systems in 17 states in 1968 to become the fourth largest CATV company in the business. Biggest is H&B American, which also took a giant step in 1968 by acquiring the cable interests of Jack Kent Cooke; its combined operations now embrace 56 systems serving 210,000 subscribers in 101 communities."[39]

Only large corporations could afford to absorb the losses incurred by major-market operation during this period of cable restraint. They persisted in hopes of long-term profit once the FCC rules were relaxed. There were few franchises available in top-100 markets, however, and when a rare opportunity such as Beaumont, Texas, opened up, giants of the magnitude of Time-Life and Gulf and Western met head-on, pushing even the larger cable corporations aside. As a result, a substantial amount of pent-up capital within the industry began to seep into smaller markets, seeking out almost any cable system in operation: "CATV companies have been trying to grab off as many franchises as possible, as quickly as they can. . . . Most of the competition between the big companies . . . is . . . for smaller existing companies which already have franchises. The going rate for these is . . . $400 per subscriber, which is more than double the normal cost of selling and installing a system from scratch."[40]

Ironically then, the "Second Report and Order," enacted to protect potential community-oriented television service in the major markets may have had the unforeseen side effect of lessening the capacity of cable to provide a similar service. If, as the FCC has often maintained, local owners are generally far more sensitive to the needs of their audiences than conglomerate managers, this period of restraint, by encouraging the assimilation of locally owned cable systems, diminished the responsiveness of the local-origination channel it authorized for cable operation in 1969. Thus it would seem that, in enhancing the community orientation of one class of communication service, the agency had unknowingly impaired that quality in another. Yet, as one commission policy accelerated the tendency toward CATV system consolidation, another was protecting the cable domain from annexation by an even more formidable group of corporate owners, the telephone common carriers.

The Challenge of Telephone Common Carriers and FCC Reaction

The telephone common carriers, with annual earnings nearly five times those of the entire broadcast industry, had generally over-looked scattered CATV operators attaching cable to their poles prior to 1965; they were more concerned with avoiding damage arising from these activities than with collecting a share of their profits. As this era began, however, the rapid growth rate of these systems attracted the attention of even the giant Bell network, which by May of 1965 had filed tariffs for full CATV service in twenty-six states, including New York, Illinois, Pennsylvania, Texas, and Ohio.

Bell was barred, by the terms of a consent agreement entered into with the Justice Department in 1956, from engaging in any business not subject to state or federal common carrier tariff.[41] Since the operation of cable systems did not come within these terms, Bell could not own a CATV facility, but on the other hand, it could not be compelled to provide pole space for cable operators. Instead, Bell began to construct its own elaborate and expensive cable or "wire-grid" systems and insisted that CATV franchise holders rent or "lease-back" these lines rather than pay the lower pole-rental charge and install their own lines.

Telephone carriers not restrained by federal decree began to enter the cable field directly. United Utilities, the third-largest inde-pendent telephone carrier, announced plans to introduce CATV service in all of the 500 communities in which it operated, and the largest independent, General Telephone and Electronics, formed a subsidiary, GT and E Communications, for the exclusive purpose of operating cable systems.

In mid-1965, as the telephone carrier movement began to assume the dimensions of an invasion, the NCTA asked the Justice Department to investigate possible anticompetitive aspects of this type of ownership. It was the FCC, however, which took the first positive federal action in this area; it issued a letter in September 1965 to the attorney general of each state, inquiring whether telephone carriers furnishing CATV service were being instructed to file tariffs, or tables of rates and services, with the FCC, rather than with that state's public utility commission. The letter reminded these officials that Bell companies engaged in "television signal distribution" had been held to be "engaged in interstate commerce by wire or telephone," and thus subject to federal, rather than state, jurisdiction.[42]

Apparently disappointed with the results of this indirect approach, the commission, on 6 April 1966, ordered AT & T and General Telephone to thereafter file all proposed tariffs for CATV service with the FCC rather than with the utilities commissions of the states in which the services were to be provided. Both carriers objected, maintaining that state agencies had by custom been accorded concurrent authority with the commission over intrastate carrier activities, but on 22 June 1966 the FCC dismissed these objections.[43] In doing so, the agency reiterated the rationale used only three months before in asserting jurisdiction over all cable systems—that the interstate nature of television signals made any carriage, even within the borders of a single state, subject to federal control.

Four months later, on 21 October 1966, the commission issued a new order warning all telephone carriers that any further construction of cable systems without prior FCC approval would be at the carrier's own risk because the agency had taken under consideration a proposal to bring such activities within the purview of section 214 of the Communications Act.[44] This threat to invoke a provision compelling telephone carriers to establish, to the commission's satisfaction, the public interest, convenience, and necessity to be served by each proposed CATV system prior to its construction or operation deprived the "telcos," or telephone company cable subsidiaries, of a primary competitive advantage they had held in franchise negotiations. As the FCC explained the situation, when making section 214 applicable to all telco operations on 26 June 1968, "The telephone company is in a position to preclude or to substantially delay an unaffiliated CATV system from commencing service and thereby eliminating competition. Furthermore, construction by a telephone company for an affiliated CATV operator calls for careful scrutiny on the part of the Commission in order to insure against wasteful duplication or unnecessary construction."[45]

Both General Telephone and the Bell systems appealed this commission decision and its immediate application for cease-and-desist orders to halt further use or construction of telephone carrier cable systems which had been less than half completed on the date of the FCC's October 1966 notice and had not subsequently applied for section 214 approval. The FCC position was ultimately sustained by the federal courts, and after this affirmation, the agency began deliberations which would result in extending telco restraints still further, eventually terminating CATV functions performed within the operating territory of the parent telephone company.

Despite the rather hostile regulatory environment facing telephone CATV subsidiaries during this era, however, these companies were operating more than 150 systems, or almost 7 percent of all cable facilities, at the end of 1968, and AT and T alone had invested more than $40 million in the industry.[46] What the FCC "214" controls had accomplished, then, was not to force telcos out of the cable business, but simply to deprive them of any special competitive advantage arising from their ownership by telephone carriers. Lengthy federal procedures denied them the ability to coordinate their franchise applications with the construction activities of their parent companies and denied the carriers themselves the power to recoup applications they had lost to independent CATV operators by forcing them to lease costly, carrier-constructed grid systems in order to perform their franchise agreements.

There appears to be little question that, without commission intervention, the superior resources and bargaining power of the telephone companies would have transformed cable television into an industry dominated by common carriers within only a matter of years after their first incursions into the field in 1965. Whatever other criticisms the NCTA might make of commission policy, it was this series of actions which preserved the independent nature of the cable industry. To some extent, however, it might be argued that in preventing telephone carrier domination of cable service, the FCC was protecting broadcasting as well as cable interests.

In the eighteen months between June 1966 and December 1967, the number of broadcasters with cable interests increased by 44 percentage points, from 548 to 789, with the 1,266 systems and franchises in which they held interests serving more than 750,000 CATV subscribers, almost one-third of the entire cable audience.[47] Yet a federal district court decision in May 1966 offered promise of even more complete broadcaster predominance in cable functions than this influx of ownership could provide. In the first opinion construing the federal copyright implications of cable program carriage, Judge William B. Herlands held that CATV use without the program owner's consent constituted copyright infringement, and he allowed immediate restraint of such carriage. Thus for the next two years, while the *Fortnightly* case awaited review by the Supreme Court, it appeared that broadcasters might at last have won the cable controls they had so long demanded—signal carriage restrictions through retransmission consent.

The Copyright Hope and Disappointment

The *Fortnightly* decision rested squarely upon the court's interpretation of the term "performance" as employed in the Copyright Act of 1909, a statute predating not only CATV but even commercial radio broadcasting. The act specified each right in copyrighted literary property which a titleholder could protect against infringement; and unless the use of a property fell within these terms, the owner was powerless to prevent it. In essence, the act was designed to promote public enjoyment of creative works while prohibiting private profit by anyone other than the owner. Thus, as an example, members of the public could read a copyrighted play, but no individual could "perform" the play in public without authorization from the copyright holder. The cable defendant, in maintaining that his systems did not "perform" the copyrighted television film programming they carried, was arguing by analogy that he operated as a lending library, simply increasing the availability of material already accessible to at least a segment of the public. Judge Herlands rejected this contention. He viewed the defendant's two systems as more akin to pirate publishers, "large scale commercial enterprises, advertising and promoting television programs, and making a profit out of the exploitation of television programs. . . . Defendant's two systems . . . receive, electronically reproduce, amplify, relay, transmit and distribute television programs—operations requiring complex, extensive and expensive instrumentation. These systems function as wire television systems, only one of whose structural components consists of antennas."[48]

Again, as in the *Cable Vision* era, all CATV owners, particularly those without broadcast affiliation, would be forced to consider, when making future plans, the distinct possibility that both the quantity and the quality of their services might soon be determined by their competitors. Again, as in that period ending less than two years before, only one decision on review could protect them from this result, while either of the two more likely actions would unleash an immediate wave of copyright litigation. If the Supreme Court affirmed, CATV systems throughout the nation would face lawsuits to enforce particular rights; if it simply denied certiorari, these actions would test the position of each of the federal circuits on the copyright issue. Yet reversal seemed the least likely possibility, not only because customarily it was less often granted but also because the limited precedents available appeared to support Judge Herland's decision.

As early as 1927, broadcasters had begun challenging wired services that charged subscribers for delivery of their copyrighted radio material, and by 1934 *Uproar Co. v. NBC* had established that a radio station did not lose all right to control subsequent use of its programming simply by transmitting it to the general public.[49] Under the federal act of 1909, however, securing a copyright for the protection of programming was too expensive and too involved a process to be attempted by the average broadcaster. Instead, stations without this federal right relied upon the traditional copyright title recognized by common law as belonging to the creator of literary property—a right which arose at creation, without the need of any filing procedure. However, this right, both at common law and as reaffirmed by statute in many states, protected the creator's property interest only until the work was disseminated publicly. Station owners maintained that broadcasting a program made it public only for entertainment, not for private profit; but in *Z Bar Net, Inc.* v. *Helena Television, Inc.*, a federal court held in 1960 that the Montana copyright statute stating that "if the owner of a product of the mind intentionally makes it public, a copy or reproduction may be made public by any person without responsibility to the owner, so far as the law of this state is concerned" meant that transmission of programming waived any further right to restrict its reproduction or carriage by a cable system.[50] When it became apparent that this "waiver of right by publication" would probably be interpreted in most jurisdictions in similar fashion, broadcasters turned to the "unfair competition" and "contractual infringement" arguments of *Intermountain* and *Cable Vision*, since they were aware that the remaining remedy, federal copyright infringement, could only be successful if maintained at the national level by owners of network or syndicated programs.

Until 1965, then, there was little general industry interest in the question of CATV copyright liability for program carriage, because most broadcasters could claim no title to any portions of their most valuable network or syndicated programming, and the copyright owners of such programming were not sufficiently concerned about the rather minimal effect of cable carriage upon such properties to become involved in costly litigation to protect them. With the rejection of both the "unfair competition" and the "contractual infringement" arguments, however, broadcasters soon realized that the only immediate legal restraints upon cable still possible were through copyright law. Thus attention began to center on the only copyright holder commencing an action during this period, United Artists, which was pressing its claim against defendants whose interests would soon be purchased by the Fortnightly Corporation.

The *Fortnightly* case had actually begun in 1960 when United Artists, after paying ZIV Television Productions more than $20 million for a library of feature films it hoped to lease to UHF stations, attempted to establish its exclusive right to control distribution of this costly programming investment. The two West Virginia community antenna systems selected as defendants were each delivering several television signals carrying the copyrighted film material to subscribers located outside the broadcast markets authorized by United Artists. While neither system imported signals by microwave, United Artists contended that even an antenna and amplifier, if used to extend the range and strength of a broadcast signal for commercial purposes, constituted a "performance" of its programming. It cited *Buck v. Jewell-La Salle Realty Company*, a 1931 U.S. Supreme Court decision which had imposed copyright liability upon a hotel owner who piped broadcast music into each guestroom in his hotel.[51]

In December 1964 CBS commenced a similar copyright-infringement action against TelePrompTer, using the argument that, even if relatively passive reception and distribution through a "Fortnightly type" system were ultimately found not to be a "performance" of a broadcast program, the added elements of microwave importation of that signal and its dissemination in conjunction with other communications services might alter the nature of its cable usage. CBS, however, did not seem as completely committed to preserving its title as United Artists, for when a federal district court in New York refused to consolidate the two cases, or grant CBS a judgment on its pleadings, the network did not press on to trial but asked only for leave to file supplemental pleadings. In effect CBS was allowing time for this crucial issue to be decided in another arena. There was certainly strong justification for the network's hesitancy to expend great effort in achieving a clear judicial definition of cable copyright liability, for from the summer of 1965 onward it appeared that Congress might at any time make all definitions academic by adopting certain revisions in the Act of 1909 submitted by the Copyright Office.

"Performance" might have been an adequate description of an infringing use more than a half-century ago, but if technology now clouded its meaning, nothing prevented Congress from redefining this purely legislative right to the extent necessary to encourage continued literary and artistic efforts. Thus, among the provisions of a revised copyright bill considered by subcommittee number 3 of the House Judiciary Committee, was section 106(b), which would have broadened the term "performance" to include CATV "transmissions": "To perform or exhibit a work publicly means: ... (B) to transmit or otherwise communicate a performance or exhibition of the works to the public by means of any device or process."

Section 109(5) would have allowed exemption from copyright liability only if "the further transmission is made . . . without any purpose of direct or indirect commercial advantage and without any charge to the recipients of the further transmission."

In effect, then, only the true cooperative master antenna would have escaped copyright controls, since section 101 clearly brought CATV carriage within the terms of the act: "To transmit a performance . . . is to communicate it by any device or process whereby images or sounds are received beyond the place where they are sent."

However, if Representative Robert Kastenmeier, the subcommittee chairman, believed that his portion of the deliberations on copyright revision could be limited solely to the proposals advanced by the Copyright Office, he was soon to be disappointed. The House Commerce Committee, already angered by the recent FCC usurpation of the group's regulatory role, pressured for a voice in these hearings, and the Justice Department indicated grave concern about the possible anticompetitive effects of such broad restrictions of CATV carriage. After a full summer of hearings the Kastenmeier subcommittee adjourned in September 1965, reconvening the following spring to consider a new, less drastic set of cable copyright controls.

By May 1966 the subcommittee had emerged with a bill, H.R. 4347, designed to base the fees for copyright licensing of CATV carriage upon the degree of impact such carriage would have upon the market value of the copyrighted programming. The CATV carriage areas were classified as (1) "white" areas, in which CATV systems simply filled in the B contours of existing local stations (the cable operators were exempted from licensing charges because the copyright owners had already been paid for performance by the broadcast services in the markets); (2) "black" areas, into whose markets programming that had not yet been broadcast was imported (the cable operators were subject to full copyright liability); and (3) "grey" areas, in which there was no existing broadcast service (the cable operators paid reduced fees in recognition of the fact that the copyright owners had lost no markets but had nevertheless experienced exposure for which they had not been compensated.

The plan appeared to have considerable merit, but before the month had ended Judge Herlands had made all CATV carriage areas "black" with his *Fortnightly* decision. Yet the outlook was not altogether black for the cable industry during the summer of 1966, for the NCTA began negotiations with a NAB committee, a motion picture association, and a copyright group with a view to determining reasonable copyright license fees for cable use. Congress could have reversed *Fortnightly* at any time simply by legislatively redefining the term "performance" or by imposing a fee schedule that would limit the broadcasters' bargaining power. Although neither of these actions seemed likely, they gave the NCTA some room for negotiation, a position bolstered by a strong Justice Department statement declaring that copyright could not be used as an economic weapon to damage CATV systems.

The private copyright negotiations having failed to achieve any significant progress by March 1967, the House Judiciary Committee grew impatient and decided to report out a bill substantially similar to the one proposed by Representative Kastenmeier the year before. The chairman predicted speedy passage of the measure, apparently unaware of the depth of the jurisdictional jealousy occasioned by the virtual bypassing of the Commerce Committee during the deliberations. After an extensive floor battle the Judiciary Committee was able to engineer the passage of a major portion of its copyright-revision legislation in April 1967, but only by agreeing at the last minute to strike all CATV provisions from the act: "Only a series of House floor concessions . . . staved off a grave challenge to the entire bill by an alliance of forces opposed to one feature or another. . . . To resolve the jurisdictional dispute, Chairman Celler of the Judiciary Committee agreed to drop the bill's section dealing with community antenna television. Commerce Committee Chairman Staggers contended the bill's intricate standards for determining CATV copyright liability would have intruded on his panel's sway in the CATV field."[52] These compromises were unable to salvage even the basic bill in the Senate; and, with private negotiators entrenched in firmly opposed positions, all major efforts to achieve a CATV copyright compromise ended in December 1967, when the Supreme Court agreed to accept certiorari in the *Fortnightly* case.

On 17 June 1968 the court handed down its opinion, a 5 to 1 decision reversing the lower court's holding on copyright liability, with Justice Stewart speaking for the majority and Justice Fortas dissenting. Although Fortnightly had not employed microwave relays in its operation, the opinion made no attempt to limit its holding solely to master antennas, declaring, "At the outset it is clear that the petitioner's systems did not 'perform' the respondent's copyrighted works in any conventional sense of that term, or in any manner envisaged by the Congress that enacted the law in 1909. . . . We conclude that CATV falls on the viewer's side of the line. Essentially, a CATV system no more than enhances the viewer's capacity to receive the broadcaster's signals; it provides a well located antenna with an efficient connection to the viewer's television set."[53]

Justice Stewart acknowledged that "performance" had been chosen by Congress as the actionable term in copyright infringement long before the functions of cable or even of commercial television were known, but he pointed out that Congress had possessed knowledge of these functions for at least a decade without amending or clarifying the term. Therefore, he stated, since copyright relief was purely statutory in nature, Congress, not the courts, should modify its meaning, for judicial action without legislative explanation might distort "performance" to the extent that even manufacturers of television receivers, whose sets enhanced reception, might be found to be infringing upon broadcaster copyrights.

Justice Fortas declared in his dissent that the case called, "not for the judgment of a Solomon but the dexterity of a Houdini," in trying to piece together congressional intent from the fragments of legislative history available. He saw the copyright owner's complaint in basic terms ("The operations of CATV systems are based upon the use of other people's property. The issue here is whether, for this use, the owner of copyrighted material should be compensated") and likened efforts to apply more esoteric jurisprudential approaches to attempting to "repair a television set with a mallet."

Though perhaps stirred by his wit, his fellow justices were unmoved by his reasoning, and despite the fact that Justices Douglas, Harlan, and Marshall had not participated in the original decision, the copyright holder's petition for a rehearing was denied three months later. This effectively ended any further speculation about the possibility of establishing cable television's copyright liability under existing law. In 1968, as in 1965, the hope of private solution vanished almost without warning, again isolating the commission as the lone force protecting major markets from cable penetration.

Challenges to Commission Jurisdiction, 1966–68

While the cable industry fought defensively against the incursion of telephone carriers and copyright controls, it did mount one legal offensive during this era; it challenged the authority of the FCC to exercise the broad powers of the "Second Report and Order" without having received a congressional extension of its regulatory jurisdiction. Black Hills Video, a microwave-served CATV system which had contested the 1965 restrictions, was joined by other operators in an action consolidated for trial in one federal circuit court; Buckeye Cablevision was charged by the FCC with failing to abide by its rules in another; and Southwestern Cable, a San Diego system, was successful in obtaining a court order restraining the FCC from enforcing an interim ban on the importation of signals in a third.[54]

It was the *Southwestern Cable* case which would ultimately establish the commission's authority over cable television and which would provide the justification for the still more drastic restraints imposed in December 1968 upon the importation of the signals of top-100 markets. As the commission stated at that time, "The San Diego proceeding established that potential CATV penetration is likely to be substantial. . . . We are also convinced that a penetration of that order could pose a real threat to UHF development and that the unfair competition would be significant."[55]

The FCC intervened in the San Diego market, which was ranked fifty-fourth in the nation, at the request of Midwest Television— AMST member, vigorous cable opponent, and owner of one of the area's three VHF stations. The Midwest petition, filed on 17 March 1966, less than two weeks after the issuance of the "Second Report and Order," alleged that the importation of Los Angeles television signals by Southwestern and two other cable systems threatened both existing local service and further UHF development in that market. The local service Midwest sought to protect was provided by its own network affiliate and two other VHF stations, one located in Tijuana, Mexico. The only UHF station in the market, KAAR-TV, had indicated that CATV carriage might enhance its economic position, but the commission was apparently more impressed by the opposition of a prospective UHF operator, Jack Gross, whose station was not yet in operation at the time of the *Southwestern Cable* decision more than two years later.[56]

The cable systems maintained that they were not "importing" signals from Los Angeles, since San Diego was within the grade B contour of the Los Angeles stations. The FCC did not deny this fact, but invoked the "footnote 69" exception, designating only the San Diego signals as being "local" in that market. However, when the commission attempted to impose an immediate ban on this importation, a California federal court of appeals entered an order, at Southwestern's request, restraining the FCC from exceeding what the court declared to be its statutory authority.

After this setback the commission assigned a senior hearing examiner to hold a full hearing on the issue of the cable threat to local broadcast service in the San Diego market. This was the only extensive investigation of this type authorized by the FCC during this entire era. The examiner conducted a broad inquiry, collecting several weeks of testimony, numerous documents, and a broad range of arguments from various parties. On the basis of this investigation, he wrote an initial opinion declaring that no need existed for immediate restrictions of cable importation because San Diego CATV systems did not pose a present threat to the capacity for local service of its television stations: "There is no evidence that CATV-produced competition, to date, has had any effect whatsoever on the service offered to the public by the San Diego television stations or the ability of those stations to continue to offer that service." Nor did he see any long-range threat as long as same-day nonduplication rules remained in effect: "It is reasonable to expect that, if the program exclusivity rules are given full play, CATV will have little or no effect on the San Diego audience for locally transmitted network programming."[57]

While the FCC had been unsuccessful in *Southwestern*, the Court of Appeals for the District of Columbia had affirmed its "Second Report and Order" powers in Buckeye. It declared that the commission had chosen "an eminently reasonable course" and that its rules imposed no greater restraints upon CATV than those "required to effectuate public interest requirements."[58] With this division of opinion at the level of courts of appeals, and with *Black Hills* yet to be decided, the Supreme Court agreed in October 1967 to accept certiorari and review the *Southwestern Cable* case.

On 10 June 1968, one week before *Fortnightly*, the court issued its opinion, a 5 to 0 decision reversing the lower court and affirming the FCC's authority. Justice Harlan, however, in speaking for the majority, made it clear that this judicial support was not absolute: "We must first emphasize that questions as to the validity of specific rules promulgated by the Commission for the regulation of CATV are not now before the court. The issues in these cases are only two: whether the Commission has authority under the Communications Act to regulate CATV systems, and if it has, whether it has, in addition, authority to issue the prohibitory order here in question. . . . Nothing in the language . . . of the Act . . . limits the Commission's authority to those activities . . . and forms of communication that are specifically described by the Act's other provisions. . . . We have elsewhere held that we may not, 'in the absence of compelling evidence that such was Congress' intention . . . prohibit administrative action imperative for the achievement of an agency's ultimate purposes.' . . . We therefore hold that the Commission's authority over 'all interstate . . . communication by wire or radio' permits the regulation of CATV systems."[59]

Thus, the decision did not rest solely upon the merits of the case but was partially influenced by the theory of judicial restraint in the field of administrative law dictating that agency actions should be deemed authorized unless clearly beyond the scope of their statutory powers. Whatever the actual breadth of the commission's authority, the agency began, only a week after the Supreme Court's action, to assert its newly affirmed jurisdiction by overturning the *Southwestern* initial decision, which had gone unchallenged for nine months. Commissioners Loevinger, Bartley, and Wadsworth dissented, with Loevinger declaring that the majority had rejected the hearing results simply because the findings did not conform to their prejudices. UHF advocate Commissioner Robert E. Lee, in an opinion supported by Commissioners Hyde, Johnson, and Cox, stated that each of the five cable systems operating in the San Diego market area had to be prevented from importing Los Angeles television signals because "unlimited CATV expansion would seriously impair whatever chance UHF might have to succeed in the 50th market and would probably discourage prospective UHF operators from even undertaking such formidable odds."[60]

A combination of VHF stations, over the protestations of the only UHF broadcaster in their market, had succeeded in having a full evidentiary hearing reversed and a federal court injunction dissolved. Ultimately, after the protracted siege of freeze and litigation, the stations were able to eliminate their strongest cable opponent. In June 1968, as the Supreme Court was handing down its *Southwestern* decision, Southwestern became the property of Time-Life, owner of a San Diego VHF television station.

Soon afterward, the *Black Hills* action was dismissed in conformance with the Supreme Court's mandate, and the era of major challenges to the commission's jurisdiction arising from the "Second Report and Order" had ended.[61] The Supreme Court, in establishing the agency's regulatory rights over cable without allowing supporting private copyright controls, had effectively determined its future course of action: "CATV interests now face the prospect of an onrush of rulemaking. FCC Chairman Rosel H. Hyde said last week that the Supreme Court had clarified both the Commission's jurisdiction and its responsibility. 'We will take another look at the whole problem,' he said."[62]

The prospect was hardly one to be greeted with great joy by the cable industry. There seemed little reason to believe that the "new look" would furnish a broader vision of CATV as an entity as well as a threat. The commission had made one effort in this direction when it created the CATV Task Force in August 1966. Yet this ad hoc section of staff members on temporary assignment seemed better suited to act as a buffer for criticism previously directed at cable administration by the Broadcast Bureau than as an independent unit for CATV supervision and research.

The task force had been established to absorb the bureau's cable functions, but it had been assigned a staff less than one-tenth the size of the bureau's. As a result, by September 1967, CATV matters alone accounted for one-third of the FCC's entire backload of cases. Nor was a cable applicant's patience likely to be rewarded. A survey of the requests for hearings or hearing waivers by top-100 markets during the fiscal year 1968 revealed a denial rate of almost 70 percent, with 469 requests denied without hearing, as the total backlog of all cable proceedings swelled from 1,089 to 1,133.[63]

The task force had no more success in the field of research. The commission not only denied it sufficient funds to collect its own empirical data but even refused its request for controlled industry studies of the economic impact of CATV systems, which had been proposed by the NCTA. *Broadcasting* reported, "The FCC made it clear it is·not persuaded that specially designed experiments to measure the impact of CATV systems in major markets are of much value. It instructed the staff last week to draft orders denying requests for such experiments in Philadelphia and Goshen, Ind. . . . Basically, both tests, their proponents say, would provide the kind of empirical data it needs to assess the impact of CATV systems importing distant signals on major-market UHF stations. The same four member majority . . . Chairman Rosel H. Hyde, and Commissioners Robert E. Lee, Kenneth A. Cox and James E. Wadsworth—were against the revised plan."[64]

Although the backlog of cable television cases continued to increase, the commission, while requesting two new attorneys for its Broadcast Bureau in 1968, asked for no additional personnel for either the rule-making or research sections of the task force. Yet in the same request the FCC observed, "The time required to process top-100 market applications is expected to increase because of the increasing complexity of factual situations as proposed CATV operators move into the major market areas. And, as the Commission actions continue in this area, the arguments and rebuttals presented will become increasingly sophisticated."[65]

For a time this willingness, on the one hand, to admit increasing administrative difficulty in handling CATV matters without making any effort, on the other, to augment its cable staff seemed illogical. Then on 9 December 1968, at a commission meeting held without prior notice, the FCC revealed the logic behind its conduct: it approved new rules which allowed the agency to prevent cable penetration of major markets without need of extensive staff involvement.

Notice of Inquiry on Docket 18397:
Retransmission Consent

The "Notice of Inquiry and Notice of Proposed Rulemaking on Docket 18397" issued by the commission on 13 December 1968 was a model of administrative efficiency and political expediency.⁶⁶ Its adoption process, implementation procedures, and manner of release to the public were managed with consummate skill. The Administrative Procedure Act governing all agency rulemaking actions required that all parties to be affected by any rule be given the opportunity of filing comments on the proposed regulation prior to its enactment. The FCC bypassed this procedure and the adverse publicity it might have caused by simply labeling its rules "interim," which allowed immediate enforcement without debate.

In similar fashion the commission was able to transform the breakdown in CATV administration into an asset, by using the backlog of cases as justification for imposing the broadcaster-controlled regulation of retransmission consent it had sought for more than a decade. As the FCC pointed out in the notice, shifting the authority for the control of program use to the television stations would allow the commission "to close down the burdensome major market hearings except those few involving issues other than impact upon local broadcast stations . . . and to proceed to elimination of the unfair competition aspect. . . . The proposed major market rules would apply across the board and do away with the necessity for case-by-case consideration in evidentiary hearings or upon petition for waiver."⁶⁷

Thus, by terminating all proceedings concerning major-market CATV importation in process of either hearing or waiver, denying all those not yet granted, and imposing an entirely new private obligation on the parties involved, the FCC was able, in a single day, to dissolve the greater portion of the cable backlog. Thereafter, all systems operating within thirty-five miles of the downtown area of a city in a top-100 market could not import signals without the consent of the station from which the signal was obtained. Systems operating within this proximity of cities in markets ranked from 101 to 200 could import only sufficient signals to carry the three networks and one independent channel without consent, and all systems were still subject to "Second Report and Order" restraints such as nonduplication protection, mandatory local carriage, leapfrogging prohibitions, and all other provisions not expressly superseded by the new rules.

At first it seemed, and perhaps this was the FCC's intention, that the prospects for the growth of cable systems in major markets had been enhanced, for few stations were likely to object to extending their coverage into other markets unless a reciprocal market-protection arrangement existed. However, with the FCC "clarification" of 17 January 1969, this hope ended. The commission declared that blanket approval of station carriage would not satisfy the rule; it demanded instead that the importing cable system obtain program-by-program approval from all parties holding any ownership interest in each segment broadcast.[68] Thus, a major-market CATV owner could not import any distant signals unless he obtained in advance an agreement—not only from an affiliate, but from its network, film syndicators, and all other program suppliers—specifically granting him the right to carry their portions of the station's transmissions during a particular twenty-four-hour period. This new technique—substituting retransmission consent for a hearing to establish the lack of economic impact—had lessened the staff's caseload but had replaced a standard difficult to prove with a requirement impossible to discharge.

Perhaps the most remarkable aspect of the FCC's action was the agency's ability to engineer support for rules which, in effect, reversed the Supreme Court's *Fortnightly* decision and ignored a decade of congressional opposition to control of retransmission consent. The retirement of Commissioner Loevinger left Commissioner Bartley as the lone opponent of these broader restraints. In his dissent, Bartley scored both the enactment tactics of his colleagues and the terms of the regulation involved: "I believe . . . the new 'interim' rules are fatally defective because . . . the Commission makes no showing . . . that the 'situation is one in which the agency for good cause finds . . . that notice and public procedure thereon are impractical, unnecessary or contrary to public interest.' It appears to me . . . the 'interim' procedures will either compound the administrative quagmire the Commission . . . got itself into with the Second Report and Order or they will completely stifle further development of CATV. I am satisfied that the latter is a distinct possibility."[69]

Bartley's criticisms, however, were submerged in the flood of documentation released by the FCC on 13 December 1968, as the CATV notice was issued simultaneously with the long-awaited commission proposals on subscription, or "pay-TV." Even the organization of the notice seemed artfully designed to obscure cable restrictions within a set of visionary projections of wired-system growth, proposals for future CATV studies, and authorizations for cablecasting on a limited basis pending further consideration.

This barrage of information was also effective in drawing attention away from a preliminary report of the Presidential Task Force on Telecommunications being released to the press the same week. This report was enthusiastic about cable television and extremely critical of the commission's repressive CATV policy. Even Jack Gould, knowledgeable television reporter for the *New York Times*, seemed to mistake the FCC promise for performance; he called the notice "the most vital communiqué to come out of the Commission in many years" and added, "While the President's Task Force on Communications has been brooding for months over purely advisory recommendations on the . . . revolution in electronics, the FCC has upstaged the Presidential force by spelling out in substance and fixing deadlines for dealing with the imminent upheaval in communications technology."[70]

The following week Gould elaborated on his analysis with the comment, "In a nutshell, the FCC came out as a champion of cable TV, but with a number of provisions that may require months to resolve. . . . Pending submission of torrents of legal verbiage the FCC is imposing a semi-freeze on cable TV proceedings in all major cities. . . . Within this framework, however, many operators can conditionally expand, which should ease much of the anguish on Wall Street."[71]

Broadcasting, perhaps more jaded after years of experience in dealing with commission verbiage, appeared better able to distill the basic essence of the notice: "This proposal is a kind of jerry-built substitute for the decision the Supreme Court did not hand down last summer when it held that CATV systems do not incur copyright liability when they pick up and retransmit programming. It is a substitute also for legislation making CATV subject to copyright laws that Congress considered but did not enact this year."[72]

The ultimate proof of the FCC's skill in handling this round of cable restrictions was the way it managed to neutralize the now almost customary congressional response to its actions. The House Communications Subcommittee did react some four months later, holding an abbreviated set of cable hearings, but the sessions were suspended without any action being taken.[73]

Thus, as the year 1969 began, the commission raised a series of broadcaster-controlled barriers to major-market importation which could only be surmounted by industry-wide agreements on copyright licensing. As Supreme Court decisions had dictated the agency's tactics, its tactics in turn now dictated the subject matter of both private negotiations and congressional deliberations.

CATV 1969: The Status of a Pending Industry

The FCC's efforts to induce a copyright compromise in 1969 were ineffective for the same reason its efforts to achieve compromise cable controls had failed in 1964. Again, the commission was directing its threat only at CATV interests, and thus encouraging the most recalcitrant of cable foes to demand impossible conditions. They could be confident in the knowledge that a collapse in negotiations would damage cable far more severely than broadcasters.

In May 1969 the NCTA made what seemed to be significant concessions during bargaining sessions with the NAB. The cable association had already agreed to pay for program carriage, on the basis of a fee schedule to be set by Congress; to protect the exclusivity of certain programming, typically, sports; and to abide by all existing FCC rules concerning nonduplication, leapfrogging, and local carriage. Now it offered to waive additional rights: "The CATV industry appears willing to give up ... such long range growth possibilities as a cable-TV entertainment network, in return for the near-term right to expand into additional U.S. cities. . . . Existing on-the-air stations in the 50 largest TV markets would be insulated from CATV competition, protected by contracts giving them exclusive rights to show programming they've purchased."[74]

A *Broadcasting* article reflected the confidence of the industry negotiators who felt that the new terms made a mutually satisfactory solution imminent: "Staff executives of both the NAB and NCTA expected resistance from the more extremist elements on each side ... but they believe they have arrived at a compromise that will attract support from the mass of broadcasters and cable operators."[75]

The NCTA board promptly approved, by 17 to 2, the proposed copyright agreement, but as the NAB circulated the proposal among its membership, AMST was convening an emergency meeting. Two weeks later *Broadcasting* reported, "In a series of letters and memos, AMST, All Channel Television Society (UHF), ABC Radio, ABC-TV . . . and National Association of Theater Owners . . . announced . . . criticism of the agreement. . . . The comments were overtly aimed at persuading the NAB board, meeting this week in Washington, either to drop the agreement entirely, or at least direct the NAB staff to continue talks keeping in mind the arguments being offered by various groups."[76]

Again it was the extremists among the trade group rather than the moderates who would prevail. The NAB board rejected the copyright pact and, while suggesting further negotiations, appointed a bargaining team composed entirely of members opposed to cable. After three months of virtual stalemate these meetings ended, and with this adjournment, the last chance for private copyright agreement during the decade.

The search for a cable copyright route into the protected top-100 markets was now taken over by the Senate Judiciary Committee, whose proposal S. 543 provided access through a compulsory copyright licensing system for CATV. Each cable owner, for a fee progressively increasing from 1 percent of his first $40,000 in gross subscriber revenues to a maximum of 5 percent of all revenues in excess of $160,000, was entitled to carry sufficient broadcast signals to achieve "adequate service" without additional charges, and irrespective of FCC rules. "Adequate service," as defined by S. 543, meant all network-affiliate and three independent signals in top-50 markets, and one fewer independent signals in all markets below that rank.

While FCC authority to prevent same-day duplication and leapfrogging was preserved, and copyright agreements were protected in top-50 markets during their existing terms, the rigid barriers of "footnote 69" were breached by a provision declaring all stations placing a B contour over a system to be "local." Thus, especially in markets designated 50–100, the passage of this amendment would have encouraged almost immediate cable penetration. As the *New York Times* described it, "The prospects for cable television's expansion into the nation's urban markets—changing through the years like images in a kaleidoscope—has shifted again into a bright new focus. . . . As Wall Street measures the news, the major cable stocks continue to hold in a sagging market."[77]

Cable prospects seemed even brighter in October 1969 when the commission released its "First Report and Order on Docket 18397," its last cable pronouncement of the decade.[78] This first phase of the broader CATV inquiry dealt only with the issue of cablecasting. The FCC declared that "program origination on CATV is in the public interest" and limited such origination to one channel for each system. Fairness and equal-time provisions were made applicable to such cablecasting, and advertising allowed if inserted only "at the beginning and conclusion of each cablecast program and at natural intermissions or breaks within a cablecast."

More than two hundred CATV systems were already originating live programming at the time of the commission's authorization, and as Robert Shayon pointed out, "the opportunity of selling commercials and earning revenue by origination . . . might conceivably mean the difference between entry and non-entry into a market. . . . One cable TV operator said that if such a pattern were to develop in the lower 80 of the top 100 markets, it would inevitably lead to the inclusion of the remaining twenty markets in a national wired pattern."[79]

Yet such brave projections were dependent upon the passage of a bill still in Senate committee, and no cable legislation had as yet emerged as law. This proposal was even more vulnerable than the others because in threatening the existing copyright structure it challenged the very pricing mechanism of broadcast programming. Through copyright agreements syndicators could release material on a market-by-market basis, exposing film and series packages selectively to various audiences over an extended period of time. Cable importation as authorized by S. 543 would have allowed cable in most areas, and ultimately even in top-50 markets, to contaminate protected audiences, by eroding "first run" prices and lessening the value of reruns being held for later release. Thus, the thrust of the copyright proposal had forged a major alliance of broadcasters and film producers that seemed capable of either defeating the bill on the floor of the Senate or dismembering it through jurisdictional disputes. In the latter tactic, they could rely upon the support of certain Senate Commerce Committee members. Lyden wrote, "The move to the Commerce Committee has political . . . rationale. . . . Senator Warren G. Magnuson . . . and John O. Pastore . . . the senior Democrats on the Commerce Committee and both powerful, sympathetic experts in the broadcasting industry—might find a way to offer significant amendments. . . . Further stalemate—compounding the rivalry between cable and broadcast TV with a jurisdictional dispute between Senate Committees—is still considered as real a possibility as a decisive victory for either side."[80]

The copyright bill was trapped in committee as the decade ended, with FCC restrictions upon cable operations in major markets continuing unabated. However, while copyright legislation might eventually release cable from its bondage, its immediate destiny would continue to be in the hands of the FCC.

A Nielsen survey conducted in November 1969 revealed that almost 35 percent of the nation's 3.7 million homes were clustered in small communities, another 24 percent in predominantly rural areas, and less than 2 percent in major cities. Only ten cable systems could claim more than 15,000 subscribers, with the average system serving only 1,500 homes.[81]

As the decade ended, TelePrompTer, the owner of the largest cable group, was serving only 10 percent of all cable subscribers, and thus less than 1 percent of all television homes, even after its merger with the previous leader in the field, H and B American. In comparison, the five television stations owned and operated by ABC, the smallest television network, claimed an approximate weekly circulation of 14 million households, or 25 percent of the total television audience. In fact, the combined subscriber figure for the fifty largest cable systems, serving almost 60 percent of all cable households, constituted less than one-sixth of the weekly coverage of the ABC-owned outlets. Similarly, the gross revenues of the entire cable television industry in 1969 was exceeded by the gross broadcasting revenues earned by these five stations.[82]

Viewed within this comparative framework of audience, corporate strength, and revenues, the cable industry of 1969 hardly seemed to represent an immediate threat to the survival of television broadcasting in this nation. From the beginning, however, both supporters and opponents of cable have tended to confuse potentiality with actuality, and thus, ironically, the confusion which stimulated the interest of investors and the imagination of the public became in time the primary basis for those regulatory restrictions which were now denying cable its promise.

Docket 18397: Cable as a Captive Challenger

During the extensive proceedings in Docket 18397 the commission for the first time was able to examine the full dimensions of the cable controversy. The efficiency of its controls over retransmission consent allowed the FCC adequate opportunity to consider all of cable's characteristics without the continual compulsion to react to its particular perils. By 1970 the agency had gained sufficient confidence in its projective techniques to declare that, according to its own assessment, the magnitude of the cable challenge had in the past been vastly overstated.[83]

Yet, through its success in achieving its decade-long objective of delegating cable control to the broadcast industry, the commission appeared to have substantially altered its relationship with this media challenger by bringing cable within the process it had previously threatened. In this sense, then, the regulatory behavior of the FCC after December 1968, and especially after the limited nature of the cable threat became apparent to the agency in 1970, no longer seems as indicative of the commission's capacity to react constructively to future media innovation. The commission from this point onward would be "releasing" cable, as the situation warranted, from restraints which had blunted its competitive force; and thus the commission would be supervising an evolutionary process within its own domain rather than protecting itself from an alien challenge. There can be no guarantee that innovation in the future will be so amenable to FCC control, and so any modification in restrictions which seems attributable to the lessening of the cable peril will have no relevance in indicating the FCC's probable reaction to the next communications challenger.

Through its successful assertion of jurisdiction over all major aspects of the operation of cable television, the commission assumed broad responsibilities for enhancing each cable function of benefit to the public. For this reason it seems proper in the following chapter to begin judging the effectiveness of cable regulation, no longer simply in terms of severity or leniency, but in terms of the agency's apparent capacity to provide positive guidance in encouraging those cable services more responsive to the needs of its audiences.

Finally, whatever the ultimate resolution of the cable controversy, its value must be balanced against the cost in vital services denied the public during the seven years of restraint preceding March 1972. To the extent that future controversies can reasonably be expected to require similar periods of time for resolution, this element of societal loss appears to be a vital factor to consider when determining the need for a government mediator during the next phase of communications challenge.

Although technology had expanded the capacity of cable communication by 400 percent during the 1960s, government controls discouraged the development of additional channels and compelled major-market systems to function as master antennas long after they had attained the potential to provide a broad range of message services. CATV managed to survive FCC control, but only at the price of continued adolescence during a time when the existing three-channel system of television distribution seemed unable to convey the diversity of the 1960s to American audiences. Perhaps a broader range of channels for discussing or debating the issues dividing the nation would not have lessened the anger of the era or prevented some from gaining the access they coveted with torches or guns, but in a time when the need for information appeared so great, any artificial restraint upon its dissemination, no matter how sincerely motivated, seems to have been particularly unfortunate. Since there is no reason to believe that that need has abated or that the flow has increased, the price for administrative lag in the field of communications still appears to be excessively high.

IV

The Cable Experience: Epilogue and Prologue

This case history of the regulation of cable television concludes with the industry beginning to emerge as an integral part of the structure of the electronic mass media it once challenged. It ends at this point, not because all questions concerning the ultimate fate of its wired systems have been answered, but rather because answers from this time onward no longer seem to relate as directly to the crucial question of future governmental capacity to encourage advances in competitive media functions and services. While there is need to follow the continuing expansion of cable television now that it has gained a degree of regulatory acceptance, there seems a far more urgent need to begin considering factors preventing this innovative medium from realizing its full public interest potential before the communications revolution enters its next cycle of media emergence and decline.[1]

There is no reason to believe the cable industry any more impervious to challenge than the newspaper, film, radio, or television industries which preceded it during this century, for as a recent media study observed, "while the exact forms of the new media to come cannot be predicted, the conclusion that they will inevitably arrive seems inescapable."[2] Therefore, it seems that the most demanding, and at the same time the most crucial, responsibility of the communications regulator in the years ahead will be to manage evolving and expanding media functions in a manner best serving the varied and various interests of the public. If cable represents only the first in a series of ever intensifying challenges to the electronic media, then the particular questions raised during this era would appear less significant than the more universal questions it has revealed. It is the implications of these broader questions, then, that will form the focus of this final section.

187

The "epilogue" portion of chapter 8 will follow the course of regulatory proceedings beyond the "Third Report and Order in Docket 18397," while the "prologue" will consider the probable effects of this type of control or of alternative techniques of supervision upon the continuing process of media evolution in the United States.[3]

8   Cable: The Once and Future Challenger

Since the balancing of interests is an integral part of the political process, a victory too complete may at times be as damaging as defeat. Thus cable, successful in escaping even minimal federal control in 1960, may thereby have increased the severity of regulatory reaction in 1966. In the same fashion major-market broadcasters, granted FCC protection in March 1966, and broad control over their rivals in December 1968, soon had reason to wish their authority had been made less than absolute. During 1969 and 1970 criticism of this government-industry communications cartel, encouraged by cable leaders who could promise without fear of having to perform, became increasingly more strident.[1] Congressional spokesmen began to repeat the criticism, and pressure was mounting for some type of commission action which would reaffirm the agency's declaration in 1968 that these restrictions were only a temporary expedient until permanent cable policy could be formulated. In essence, what seemed necessary was an immediate gesture, without concern for its long-term validity, to neutralize pressure while conveying to broadcasters the need for conciliation. In June 1970 the FCC produced such a gesture—the "public dividend" plan—which, whatever its operational defects, reflected the high level of pragmatic administrative skill which would be the hallmark of all FCC cable actions under the leadership of its new chairman, Dean Burch.[2]

Epilogue: Cable Control—The End of an Era, 1970–72

During an earlier period, when the FCC was asserting cable controls it had previously rejected, Commissioner Lee Loevinger had observed that the agency's shift in position did not seem to reflect a

189

change in law or fact, but only a change in personnel.[3] To the extent that the preexisting attitudes of the seven commissioners are a prime factor in determining agency decisions, the success of the chairman in winning adoption of a major-market cable proposal favorable to the cable industry in June 1970 emerges as a real tribute to his tactical skill.

Burch himself, former chairman of the Republican National Committee during the Goldwater era, seemed to have no preconceptions concerning the cable controversy when he assumed the chairmanship upon the retirement of Rosel H. Hyde in October 1969. During questioning by the Senate Commerce Committee prior to his confirmation, he indicated that because of his lack of experience in either broadcasting or cable he had "no great familiarity with the relative interplay between CATV and free TV. I think the only way I could approach that and other problems would be the charge of the Communications Act that the United States wants the best communications system available."[4]

Robert Wells, the Kansas broadcaster appointed to replace James Wadsworth on the commission, appeared with Burch before the committee. He was equally noncommittal in regard to his philosophy concerning cable regulation, but cable leaders judged correctly that in Wells the broadcast industry had found a replacement for Commissioner Cox, who would be retiring in August 1970.[5] In reality, however, Cox represented far more than one anti-CATV vote. His opposition to closed-circuit dissemination extended backward more than a decade to his report in 1958 to the Senate Commerce Committee, in which he advocated CATV licensing. He later applied this principle while chief of the Broadcast Bureau during the Carter Mountain case; and, playing his major role, he designed cable restraints in 1965, 1966, and 1968. In addition, his stature as a commissioner tended to attract other commissioners such as Robert E. Lee, a staunch UHF supporter, and Nicholas Johnson to his position on cable television.[6] While Johnson seemed, from his public pronouncements during 1970, to be retreating from his vote supporting the restrictions imposed in December 1968, and strict application of "Second Report and Order" rules in the *Midwest* case, Commissioner H. Rex Lee, the former governor of American Samoa who had replaced Loevinger in 1968, was said to be sympathetic to the Cox position.[7] Cox maintained that cable threatened educational as well as commercial television; Lee, on the basis of his experiences in Samoa, was a strong advocate of educational broadcasting.

Thus, until Kenneth Cox retired, there seemed little chance that Chairman Burch could make a dramatic move to reduce criticism of the commission's cable controls, since he needed four votes and could only hope for three: his own; that of Robert Bartley, the unreconstructed Doerfer-era commissioner who was unswerving in his opposition to government interference in the economic affairs of the industry; and possibly the vote of Nicholas Johnson. Yet in June 1970, two months before Cox retired, the commission approved by a 4 to 3 vote a proposal which, if ultimately adopted by the agency, would open every major market in the nation to cable penetration. This "public dividend" plan proposed ending "footnote 69" restraints which allowed each cable system located within two major markets to carry only one market's signal as "local." In addition, it proposed granting each system the right to import four non-network television signals from other markets.[8] Its effect would have been to expand the number of channels of television programming many urban operators could offer from four or five to as many as fifteen to eighteen if the systems were located in regions such as the Northeastern Corridor where contours overlapped.

In return for these rights all major-market systems availing themselves of these privileges were to be required to pay 5 percent of their gross annual subscription revenues to the Corporation for Public Broadcasting, to make copyright payments to program owners pursuant to a schedule to be set by Congress, and to allow local UHF stations to insert their own commercial messages into programming imported from other markets. To most cable owners, many educational broadcasters, and a few UHF operators the proposal sounded too good to be true, and in fact it may have been.

Broadcasters immediately declared the plan for UHF commercial substitution to be unworkable, and the tax for a quasi-public corporation to be unconstitutional. They described the complex design as "harebrained," "mind boggling," and a "Rube Goldberg device."[9] Commissioner Bartley, claiming that the FCC should become less rather than more involved in cable control, joined these critics; but by sacrificing one vote, Chairman Burch gained two others. Commissioner Robert E. Lee favored the extension of UHF commercial coverage, while Commissioner H. Rex Lee favored the provision of additional funds to educational broadcasting. With the support of Johnson, who by now had become firmly committed to the cause of cable freedom, and with his own tie-breaking vote, Burch was able not only to still demands for immediate action but also to indicate quite clearly to broadcasters that the time for compromise on protection for top-100 markets had come.

Judged solely as a regulatory program, the "public dividend" plan was a failure because in time the commission was forced to admit that it was too cumbersome to administer.[10] However, viewed more realistically as a forceful effort by the chairman to reopen all elements of cable debate, it was extremely successful, for it laid the foundation for the compromise that would be achieved the following year.

During this same period the commission, as a part of its broader study of the ownership of the media, issued the "Second Report and Order on Docket 18397" prohibiting joint ownership of a television station and a cable system located within the station's grade B contour, or network ownership of any domestic cable system. Divestment was required by August 1973,[11] later extended to August 1975. This restriction did not prevent broadcasters from purchasing cable systems in other areas, however, and the proportion of cable systems owned by broadcasters increased from 30 percent to 38 percent between 1971 and 1972. The primary purpose of the rule was not to discourage investment in cable, but simply to prevent a media owner in a particular area from holding either an anticompetitive or a news-monopoly position by virtue of his ownership control. With respect to newspaper or radio ownership of cable, this issue was still being deliberated two years later.[12]

In March 1971 the commission went even further in its efforts to stimulate debate on cable policy. It held a series of unprecedented public hearings in Washington to assess the positions of various broadcast and cable representatives, copyright spokesmen, and members of public interest groups concerning the merits of the "public dividend" plan and of alternative forms of cable control.[13] Few of the witnesses ventured beyond statements given at other times, and panel presentations seemed remarkable for their lack of originality, but the cable industry was at least accorded the opportunity it had sought without success for almost a decade—a formal appearance before the agency controlling its destiny.

In June and July 1971 the commissioners themselves were called to appear as witnesses before the Senate Communications Subcommittee and the House Communications and Power Subcommittee for a review of their regulatory activities in general, with particular emphasis upon the proposals they were considering for cable television. During each appearance Chairman Burch pledged that the FCC would deliver a comprehensive proposal for cable regulation to Congress within sixty days. He kept his promise with the issuance of the now famous "letter of August 5, 1971."[14]

The letter, directed to the chairman of each committee, described the program as one the commission planned to adopt by 1 March 1972 unless Congress intervened to create other policies by statute. Again, as in its "public dividend" plan, the focus was on top-100 markets, with audiences outside these areas gaining none of the benefits proposed. For those cable systems located within 35 miles of a community in which a top-50 television station was licensed, the FCC plan provided for mandatory carriage of all "local" signals including those "substantially viewed" in the cable community and set "minimum service" at full three network coverage plus three independent signals. For those cable systems located within 35 miles of a community in which a television station in markets 51–100 was licensed, "minimum service" was defined as full three network coverage plus two independent signals, while in the case of similarly located cable systems in markets 101 and above, "minimum service" meant full three network coverage plus one independent. Systems more than 35 miles from the nearest licensed television community would be exempted from "minimum service" provisions, but remained subject to "leapfrogging" and "mandatory carriage" rules where applicable.[15] If a system in any market could satisfy its "minimum service" requirements with "local" or mandatory signals, it could import two additional or "wild card" signals, subject to new "leapfrogging" rules pertaining to such importation. In essence, the proposal, while as intricate as a

Chinese puzzle, seemed to offer sufficient broadcast signals to make major market cable operation possible.

This plan, unlike the "public dividend" plan, was based upon benefit, not to any special-interest group, but to the public in general in the form of nonbroadcast services. The commission envisioned these services as creating new outlets for local expression, promoting added diversity in television programming, advancing educational and instructional uses of electronic media, and increasing the flow of information concerning local issues and local governments. To guarantee this message potential, each new system was to have at least a twenty-channel capacity, with three channels dedicated to free access—one by the public, a second by educational groups, and a third by local and state governments. In addition, for any leased channel in use for a three-hour period at least 80 percent of the time during a six-week period, a second channel was to be opened under the agency's "$N + 1$" formula to insure a continual expansion of this nonbroadcast service.

The regulations were to be enforced through a "request for certification of compliance" requiring each cable operator to file with the commission a copy of his franchise agreement, a list of the stations to be carried, a list of all stations placing a grade B contour over the cable community, and a statement disclosing all ownership interests in the system. The FCC, upon receipt of this material, would issue public notice of the application, and interested parties would be allowed thirty days in which to notify the agency of any objections to certification. While the FCC preempted jurisdiction over signal carriage, technical standards, program origination, and cross ownership, it admitted that the licensing of cable systems would impose an impossible administrative burden upon the agency. It therefore requested state or local authorities to retain the responsibility for establishing franchise boundaries; selecting the licensees from the franchise applicants; and determining terms of service, rates of expansion, and franchise fees—all subject to certain minimal federal standards.

This "letter of intent" has been outlined in great detail because each of its basic provisions was adopted without significant modification in the "Third Report and Order on Docket 18397."[16] Subsequent debate has tended to obscure the fact that the only substantial difference between this letter and the order enacted involved program exclusivity, a factor not clearly defined in the letter.

The letter was adopted in a 6 to 1 decision, with Thomas Houser, who had replaced Kenneth Cox on the commission and would soon be replaced in turn by Charlotte Reid, voting with the majority. The lone dissent was filed by Robert Wells, who would resign from the commission three months later. Commissioner Robert E. Lee voiced no concern about the threat this proposal would pose to major-market UHF stations; Commissioner H. Rex Lee entered no complaint about the lack of protection for educational broadcasters or about the single channel dedicated for educational use; Commissioner Robert Bartley did not challenge the added burden the FCC would be assuming; even Commissioner Johnson had no additional comments for the record.

Although the chairman may have achieved another masterpiece of consensus negotiation, the broadcasters were not overwhelmed by his leadership. The commission's action on Docket 18397 had shifted the traditional burden of proof in broadcast-cable regulatory conflicts, with that faction of broadcasters still opposing major-market cable growth now compelled to convince Congress of the wisdom of halting a proposal already in motion. The lethargy of the legislative branch, which had previously worked to broadcaster advantage, had become a serious handicap; but a new force, the Office of Telecommunications Policy, had emerged in the executive branch during this period which, by the nature of the political process, seemed likely to be useful to opponents of a congressional agency's proposal.[17] President Nixon himself had already entered the cable controversy in June 1971 by creating the Cabinet Committee on CATV, which was chaired by Office of Telecommunications Policy director Clay Whitehead and included HEW's Elliot Richardson, HUD's George Romney, Secretary of Commerce Maurice Stans, Executive Director of Communications Herbert Klein, and presidential advisors Leonard Garment and Robert Finch. While Dean Burch declared that he had received "personal assurances that the President's committee . . . will not slow the Commission's pending rulemaking,"[18] he had no guarantee that the OTP chairman, as head of an executive office, would stand aloof from the conflict. In time it became apparent that the cabinet committee was created more as a gesture of presidential interest than as a full-scale effort to generate policy, but the OTP itself seemed to have a broader vision of its role. In July 1971 Whitehead called cable, broadcast, and copyright spokesmen to his office "to explore the possibilities" of an interindustry settlement of copyright and importation differences without need of cumbersome regulation. In fact, the NCTA had been negotiating privately with copyright representatives for several months prior to the OTP meetings and in June 1971 had entered into an agreement to support both compulsory copyright licensing of all cable systems and market-exclusivity protection effectively denying cable access to top-50 markets in return for access to markets 51–100. Alfred Stein, chairman of the NCTA Copyright Committee, admitted that his group had bargained away top-50 opportunities with this pact but added, "This agreement does crack the second 50 markets and there is a lot of business in the second 50 markets."[19]

Broadcasters had pressed for the OTP meetings because they had not been parties to the cable-copyright agreement and felt their interests had not been adequately considered. After the release of the FCC letter of 5 August 1971, however, the NCTA group no longer seemed as concerned about the progress of these "unofficial" sessions, for, like the NAB in a previous era, it saw little reason to concede any point it had already won. Thus, when pressure began to build late in August 1971 for a joint statement by the two trade associations disavowing provisions of the commission's letter relating to signal importation and leapfrogging, the NCTA group could walk out of the meetings with association chairman John Gwin declaring, "We cannot negotiate downward."

"Cannot" in one sense seems to have been an extremely descriptive word, for again, in a fashion parallel to that of earlier NAB experiences, the favorable terms of the FCC proposal had splintered rather than unified cable factions. Some were already demanding withdrawal from the copyright agreement of June 1971, and others insisting that the NCTA boycott any further discussions until the FCC proposals became law. The NCTA committee refused to return for further negotiations, even though the OTP let it be known that Clay Whitehead might consider this a lack of good faith and might, therefore, request extensive hearings or more stringent safeguards for broadcasters during his scheduled appearance in October before the Senate Commerce Committee. John Gwin, the NCTA chairman, actually had little choice in his actions, since he was only a spokesman for, rather than a leader of, the organization he headed. Gwin had been chosen only six months before to replace Ralph Demgen, who, charging that continued interference by a narrow clique of association members made his job impossible, had resigned suddenly. Gwin's selection was greeted rather unenthusiastically by that same group, which had wanted someone of greater prominence. After NCTA president Donald Taverner, followed by some of his key staff members, resigned under pressure in July 1971, the major problem confronting Gwin was, not the issue of cable regulation, but simply the maintaining of some degree of unity within the organization.

Since Gwin could not risk alienating the membership by further meetings with the OTP, Chairman Burch made his own attempt to bring the groups together in October 1971. This time it was the broadcast interests that terminated the discussions, and NAB president Vincent Wasilewski, who had had his own problems with dissidents on the cable issue, was said to have informed Burch that his group could not accept the letter of intent and would not be interested in further discussions unless substantial changes were to be made in its provisions.

At this point the OTP pressed both sides for a resumption of the discussions broken off in August. Rumors began emanating from NCTA leaders indicating that failure to cooperate could place the entire commission proposal in jeopardy. Clay Whitehead had in the interim postponed his presentation before Senator Pastore's committee from October until mid-November, and association officials maintained that, unless a satisfactory solution to the problem of program exclusivity was achieved by that time, Whitehead might urge a continuation of the existing freeze until this issue could receive further study.

There did seem to be substantial cause for considering such protection prior to putting the commission's proposals into operation, for unrestricted importation could have had a serious impact upon the value of the copyright owner's and the broadcaster's investments in program properties. "First run" programming is generally considered to be far more attractive to audiences than "rerun" programming; and if a television station is denied exclusive protection to show the feature films and syndicated programming it has purchased for its own market, local cable systems importing those same films or series from another market prior to their scheduling by the local station will reduce them to reruns for all the station's cable subscribers. Similarly, importing programs from market "A" to market "B" will reduce their "first run" value in "B" when the copyright owners seek to sell them in that market.

Perhaps in this single area Chairman Burch had been too pragmatic in his efforts to put together a massive majority of commissioners favoring major-market cable operators. Rather than attempt to spell out such protections, and transform Nicholas Johnson into a volatile and vocal opponent, or reject them and add Robert E. Lee and possibly H. Rex Lee to the list of dissenters, the commission sidestepped the issue with the comment, "We intend to study whether present or future considerations call for altering our existing CATV program exclusivity rule (Section 74.1103) which in effect protects only the network programming of network affiliates."[20]

During the first week of November 1971, Clay Whitehead delivered to representatives of NCTA, NAB, and AMST (now called MST) what was later termed a "take it or leave it" compromise requiring the cable industry to accept two minor amendments and one major addition to the commission's proposals of 5 August 1971 and requiring the broadcasters in turn to pledge their support of the proposal as modified. The minor amendments simply increased from 1 to 2 the percentage of viewing necessary for out-of-market independent stations to be classified as "local" signals and modified the "leapfrogging" rules to prevent a blending of programming from several distant stations on a composite channel. The major addition was a rule on program exclusivity designed to protect non-network as well as network programming in major markets by preventing any cable system in a top-50 market from importing programming under exclusive contract to a local station for the duration of the contract. In markets 51–100, the maximum period of contract exclusivity could not exceed two years, while below market 100, no program exclusivity was to be granted.[21]

Since the five to seven stations classified as "local" in most top-50 markets would collectively have under contract a substantial percentage of all the programming available from other markets, the practical effect of this exclusivity compromise was, as in the NCTA copyright pact of June 1971, that 75 percent of the potential cable audience was traded off for a gain of an additional 15 percent of that audience, which more than doubled the 10 percent then available outside top-100 markets.

Within a week after the OTP compromise was advanced the NCTA board of directors agreed to it, and only two weeks later the NAB and the AMST followed suit. Why did all factions surrender so rapidly after having vowed to fight these issues if necessary through Congress and the courts? Each trade association had an answer. The NCTA maintained it acted "in the face of strong pressures from the OTP and FCC"; the NAB declared it "reluctantly accepted" the "best . . . present available package"; while the AMST claimed it agreed "to avoid what could have been a very bitter and destructive battle."[22] But to portray the OTP as so potent a force or the situation so critical seems somewhat inaccurate. While there is no way of determining the actual degree of pressure each trade group felt as it received the OTP edict, there is no question that the presence of this new body and the aura of mystery surrounding Clay Whitehead's influence were of great value to the leaders of each trade group as they attempted to explain to their own organizations the concessions they had made.[23] Thus, there may be reason to argue that the most significant role the OTP played in the consensus agreement of November 1971 was that of scapegoat; it allowed negotiators to blame an omnipotent third party for a settlement all realized was ultimately necessary but which was too unpopular to risk without adequate justification.

After the infighting which preceded the November compromise, and the skirmishes which continued even after its acceptance, the issuance of the "Third Report and Order on Docket 18397" on 3 February 1972 seemed almost anticlimactic. *Broadcasting* described the document as "the FCC's magnum opus on CATV, . . . some 500 pages of report and order, rules and appendices, separate opinions of the commissioners, plus collateral items including notices of proposed rulemaking dealing with issues not treated in the main document."[24] The rules, which became effective on 31 March 1972, were basically a regulatory description of the terms contained in the commission's letter of 5 August 1971, as modified by the November compromise. Chairman Burch, while indicating that the terms of the report should "regularize and validate an industry that never knew what its future was," admitted that without accompanying copyright legislation from Congress the agency's problems in supervising its operation might be acute.[25] Although Charlotte Reid, who had replaced Robert Wells on the commission, voted in support of the proposal, approval was not unanimous, since Robert E. Lee returned to his former position of opposing the cable threat to the "quality and quantity of local television service." Commissioner Johnson also dissented to one portion of the rules, the exclusivity provisions inserted by the November compromise. Johnson soon expanded upon his initial comments with a rambling discourse challenging the entire process employed to incorporate the industry compromise into the order. Describing the consensus agreement as one dictated by "fat cat" broadcast interests and as "forced down the throat" of the commission, Johnson charged that audiences had been bartered among private entities without protection from the agency. While he did raise significant questions concerning the right of public participation in matters affecting public rights, the tone of his attack tended to moralize rather than analyze the differing weights he and the chairman seemed to accord pragmatic and philosophical values.[26] Burch responded to the attack, Johnson responded to the response, and the essay contest ended without clarifying the central issues involved.

One of the rare points of agreement in these statements concerned the impact two cases then pending in the federal courts could have upon the rules adopted. If, in *CBS v. TelePrompTer*, modern cable systems were found to be copyright infringers, the new importation rules would be overridden by private controls; while if, in *United States v. Midwest Video*, the FCC was found to have no authority to compel program origination, all nonbroadcast obligations imposed by these same rules would be in serious jeopardy.[27]

The *TelePrompTer* decision was rendered first, with a New York federal district court finding that the additional functions of microwave importation, interconnection, and origination of sponsored programs did not alter the status of a cable system according to the "functional" definition of the *Fortnightly* case. After holding that in itself no single function of the modern broadband system would transform the system from a passive antenna into an active "performer," the court, in viewing all these functions together, declared that "if a CATV is like a viewer and a viewer by his choice of equipment can determine the range of a broadcast then there seems to be little limit to what can be done with broadcast signals by CATV's."[28]

While CBS immediately indicated its intention to appeal this decision, the defeat again denied the broadcast industry any leverage in the interim between negotiations concerning copyright legislation which the consensus agreement required be proposed and supported by all parties before Congress. Even if such a universally acceptable proposal could be drafted, hope for rapid enactment into law seemed rather dim when Senator John McClellan, chairman of the Subcommittee on Patents, Trademarks and Copyrights, in introducing a joint resolution to extend copyright protection under existing law, declared, "Because certain provisions of the bill are highly controversial it is uncertain if it can be enacted into law during the first session of the 93rd Congress. . . . It will also be necessary to allow the Copyright Office a period of time to prepare for the new law . . . and consequently the effective date of the legislation will have to be several months after its enactment."[29] Thus, while the TelePrompTer case did not have the impact upon major-market importation rights feared by the commission, neither have efforts to gain passage of copyright-licensing legislation progressed as hoped. Since copyright has aptly been termed the "glue" holding the consensus agreement, and thus the "Third Report and Order," together, a certain reluctance to commence major-market cable construction has remained despite the brave promise of the commission's report.

The *Midwest Video* case posed an even more direct threat to the commission's rules, in that it challenged the agency's right to enact or enforce any cable regulations not directly related to the protection of the broadcast industry. In February 1971 the U.S. Court of Appeals for the 8th Circuit issued an injunction restraining the FCC in its efforts to compel Midwest Video, a cable system serving more than thirty-five hundred subscribers, to originate programming in accordance with the terms of the "First Report and Order on Docket 18397."[30] The court, in granting the injunction, declared that, since Congress had not acted to extend the cable jurisdiction of the commission, the only authority it could exercise was that reasonably related to broadcasting—restricting cable services which threatened the quality of the broadcast service provided the public. Program origination had no relationship to the objective, and therefore no matter which rule the FCC might choose to adopt concerning this service, it would be "without authority to impose it."[31]

In June 1972 the U.S. Supreme Court reversed the lower court's decision and thereby may have saved the entire nonbroadcast segment of the "Third Report and Order," which seemed similarly remote from the objective of protecting broadcast service. It did so, however, by the narrowest of margins, a 5 to 4 decision in which Chief Justice Burger in his concurring opinion declared, "Candor requires acknowledgement for me, at least, that the Commission's position strains the outer limits of even the open-ended and pervasive jurisdiction that has evolved by decisions of the Commission and the courts."[32]

Justice Brennan's opinion, joined in by Justices White, Marshall, and Blackmun, held that *Southwestern Cable* had established general FCC jurisdiction over cable television and that, since cablecasting appeared to "promote the general interest" within that context, it was a logical extension of that authority.[33]

In the dissent of Justice Douglas, concurred in by Justices Stewart, Powell, and Rehnquist, the plurality opinion was described as having performed the "legerdemain" of adding a provision to the Communications Act transforming "CATV carriers" into "broadcasters." Instead of judicial action, the opinion maintained, "That requires a brand new amendment to the broadcasting provisions of the Act which only Congress can effect. The Commission is not given *carte blanche* authority to initiate broadcasting stations; it cannot force people into the business."[34]

Although the authority of the commission was thus sustained, it can be argued that the assessment of the lower court was perhaps the more accurate, in terms of the primary emphasis and focus of FCC regulatory activities. While consistently professing its dedication to the principle of extending the range of media services available to individual communities, the FCC, from its initial microwave rules in 1962 through its third report a decade later, has used only one basic technique—restriction of cable signal carriage—to achieve one goal—protection of the broadcasters' economic markets. In that sense the third report differs from the second report of

1966 only in degree; it allows a greater number of signals to be carried into a broader range of markets.

The scope of program options and nonbroadcast services available to each community, then, has no relationship even today to its own distinct needs or to the desires of its citizens, but only to its location within the boundaries of a private audience-survey unit designed for the sale of broadcast time. Because the FCC has chosen to rely upon a broadcast standard to determine audience rights in cable service, the factors dictating public interest are demographically rather than democratically oriented, with the cities, towns, and unincorporated areas of several counties considered by the commission, as by sponsors, to be a single, undistinguishable mass of population.

While it may still be somewhat premature to make any long-term judgments about the future value of cable communications services, it must be remembered that radio, once released from its constraints in 1927, had within a year assumed nearly all the characteristics which would dictate the function of electronic mass media for the next half-century. Therefore, it may be of some value to consider, in broad perspectives, recent trends in cable evolution in an effort to determine to what extent these systems, under the commission's guidance, appear to be moving toward realizing the public interest potential inherent in their multichannel, audience-supported, two-way communications functions. If the FCC, by continuing to place undue emphasis upon the competitive aspects of cable signal carriage, should thereby be failing in its obligation to guide the development of cable's nonbroadcast service, the damage caused by repressing this medium in the past may only have been compounded by releasing it prematurely in 1972.

The Emerging Broadband Communicator

Perhaps because cable television has for so long enjoyed the status of a promising pending medium, scandals which would have severely damaged the image of a mature industry have generally been dismissed by a tolerant press and public simply as instances of boyish enthusiasm. Thus, neither "blue sky" projections, which have become a trademark of the industry, nor even documented examples of improper practices, such as those revealed by the New Jersey hearings or those involved in the recent conviction of Irving

Kahn, TelePrompTer chairman and president, have prompted any widespread criticism of either the good faith or the maturity of cable operators generally.[35]

Even more surprising has been the almost universal acceptance by newsmen of such traditional publicity ploys of cable promoters as the "joint venture" agreement or projections of astronomical numbers of cable channels. "Joint venture" dates from the earliest era of cable franchising when applicants began to realize that influential citizens in a community would support a proposal in which they had an ownership interest. Today as in the past the local interest is seldom a controlling one, and the only modification in recent times is the substitution of racial or ethnic minority leaders for the lawyers and bankers offered equity interest prior to 1970.[36] Projected systems of forty, forty-eight, or sixty-four channels are often created by the same process challenged by the FCC in the case of "diet" bread—simply the slicing of existing frequencies into greater numbers of thinner radio or FM audio circuits. While a scarcity of risk capital and an unsettled situation in copyright licensing have limited major-market construction since the issuance of the "Third Report and Order," there is as yet little evidence of long-range industry planning for transforming the promises of the past into reality.

Perhaps because the uncertain and at times hostile regulatory environment has encouraged the emergence of the promoter-salesman rather than the operator-manager cable leader, the industry appears content with only the image of broadband service and in general provides cablecast programming without strong conviction and "public access" channels without deep commitment. TelePrompTer and Sterling, for example, have both opened production facilities for public access programming, but since making this gesture, neither has made a major effort to promote this service and thus assure its viability, or even its visibility.[37] The fact that this new function of "narrow"- rather than "broad"- casting runs counter to a half-century of industry experience and audience conditioning and therefore demands an extremely high level of support and guidance during this formative era seems to trouble neither the cable leaders nor the commission.

The New York experience can be criticized because it exists, but far more telling criticism can be directed at systems in other urban areas which have not even made the attempt to expand their non-broadcast services in similar fashion. The FCC has provided little incentive for innovation in nonbroadcast programming, and no guidance for those seeking to expand such service on their own. The New York services grew from local, not federal, requirements; and although insisting upon the preemptive right to allocate basic major-market cable channels, the commission has in effect delegated the responsibility for achieving effective nonbroadcast service to the local franchising body.[38] While this might in one sense indicate an enlightened reliance upon "federalism" on the part of the agency, it might also, in view of the rigid controls retained over broadcast elements of such cable operations, simply reveal a lack of interest in any aspect of cable operation not directly related to the competitive impact upon broadcasting.

In any case, neither the commission nor the industry appears to have any marked interest at present in learning to what extent "public access" channels must be structured, provided production facilities, and promoted in order to attract interest and to prevent their deterioration into a service whose image would make it valueless for those sincere in seeking to convey a mood or an idea to others. Yet once the reputation of these public access channels, as well as that of other dedicated services, has been firmly established in the public mind, the task of altering that image may be even more demanding than the initial problem of structuring their operation for the most effective service.

If multichannel systems are to offer broad public participation in the mass communications process, an extension of educational functions, and an increase in knowledge about local and state government, it seems apparent that the era of promise has now become the time for performance, with respect to both FCC policy and industry action. At present the only unique element of cable communication which seems to be stimulating much interest on the part of its operators is "audience support," and this interest extends not to the creating of programming, but only to the delivering of existing entertainment material by means of leased pay-TV channels. At the first NCTA convention, after the "Third Report and Order" made major-market broadband communications feasible in many areas, the major topic of discussion was not cablecasting or "public access" operation, but pay-TV. According to *Broadcasting*, "They were calling it by several names ... 'premium TV,' 'public-choice TV.' Some came right out and said it: 'Pay TV.' But by whatever name, it emerged as the expected wave of cable's future."[39] Broadcasters had maintained from the beginning that wired systems would not augment entertainment and news available to audiences but would simply levy a distribution charge upon programming already in existence. While program creation for cable, like that for broadcasting, will be dependent upon some method of national distribution to broaden its audience base, the stress upon this one leased-channel service to the virtual exclusion of all others does seem an indication that cable television, lacking countering incentives or requirements, is well on its way to finding its own lowest common denominator.

The third distinctive element of cable communication systems, their two-way potential for allowing audiences to react to and eventually to direct the mass communications process, is also at present being developed more extensively for use in pay-TV circuits. Studies indicate that subscriber-initiated services may be more than a decade away, but on the basis of past experience, it seems likely that the development of this "hardware" will advance more rapidly than the development of techniques for operating it in conjunction with other cable attributes in a truly effective system of broadband communications.[40]

All projections concerning future broadband services share one seldom stated basic assumption: that the services will be applicable only in regions of reasonable population density. A study prepared in 1968 for the President's Task Force on Telecommunications Policy predicted that it would cost some $125 billion to wire all the 100 million homes expected to exist in the United States in the year 2000, but only $5 billion to wire the 50 percent of them located in the areas of greatest population.[41] Thus, unless the FCC can soon discover some method of extending the breadth of these services, through either incentives or requirements, the broader dimensions of both service and cost will in the future make the "white" areas of the radio and television eras seem almost infinitesimal in retrospect.

From this brief survey it appears that history is about to repeat itself in almost every respect during the cable era, with the lowest common denominator of mass entertainment already beginning to take root in its urban environment. Cable seems to have been released, as it was previously repressed, not because policy had been developed to guide it in performing communications functions essential to the American public, but simply because a process of legal and economic assimilation had blunted its threat to. the broadcast industry it once challenged. On the basis of the cable experience, then, it seems essential to begin considering alternative methods for integrating new communications techniques into the existing electronic media system before this process begins again.

It appears that a regulator almost uniquely without responsibility for the economic stability of its clientele industry has voluntarily assumed that obligation simply because it has lacked broader vision or more progressive goals. Since the FCC has since its inception been denied sufficient research facilities to enable it to look beyond its regulated industry, and the autonomy necessary to the formulation of policy, there seems little reason to expect that its future reaction to communications innovation will differ in any marked respect from its reaction in the past.

Whether by force of law or by custom, the FCC as presently structured is not a mediator in the field of mass communications, but simply a supervisor of industry activities. As such it has the capacity to measure the benefits to be derived from broader media service only in terms of its compatibility with existing services. Thus, the agency appears capable of encouraging innovation only to the extent that the interests of the industry and the public seem to coincide; and since the industry can be presumed willing to encourage innovation serving its interests, the agency's present role in this process might be described as at best superfluous and at worst repressive.

Prologue: Communications Control Beyond the 1970s

Continuing communications innovation appears inevitable, but the regulatory response to it need not be immutable. Media technology might in the future be freed of government restraint, and evaluated by a more expert, independent body; or it might be supervised with greater flexibility through a confederation of federal, state, and local administrators. While none of these general approaches can promise ultimate effectiveness in matching expanding communications capacity with growing public needs, each might to some extent be preferable to the perpetuation of a system whose past performance provides little reason to hope for future success.

An Independent Innovation Process

Why should the communications industry be granted an additional layer of legal protection from technological competition—this administrative body empowered to restrain activities deemed lawful by the courts and Congress? Broadcaster claims of "unjust enrichment," "unfair competition," and "copyright infringement" were rejected by the courts and ignored by Congress; yet the industry was sucessful in preventing the functioning of legitimate cable operations, desired by the public, through the actions of its regulator.

On the basis of this record of regulatory conduct, it seems justifiable to argue that technological advances in electronic mass media should be able to prove their worth in the marketplace, free of government restriction. Yet it might also be argued that vital societal needs could be swept aside by the sheer force of innovation or of economics, and that if "public interest" cannot be equated with broadcast interest, neither can it be measured solely in terms of channel capacity.

The success of competing communications systems might be determined by economics if the public had the option of selecting from among clearly defined alternative types of service. However, if the history of technological progress serves as a guide to its future, no such clear choices will be possible, for innovation will not be advanced in concert by a united industry but will emerge sporadically in various stages of development, championed by a wide array of rival enterprises. Each faction will advocate its own distinct mixture of communications features, related only incidentally to public needs and often to some extent incompatible with other techniques already in operation.

If a force other than the lowest possible delivery cost is to determine whether a wired system featuring locally oriented cablecasting, for instance, is to be replaced by a more effective direct-to-home satellite linkage, it would appear essential that the owners of such systems do not exercise absolute right of control. Yet no single set of statutes or rules can ever permanently resolve questions raised at all stages of communications evolution, for the proper response to each question will be dependent upon constantly varying relationships between the extent of public demand for each of a variety of communications services and the capacity of various evolving media to satisfy each need.

Thus, while free competition among electronic media might provide the incentive for technological advances far more beneficial to audiences than mere industry stability guaranteed by law, an even greater range of social benefits might be realized through consistent and perceptive guidance of these advances on behalf of the American public. However, consistency and perception during an era of industry transition and expansion will demand one attribute the FCC has never possessed, the capacity to create and enforce broad and comprehensive long-range communications policy. Without this capacity the agency can only react to events rather than achieve objectives; it is the prisoner of the process it would supervise. Therefore, the decision whether the public would be better served by a medium freed of competitive restraints, or subject to continuing controls, seems dependent on one central factor—the ability of the government to create a regulatory body truly independent of particularized pressure and capable of gathering and analyzing sufficient information to select and pursue goals based on only one standard, the interests and needs of the public.

A Strong Federal Role

In 1926 Senator Dill, coauthor of the Dill-White Radio Act of 1927, declared that the governmental body vested with the authority to control broadcasting must be an independent commission because "the exercise of this power is fraught with such possibilities that it should not be entrusted to any one man nor to any administrative department of the government. This regulatory power should be as free from political interference or arbitrary control as possible."[42] Yet from the inception of federal broadcast regulation this hope of impartial administration has been difficult to realize simply because it has been impossible to filter politics out of what is essentially a political process: to make what is subjective, objective; what is irrational, rational; what is particularized, universal. Eight major governmental studies have focused on weaknesses in the FCC's process of administration and policy making during the past three decades and have recommended structural modifications, either specifically or as part of a general revision of independent commission operations. Yet the latest of such studies, in 1971, could declare with reason that "obsolete organization forms limit the effectiveness of . . . commissions in responding to economic, technological, structural and social change. Inappropriate regulatory structures and cumbersome procedures impose burdens that impede good public service, sound financial and operational planning, and adjustment to changes in growing industries—contrary to the purposes of regulations."[43]

Since seven of these studies were commissioned by the president, and four of them recommended transferring at least a portion of agency regulatory responsibility to the executive branch, the reluctance of Congress to act upon their findings might be explained in terms of broader rivalries between these two branches of government.[44] Yet the fact that Congress instituted only one such inquiry of its own during this era, and terminated that study after evidence pointed to questionable associations involving two FCC commissioners and certain broadcasters, reveals a far more disquieting attitude—an apparent lack of interest in enhancing either the integrity or the efficiency of existing commission process.[45]

Unless a public heretofore uncertain of its needs and unaware of its rights can unite to exert pressure for more effective communications regulation, the prospects for major improvements in the FCC's structures or procedures seem extremely dim. For this reason, then, none of the eminently rational reports advocating broad-scale revisions in the agency's mechanisms seems as likely to achieve improvement as a narrower approach aimed solely at the crucial weakness in commission process, its inability to authorize continuous improvement in the communications systems' delivery capacity.

Not only could public attention be more easily directed to this weakness, but the remedy itself could be justified in basic terms rather than in the complex phraseology of administrative science. All that seems necessary is an amendment to the Communications Act of 1934 expressly relieving the FCC of any responsibility for the economic welfare of the electronic mass media, an obligation it now discharges on the most tenuous of grounds. This single obligation, which has formed the basis for all restrictions upon cable carriage, might be transferred to a new communications research body which would issue each prospective nonspectrum media system a certificate of "public interest, convenience and necessity" upon a showing that its proposed services would enhance rather than diminish the total communications benefits available to the audience it intends to reach. While this pragmatic technique of simply denying an industry regulator the power to stifle outside competition would not result in an ideal system of administrative organization, it could at least claim the virtue of possible legislative approval. Congress could hardly ignore unified public demand for a research and policy-making organization with a single mission so clearly in the public's interest, especially since, in the absence of congressional action, the executive branch might be encouraged to attempt to assert broader authority over this area of communications control.

Even if this type of regulatory body should be created, there is, of course, no guarantee that it would prove effective in ascertaining public needs and encouraging innovation to serve those needs. However, simply insulating the two mutually antagonistic goals — promoting industry stability and stimulating competitive progress —from contamination through intermixture in a single administrative process would seem at least a first step toward that objective.

A federal role in future media evolution appears essential because most systems will almost undoubtedly be engaged in nationwide programming and informational exchanges. Yet, despite the national focus of these activities, it seems equally important for additional controls to be operating at the other end of the communications process, where the value of media services can be directly related to their functions in each state and its communities.

A Vital Concurrent State Role

Although at least thirty states have considered regulating their domestic community antenna or CATV systems during the past two decades, their efforts have generally been discouraged by a combination of three factors: the likelihood of eventual federal preemption, the minimal extent of local concern caused by their operation, and the inappropriateness of public utility controls to remedy those local complaints which did exist. Each of these factors has been modified by recent events, and thus the fact that only six states were attempting to assert jurisdiction over cable operations as the year 1972 began seems less significant than the fact that four of those six states have asserted that authority within the past three years.[46]

The first clear inication that a state might claim jurisdiction over local aspects of cable operation concurrently with the federal government was contained in the Supreme Court's decision in *TV Pix v. Taylor* in 1970, which held that the state of Nevada could impose certain rate and franchise conditions upon all domestic cable operators because "the community antenna television business . . . constitutes the last stage of . . . transmission of television signals. . . . It is much more local than national, involving cable equipment, through public streets and ways, local franchises, local intra-state advertising and selling of service."[47] In its Third Report and Order, the FCC expressly delineated the outer perimeters of the preemptive jurisdiction it would claim; it asserted exclusive authority over issues involving the quantity and nature of broadcast signals carried by each cable system, the technical standards to be applied, program-origination rules, cross-ownership restrictions, and the obligation of offering equal employment opportunity. At the same time the agency admitted it did not have a staff sufficient to license cable systems already almost three times as numerous as television stations. It therefore asked the states or their municipalities, subject only to minimal federal supervision, to make the initial franchise or license awards; determine the franchise areas; set mandatory rates of diffusion, subscriber payments, and service standards; and establish franchise fees if necessary.

There seems reason to doubt whether the federal government can preempt even those areas specified, for state electrical codes, antitrust laws, and fair employment practices, among other statutes, have been held concurrently effective unless there "is such actual conflict between the two schemes of regulation that both cannot stand in the same area, or evidence [indicates] a congressional design to preempt the entire field."[48] Even if this broad claim of preemption should be sustained, however, there is now at least a rather clearly defined area of cable control each state can exercise without fear of eventual displacement.

In addition, there is an ever increasing need and justification for state control, since the nature of cable service is changing, and since cable exerts a growing influence over the life of each citizen.

As late as 1968 a federal district court could strike down a municipal ordinance attempting to control CATV systems as essential services. The court labeled the ordinance discriminatory because "the public has about as much real need for the services of a CATV system as it does for hand-carved ivory back-scratchers."[49]

States have no right to single out a particular business for special regulation unless its activities have some direct and substantial effect upon the welfare of their citizens. Thus, while cable's function remained primarily that of broadcast delivery, there was no constitutional justification for the exercise of any state regulatory power except that customarily applied to similar operations of common carriers. For this reason the first two states to enact cable legislation, Connecticut and Nevada, were forced to follow this public utility approach. Since most systems have been compelled, either by their nonexclusive franchises or by the availability of existing broadcast signals, to maintain reasonable rates, the primary result of controls dictated by legal necessity rather than by choice has been to increase the cost of both system operation and system administration without corresponding benefit to the public.[50]

Now, however, the transformation of the cable medium from an antenna service to a community-supported network of program originators and common carriers has greatly extended the actual or potential effect of its functions upon the citizens of each state and has thereby allowed a much broader range of regulatory powers to be employed in supervising its operations. Rhode Island, in 1969, was the first state to draft a flexible cable code, based, not upon cumbersome formulas for setting public utility rates, but upon the simple mandate "to prevent such operation from having detrimental consequences to the public interest." The code authorized the state's cable administrator to enact rules and regulations necessary to achieve this end.[51] Vermont and Hawaii have since passed similar broad guidelines for cable regulation; and with its latest model bill, the National Association of Railroad and Utility Commissioners (NARUC), the influential organization of state regulatory agencies, has abandoned its earlier common carrier approach to adopt this less rigid structure for cable administration.

Thus the authority, the need, the justification, and the technique for effective state control have coalesced in the early 1970s, and in view of the fact that some 4,500 franchises have already been granted, with another 2,800 pending, the necessity for immediate exercise of this new capacity appears extremely urgent. Municipal corporations have customarily been involved in the franchising function because cable systems have needed easements or other land rights in order to lay their cable across city-owned streets. By such grants, in return for benefits promised by the systems, cities have been found by the courts to be creating an "interest of a proprietary nature in public land."[52] The award of each franchise, then, may create a right in the franchisee or his successors to operate in that locality without concern for any subsequent cable regulation passed by state or federal authorities, since to hold otherwise could be an unconstitutional impairment of an existing contractual right.[53] Considering the growing disparity between the resources of cable corporations and the expertise available in the average community, there seems to be a compelling need for each state to intervene before additional communities are committed to agreements denying their citizens the full range of communications benefits available to all other citizens of that state.

In addition, municipalities, because of their limited administrative capacity and narrow jurisdictional base, have proved to be extremely parochial cable administrators. The emphasis in most cable negotiations has been upon revenues to be paid the city, while crucial issues such as rate of diffusion to poorer or less populated areas of the city, technical compatibility with neighboring systems, and facilities available for cablecasting and common carrier operation have been largely ignored. The fact that service customarily extends only to the outer boundaries of the franchising unit not only denies unincorporated areas any linkage with the city but also severs school districts and regional college services and in general intensifies the rivalries between urban and suburban factions.[54]

Each state could end this narrow factionalism and its accompanying waste of communications benefits by imposing broader franchise districts upon areas not already splintered by existing cable agreements; and, through provisions of mandatory coverage in the state code, at least basic service for all sections within these districts could be insured. Thus the state, rather than the community or the federal government, seems the ideal administrative unit to achieve a truly responsive, locally oriented cable service.[55]

Working in conjunction with a federal body evaluating the

potential of various media systems, and with local authorities responding to complaints of individual subscribers, the state would be well-situated to coordinate these regulatory activities into a cohesive communications policy of particular value to its citizens. The emergence of the state as a major force in the structure of media control would therefore appear to be one of the most useful elements for increasing the effectiveness of evolving communications supervision in the future.

The Alternative

Freeing communications technology from competitive controls might result in a chaos of techniques incompatible with public needs; creating a new federal agency might result only in raising another barrier of bureaucratic procedures between media and audience; strengthening the state regulatory role might result simply in balkanizing national systems into narrow sectional services. Clearly, no structure or technique in itself can guarantee that either the communications industry or its regulators will be guided by the principle of enlightened public interest in the future. Yet, to the extent that organizational structure limits the capacity of men, there seems to be a guarantee inherent in the existing regulatory process of the FCC that each new innovative force will evoke the same instinctive responses as cable. This guarantee seems to argue for experimentation before the next cycle of abrogation and repression begins.

An agency created to protect the spectrum resource now seems a primary cause of its pollution; an agency charged with the responsibility of encouraging communications service now seems a primary cause of its restriction. However diligently individual members of the commission might strive to enhance the expansion of media services in the future, an agency without the capacity to determine audience needs, and incapable of acting without reference to irrelevant industry interests, seems able to succeed only by chance and to fail almost of necessity. Considering the vital function of communications in our society, this process would seem too precious to entrust to such odds.

Appendixes

Appendix A

A Cable Chronology

An outline of comparative media growth and characteristic economic, legal, or regulatory events occurring during the past quarter-century. Cable television information prior to 1967, the first year of extensive FCC filing requirements, is based primarily upon estimates derived from *Television Digest* and *FCC Annual Reports*. For explanation of FCC and RR citations, see "Primary Federal Communications Commission Documents" in References.

1947. TV stations, 12; TV households, 14,000. The master antenna movement begins (R. W. Sanders, "Fringe Area Television Reception," *Radio & TV News*, October 1949, p. 44; or "Community Aerial Stretches TV," *Science Digest*, April 1951, p. 94).

1948. TV stations, 16; TV households, 172,000. The television license freeze is instituted, limiting operation to the 108 stations already authorized (J. A. Stanley, "No Television for Your City?" *Radio & TV News*, December 1951, p. 40).

1949. TV stations, 51; TV households, 940,000. The first extensive noncommercial community antenna is constructed in Astoria, Washington (I. Kamen, "Television Master Antennas," *Radio & TV News*, April 1949, p. 31).

1950. TV stations, 98; TV households, 3.4 million. The first commercial community antenna begins in Lansford, Pennsylvania (E. D. Lucas, "How TV Came to Panther Valley," *Radio & TV News*, March 1951, p. 31).

1951. TV stations, 107; TV households, 10.3 million. Sustained building of community antennas begins, primarily in isolated hilly regions of Pennsylvania, West Virginia, and Oregon ("Community Antenna Systems," *Radio & TV News*, October 1952, p. 8). Wisconsin is the first state to consider cable regulation (7 RR 2054).

1952. TV stations, 108; TV households, 15.3 million; cable systems, 70; cable households, 14,000. Television license freeze is ended, and FCC staff considers cable controls (FCC memos discussing such controls are published in U.S., Congress, Senate, Committee on Commerce, *Review of Allocation Problems of Television Service to Smaller Communities*, 85th Cong., 2d sess., 1958).

219

1953. TV stations, 120; TV households, 20.4 million; cable systems, 150; cable households, 30,000. Community antenna begins to expand with increasing station signals available ("Community TV Antennas: A Nationwide Survey," *Colorado Municipalities*, 1954, p. 123).

1954. TV stations, 356 (ETV, 2); TV households, 26 million; cable systems, 300; cable households, 65,000. Microwave division facilitates community antenna usage of relayed broadcast signals (*J. E. Belknap*, FCC 54-581). Other states consider and reject CATV controls: Arizona (12 RR 2094), New Mexico (10 RR 2058), Washington (14 RR 2059).

1955. TV stations, 411 (ETV, 11); TV households, 30.7 million; cable systems, 400; cable households, 150,000. The FCC decides against asserting cable jurisdiction (for a summary of the FCC's position, see J. C. Doerfer, "Community Antenna Television Systems," *Federal Communications Bar Journal* 14:4.

1956. TV stations, 441 (ETV, 18); TV households, 34.9 million; cable systems, 450; cable households, 300,000. First federal rules pertaining to CATV are enacted, simply limiting radiation level (13 RR 1546a). California court strikes down state regulation attempt (*Television Transmission, Inc. v. P.U.C.*, 301 F2d 862).

1957. TV stations, 471 (ETV, 23); TV households, 38.9 million; cable systems, 500; cable households, 350,000. CATV begins wide-scale invasion of western broadcast markets ("Collision on TV Delivery Route: CATV and Smaller Market TV," *Broadcasting*, 12 May 1958, p. 33).

1958. TV stations, 495 (ETV, 28); TV households, 41.9 million; cable systems, 525; cable households, 450,000. FCC rejects CATV common carrier controls (*Frontier*, 16 RR 1005). Congress convenes first cable hearings (U.S. Congress, Senate, Committee on Commerce, *Review of Allocation Problems of Television Service to Smaller Communities*, 85th Cong., 2d sess., 1958). Court strikes down Wyoming cable controls (17 RR 2131).

1959. TV stations, 510 (ETV, 35); TV households, 43.9 million; cable systems, 560; cable households, 550,000. FCC study discloses no existing economic threat in CATV operations ("Report on Docket 12443," 18 RR 1573). Senate holds hearings on cable control bill (S. 2653).

1960. TV stations, 515 (ETV, 44); TV households, 45.7 million; cable systems, 640; cable households, 650,000. Senate bill S. 2653 is rejected.

1961. TV stations, 527 (ETV, 52); TV households, 47.2 million; cable systems, 700; cable households, 725,000. Court rejects restrictions upon CATV carriage on the basis of "unfair competition" (*Intermountain Broadcasting v. Idaho Microwave*, 196 F. Supp. 315 [D.C. Idaho, 1961]).

1962. TV stations, 541 (ETV, 62); TV households, 48.8 million; cable systems, 800; cable households, 850,000. FCC restricts microwave service to CATV system on basis of economic injury to station (*Carter Mountain Transmission v. FCC*, 321 F2d 359 [D.C. Cir.]).

1963. TV stations, 557 (ETV, 68); TV households, 50.3 million; cable systems, 1,000; cable households, 950,000. Connecticut enacts the first state CATV regulations (*General Statutes of Connecticut*, chap. 289, sec. 16-330).

1964. TV stations, 564 (ETV, 85); TV households, 51.6 million; cable systems, 1,200; cable households, 1.1 million. Court rejects right of broadcaster to restrict CATV carriage on basis of exclusive contract (*Cable Vision v. KUTV*, 335 F2d 348 [9th Cir.]; cert. den. 379 US 989).

1965. TV stations, 569 (ETV, 99); TV households, 52.7 million; cable systems, 1,325; cable households, 1.2 million. FCC, to protect broadcasters, asserts jurisdiction over microwaves serving CATV ("First Report and Order on Dockets 14895, 15233, and 15971," 4 RR 2d 1677); also imposes freeze upon microwave importation into top-100 markets (1 FCC 2d 463).

1966. TV stations, 585 (ETV, 114); TV households, 53.8 million; cable systems, 1,570; cable households, 1.5 million. FCC asserts jurisdiction over all CATV operations ("Second Report and Order on Dockets 14895, 15233, and 15971," 2 FCC 2d 725).

1967. TV stations, 610 (ETV, 127); TV households, 55.1 million; cable systems, 1,770; cable households, 2.1 million. Telephone carrier movement in CATV peaks ("Phone Systems Active in CATV: Bring Capital, Management Skill to New and Growing Systems," *Broadcasting*, 13 February 1967, p. 52). Carrier movement stopped by FCC 214 restrictions (Dockets 16928, 16943, 17098).

1968. TV stations, 635 (ETV, 150); TV households, 57.1 million; cable systems, 2,000; cable households, 2.8 million. FCC jurisdiction over cable affirmed (*U.S. v. Southwestern Cable*, 392 US 157). Cable carriage of copyrighted broadcast programming held not to be infringement (*Fortnightly Corp. v. United Artists*, 392 US 390). FCC asserts more rigorous control over cable operations in top-100 markets ("Notice of Inquiry and Notice of Proposed Rulemaking in Docket 18397," 15 FCC 2d 417).

1969. TV stations, 662 (ETV, 175); TV households, 57.7 million; cable systems, 2,260; cable households, 3.6 million. FCC makes cablecasting mandatory ("First Report and Order on Docket 18397," 20 FCC 2d 201).

1970. TV stations, 680 (ETV, 190); TV households, 58.4 million; cable systems, 2,500; cable households, 4.8 million. FCC's "public dividend" plan proposed to allow importation into top-100 markets ("Second Further Notice of Proposed Rulemaking in Docket 18397-A," 24 FCC 2d 580). Prohibition is imposed upon ownership of cable by network and colocated TV station ("Second Report and Order on Docket 18397," 19 RR 2d 1775).

1971. TV stations, 691 (ETV, 199); TV households, 59.3 million; cable systems, 2,600; cable households, 5.3 million. FCC sends letter to Congress outlining proposal to allow importation of cable signals in top-100 markets (23 RR 2d 1755). Office of Telecommunication Policy compromise is summarized ("Third Report and Order on Docket 18397," 24 RR 2d 1501, pp. 1529–32).

1972. TV stations, 695 (ETV, 219); TV households, 60 million; cable systems, 2,750; cable households, 6 million. New rules for major markets are enacted ("Third Report and Order on Docket 18397," 24 RR 2d 1501). FCC's right to compel cablecasting is upheld (*U.S. v. Midwest Video* 406 US 649 [1972]). Microwave importation of copyrighted broadcast signals for carriage on modern cable communication system is held not to be infringement (*CBS v. Tele-PrompTer*, 173 U.S.P.Q. 778).

Appendix B

The Top 100 Markets

The material below is reprinted from "Federal Communications Commission; Cable Television Service; Cable Television Relay Service," Part II, *Federal Register* 37, no. 30 (12 February 1972): 3282.

Subpart D—Carriage of Television Broadcast Signals

§ 76.51 Major television markets

For purposes of the cable television rules, the following is a list of the major television markets and their designated communities:

First 50 major television markets:

1. New York, N.Y.—Linden-Paterson, N.J.
2. Los Angeles-San Bernardino-Corona-Fontana, Calif.
3. Chicago, Ill.
4. Philadelphia, Pa.-Burlington, N.J.
5. Detroit, Mich.
6. Boston-Cambridge-Worcester, Mass.
7. San Francisco-Oakland-San Jose, Calif.
8. Cleveland-Lorain-Akron, Ohio
9. Washington, D.C.
10. Pittsburgh, Pa.
11. St. Louis, Mo.
12. Dallas-Fort Worth, Tex.
13. Minneapolis-St. Paul, Minn.
14. Baltimore, Md.
15. Houston, Tex.
16. Indianapolis-Bloomington, Ind.
17. Cincinnati, Ohio-Newport, Ky.
18. Atlanta, Ga.
19. Hartford-New Haven-New Britain-Waterbury, Conn.
20. Seattle-Tacoma, Wash.
21. Miami, Fla.
22. Kansas City, Mo.
23. Milwaukee, Wis.
24. Buffalo, N.Y.
25. Sacramento-Stockton-Modesto, Calif.
26. Memphis, Tenn.
27. Columbus, Ohio
28. Tampa-St. Petersburg, Fla.
29. Portland, Oreg.
30. Nashville, Tenn.
31. New Orleans, La.
32. Denver, Colo.
33. Providence, R.I.-New Bedford, Mass.

34. Albany-Schenectady-Troy, N.Y.
35. Syracuse, N.Y.
36. Charleston-Huntington, W. Va.
37. Kalamazoo-Grand Rapids-Muskegon-Battle Creek, Mich.
38. Louisville, Ky.
39. Oklahoma City, Okla.
40. Birmingham, Ala.
41. Dayton-Kettering, Ohio
42. Charlotte, N.C.
43. Phoenix-Mesa, Ariz.
44. Norfolk-Newport News-Portsmouth-Hampton, Va.
45. San Antonio, Tex.
46. Greenville-Spartanburg-Anderson, S.C.-Asheville, N.C.
47. Greensboro-High Point-Winston Salem, N.C.
48. Salt Lake City, Utah
49. Wilkes Barre-Scranton, Pa.
50. Little Rock, Ark.

Second 50 major television markets:

51. San Diego, Calif.
52. Toledo, Ohio
53. Omaha, Nebr.
54. Tulsa, Okla.
55. Orlando-Daytona Beach, Fla.
56. Rochester, N.Y.
57. Harrisburg-Lebanon-Lancaster-York, Pa.
58. Texarkana, Tex.-Shreveport, La.
59. Mobile, Ala.-Pensacola, Fla.
60. Davenport, Iowa-Rock Island-Moline, Ill.
61. Flint-Bay City-Saginaw, Mich.
62. Green Bay, Wis.
63. Richmond-Petersburg, Va.
64. Springfield-Decatur-Champaign-Jacksonville, Ill.

65. Cedar Rapids-Waterloo, Iowa
66. Des Moines-Ames, Iowa
67. Wichita-Hutchinson, Kans.
68. Jacksonville, Fla.
69. Cape Girardeau, Mo.-Paducah, Ky.-Harrisburg, Ill.
70. Roanoke-Lynchburg, Va.
71. Knoxville, Tenn.
72. Fresno, Calif.
73. Raleigh-Durham, N.C.
74. Johnstown-Altoona, Pa.
75. Portland-Poland Spring, Maine
76. Spokane, Wash.
77. Jackson, Miss.
78. Chattanooga, Tenn.
79. Youngstown, Ohio
80. South Bend-Elkhart, Ind.
81. Albuquerque, N. Mex.
82. Fort Wayne-Roanoke, Ind.
83. Peoria, Ill.
84. Greenville-Washington-New Bern, N.C.
85. Sioux Falls-Mitchell, S. Dak.
86. Evansville, Ind.
87. Baton Rouge, La.
88. Beaumont-Port Arthur, Tex.
89. Duluth-Superior, Minn.
90. Wheeling, W. Va.-Steubenville, Ohio
91. Lincoln-Hastings-Kearney, Nebr.
92. Lansing-Onondaga, Mich.
93. Madison, Wis.
94. Columbus, Ga.
95. Amarillo, Tex.
96. Huntsville-Decatur, Ala.
97. Rockford-Freeport, Ill.
98. Fargo-Grand Forks-Valley City, N. Dak.
99. Monroe, La.-El Dorado, Ark.
100. Columbia, S.C.

Appendix C

Third Report and Order (Broadcast Signal Importation)

The material below is reprinted from "Federal Communications Commission; Cable Television Service; Cable Television Relay Service," Part II, *Federal Register*, 37, no. 30 (12 February 1972): 3262.

General Outline of the Rules Pertaining to
Broadcast Signal Carriage

The television signal carriage rules divide all signals into three classifications:

First, signals that a cable system, upon request of the appropriate station, must carry

Second, signals that, taking television market size into account, a cable system may carry

Third, signals that some systems may carry in addition to those required or permitted in the two above categories

These three classifications of signals are used in various market situations as outlined below:

Priorities	Cable Systems Located Outside All Television Markets
First	The following signals are required, upon request, to be carried: 1) All Grade B signals 2) All translator stations in the cable community with 100 watts or higher power 3) All educational television stations within 35 miles 4) Television stations significantly viewed in the cable community
Second	The cable television system may carry any other additional signals.

	Cable Systems Located in Smaller Television Markets
First	The following signals are required, upon request, to be carried:

1) All market signals (those within 35 miles and those located in other communities that are generally considered part of the same market) *
2) Grade B signals of educational television stations
3) Grade B signals from stations in other smaller markets
4) All translator stations in the cable community with 100 watts or higher power
5) Television stations significantly viewed in the cable community

Second   A cable system may carry additional signals so that, including the signals required to be carried under the First priority, the following total may be provided:
1) Three full network stations (subject to leapfrogging restrictions)
2) One independent station (subject to leapfrogging restrictions)

Third   Generally, the cable system may carry additional educational stations and one or more stations programmed in non-English languages.

Cable Systems Located in the First Fifty Major Markets

First   The following signals are required, upon request, to be carried:
1) All market signals (see smaller markets above) **
2) Grade B signals of educational television stations
3) All translator stations in the cable community with 100 watts or higher power
4) Television stations significantly viewed in the cable community

Second   A cable system may carry additional signals so that, including the signals required to be carried under the First priority, the following total may be provided:
1) Three full network stations (subject to leapfrogging restrictions)
2) Three independent stations (subject to leapfrogging restrictions)

Third   Generally, the cable system may carry educational and non-English language stations as described for smaller markets above.
The cable system may carry two additional independent stations (subject to leapfrogging restrictions); provided, however, that the number of additional

signals permitted under this priority is reduced by the number of signals added to the system under the second priority.

Cable Systems Located in the Second Fifty Major Markets

First   The same requirements apply as for the First Fifty Markets.

Second   The cable system may carry additional signals so that, including the signals required to be carried under the First priority, the following total may be provided:

     1) Three full network stations (subject to leap-frogging restrictions)

     2) Two independent stations (subject to leap-frogging restrictions)

Third   The same requirements apply as for the First Fifty Markets.

NOTE: Cable systems located in overlapping markets where differing amounts of service are provided for under the rules, e.g., in the overlap of a smaller market and one of the first fifty markets, must operate in accordance with the rules for the larger market.

*National audience rating services, e.g., ARB and Nielsen, recognize differing communities as being in the same market (hyphenated markets). These characterizations may be relied on for smaller markets; our new rules, however, designate specifically the hyphenated major markets.

**In the major markets, where a cable television is located in the designated community of such a market, it shall not carry as a local signal the signal of a station licensed to a designated community in another major market, unless the designated community of the cable system is wholly within 35 miles of the reference point of the other community or unless the station meets the significant viewing standard.

Appendix D

OTP Consensus Agreement

The material below is reprinted from "Federal Communications Commission; Cable Television Service; Cable Television Relay Service," Part II, *Federal Register*, 37, no. 30 (12 February 1972): 3260.

Local Signals

Local signals defined as proposed by the FCC, except that the significant viewing standard to be applied to "out-of-market" independent stations in overlapping market situations would be a viewing hour share of at least 2% and a net weekly circulation of at least 5%.

Distant Signals

No change from what the FCC has proposed.

Exclusivity for Non-Network Programming (against distant signals only): A series shall be treated as a unit for all exclusivity purposes.

The burden will be upon the copyright owner or upon the broadcaster to notify cable systems of the right to protection in these circumstances.

A. Markets 1–50

A 12-month pre-sale period running from the date when a program in syndication is first sold any place in the U.S., plus run-of-contract exclusivity where exclusivity is written into the contract between the station and the program supplier (existing contracts will be presumed to be exclusive).

B. Markets 51–100

For syndicated programming which has had no previous non-network broadcast showing in the market, the following contractual exclusivity will be allowed:

(1) For off-network series, commencing with first showing until first run completed, but no longer than one year.

(2) For first-run syndicated series, commencing with first showing and for two years thereafter.

(3) For feature films and first-run, non-series syndicated programs, commencing with availability date and for two years thereafter.

228

(4) For other programming, commencing with purchase and until day after first run, but no longer than one year.

Provided, however, that no exclusivity protection would be afforded against a program imported by a cable system during prime-time unless the local station is running or will run that program during prime-time.

Existing contracts will be presumed to be exclusive. No preclearance in these markets.

C. Smaller Markets
No change in the FCC proposals.

Exclusivity for Network Programming

The same-day exclusivity now provided for network programming would be reduced to simultaneous exclusivity (with special relief for time-zone problems) to be provided in all markets.

Leapfrogging

A. For each of the first two signals imported, no restriction on point of origin, except that if [it] is taken from the top-25 markets it must be from one of the two closest such markets. Whenever a CATV system must black out programming from a distant top-25 market station whose signals it normally carries, it may substitute any distant signals without restriction.

B. For the third signal, the UHF priority, as set forth in the FCC's letter of August 5, 1971, p. 16.

Copyright Lesiglation

A. All parties would agree to support separate CATV copyright legislation as described below, and to seek its early passage.

B. Liability to copyright, including the obligation to respect valid exclusivity agreements, will be established for all CATV carriage of all radio and television broadcast signals except carriage by independently owned systems now in existence with fewer than 3500 subscribers. As against distant signals importable under the FCC's initial package, no greater exclusivity may be contracted for than the Commission may allow.

C. Compulsory licenses would be granted for all local signals as defined by the FCC, and additionally for those distant signals defined and authorized under the FCC's initial package and those signals grandfathered when the initial package goes into effect. The FCC would retain the power to authorize additional distant signals for CATV carriage; there would, however, be no compulsory license granted with respect to such signals, nor would the FCC be able to limit the scope of exclusivity agreements as applied to such signals beyond the limits applicable to over-the-air showings.

D. Unless a schedule of fees covering the compulsory licenses or some other payment mechanism can be agreed upon betwen the copy-right owners and the CATV owners in time for inclusion in the new copyright statute, the legislation would simply provide for compulsory arbitration failing private agreement on copyright fees.

E. Broadcasters, as well as copyright owners, would have the right to enforce exclusivity rules through court actions for injunction and mon-etary relief.

Radio Carriage

When a CATV system carries a signal from an AM or FM radio sta-tion licensed to a community beyond a 35-mile radius of the system, it must, on request, carry the signals of all local AM or FM stations, respectively.

Grandfathering

The new requirements as to signals which may be carried are applic-able only to new systems. Existing CATV systems are "grandfathered." They can thus freely expand currently offered service throughout their presently franchised areas with one exception. In the top 100 markets, if the system expands beyond discrete areas specified in FCC order (e.g., the San Diego situation), operations in the new portions must comply with the new requirements.

Grandfathering exempts from future obligation to respect copyright exclusivity agreements, but does not exempt from future liability for copyright payments.

Glossary of Technical Terms

Glossary of Technical Terms

The following terms are among those most commonly employed to describe cable operation or its regulation. Those definitions marked with an (*) relate specifically to cable rules now in effect.

ACCESS CHANNELS* (*also* PUBLIC ACCESS). Those channels of a cable system made available to members of the public without charge on a nondiscriminatory, first-come, first-served basis and over which the cable operator can exercise no power of censorship.

AML (AMPLITUDE MODULATED LINK). A technique for linking cable grids or branch lines by high-frequency microwave rather than coaxial truck line. Reduces the cost of wiring rural regions or congested urban areas. *See also* QUASI-LASER.

BOOSTER. A relay device retransmitting broadcast signals at increased power on the same frequencies as those originally received. *See also* TRANSLATOR.

BRANCH. That portion of a cable television system linking the "trunk," or main line, to each "drop," or household terminal connection.

BROADBAND COMMUNICATION. Any electronic delivery system having the capacity to carry a wide range of electromagnetic frequencies. The modern cable operation would be "broadband," while telephone and telegraph circuits would be termed "narrow band." *See also* COAXIAL CABLE.

BROADCAST BAND. Generally, the medium wave (standard AM) radio broadcast frequency allocation (535 kHz–1,605 kHz). Can also apply to any other segment of such frequencies allocated for a particular broadcast service.

BROADCASTING. The dissemination of radio communications intended for reception by the public directly or through relay stations.

CABLECASTING. Term often used synonymously for any nonbroadcast signals carried by a cable system, but more accurately employed to describe only that programming produced and distributed by the cable operator on the channel authorized for such service. *See also* LOCAL ORIGINATION.

CABLE SYSTEM. By FCC definition, a facility serving a single community or a distinct governmental entity. Thus, one cable operation dis-

233

tributing signals within two separate but contiguous municipalities would be viewed by the commission as two systems, even though unified in management and operation and providing the same service to each area.

CABLE TV (*also* COMMUNITY ANTENNA TELEVISION and CATV). (NOTE: see author's distinctions, pages 6, 77.) The modern designation for a communications system which delivers by wire to those households or subscribers paying a fee for such service a number of broadcast and nonbroadcast channels of entertainment and information.

CARRIAGE. The conveyance or retransmission of a broadcast signal.

CARS (COMMUNITY ANTENNA RELAY SYSTEM) now termed CAR (CABLE RELAY SYSTEM). A microwave service owned by a cable TV system for the purpose of importing television signals for use over the system.

CHANNEL. A specified band of frequencies assigned to convey the transmissions of a particular broadcast station, which for U.S. television encompasses 6 MHz of frequencies, a range of frequencies which could also carry 600 radio or 240 FM channels.

—CLASS I CABLE CHANNEL.* Channel used to deliver broadcast signals to subscribers.

—CLASS II CABLE CHANNEL.* Channel used to deliver cablecast programming to subscriber sets without decoders.

—CLASS III CABLE CHANNEL.* Channel used to deliver cablecasting programming requiring special subscriber terminal equipment, such as encoded (pay or informational) programming, facsimile or printed message material.

—CLASS IV CABLE CHANNEL.* Return or response channel on two-way system.

COAXIAL CABLE. An extremely efficient two-conductor, common-axis design for the carriage of a wide range of frequencies (now approaching zero to 300,000 MHz, in contrast to telephone wire's 200 MHz–5,000 MHz) which provides a single conduit with the capacity to carry at least fifty channels of television dimension, or a far greater number of audio messages, simultaneously. *See also* CHANNEL.

COMMUNICATIONS COMMON CARRIER. An entity offering wire or microwave point-to-point message delivery to lessees at a specified, or "tariffed," rate.

CONTOUR. A line defining a broadcast station's coverage patterns. A grade A contour encompasses the area in which a good picture is normally available at least 90 percent of the time in the most favorable 50 percent of all receiver locations.

CONVERTER. Any device changing the frequency of a signal. A converter in the "head end" of a cable system normally changes all UHF signals received into VHF frequencies to facilitate delivery to the more effective VHF tuning band (channels 2–13) of the average television receiver. A "set top," or subscriber terminal converter, may alter band A (typically broadcast) or band B (typically non-broadcast) frequencies to double the twelve-channel VHF reception capacity; or unscramble coded signals employed in informational or "pay-TV" services.

DEDICATED CHANNEL.* A cable channel devoted to one of three uses specified by the FCC: local government, education, or noncommercial public access.

DISTANT SIGNAL. A signal carried beyond the predicted grade B contour of the station transmitting it.

DOWNSTREAM. The usual flow of signals from the "head end," or originating point, of the system to the subscriber terminal.

DROP. The final linkage of a cable system, connecting each subscriber home to the service.

DUPLICATION. Cable carriage of a "distant signal" providing the same programming as that transmitted by a "local station." *Also see* NONDUPLICATION.

EXCLUSIVITY.* The contractual right to be the sole exhibitor of a program in a particular area for a specified period of time.

FIRST-RUN SERIES.* A series whose episodes have had no national network exhibition, or no regional exhibition in the relevant television market.

FRAGMENTATION. The concept that cable's multiple-program offerings divide the viewing attention of a local station's audience among a greater number of channels, thus reducing the percentage of those watching the local station.

FRANCHISE. An agreement between a cable operator and a governmental body defining the rights and obligations of each with respect to communication service to be provided the community involved. In a technical sense, "franchise" denotes an exclusive grant, while "license" would be the more accurate term for each governmental authorization to operate a cable system on a nonexclusive basis.

FREQUENCY ALLOCATION. The reservation of a particular band of frequencies for the use of a specific broadcast service or services.

FREQUENCY ASSIGNMENT. The granting of a specific channel of frequencies to a particular broadcaster.

FULL NETWORK STATION.* A commercial television station that in weekly "prime-time" hours usually carries 85 percent of the hours of programming offered by one of the three major networks with which it has a primary affiliation.

GRANDFATHERING. A tactic commonly employed by the FCC, when it is enacting new rules, of exempting existing stations or systems from their effects, either for a specified period of time or indefinitely, to allow changes to be made without undue injury to either the operators or the audiences dependent upon their services.

HARDWARE. Actual physical equipment of a cable system, including its camera, antennas, cable, and other electronic devices.

HEAD END. The electronic control center of a cable system, usually located near the antenna or microwave relay facilities, where incoming television signals are amplified, filtered, and converted if necessary before being delivered to the subscriber home.

INCASTING. The process of sending signals "upstream" within a cable system, or from a subscriber to the "head end."

INDEPENDENT STATION.* A commercial television station that in "prime time" usually carries not more than ten hours per week of programming offered by the three major networks.

INTERACTIVE MODE. A cable system that allows two-way communication, including contact between subscriber and operator, or contacts among groups of subscribers.

LEAPFROGGING. Importation by a cable system of a broadcast signal from a distant market while bypassing the signals of a station closer to the system.

LOCAL ORIGINATION. Programming produced by the system which delivers it, ranging from automated displays of time and weather to live and videotaped features produced by the operator or members of the public.

LOCAL STATION. Any television station placing a signal of grade B contour or better over any portion of the area in which a cable system is operating. Can also refer to any television station located within thirty-five miles of any portion of a cable system.*

MAJOR MARKET. The specified zone of a commercial television station licensed to a top-100 community (see Appendix A for a list of such communities), as designated by the American Research Bureau (ARB), a private organization that conducts audience analyses.

MICROWAVE. High-frequency transmission facility used to relay messages, including television signals from point to point, by common carrier.

MSO (MULTIPLE SYSTEM OPERATOR). An entity which owns and operates a number of cable facilities.

NET WEEKLY CIRCULATION.* The number of television households without cable that view a station for five or more minutes during an entire week, expressed as a percentage of the total number of television households without cable in the survey area.

NETWORK PROGRAMMING.* The programming supplied by a national or regional television network, commercial or noncommercial.

NONDUPLICATION. Restraint imposed upon cable carriage of "distant signals" offering the same programming as that transmitted by a "local station." At various times, the FCC has prohibited such "duplication" for thirty days from time of transmission, for fifteen days prior to and subsequent to time of transmission, and for one day from time of transmission.

OFF-NETWORK SERIES.* Reruns of network series syndicated or distributed by a means other than simultaneous network distribution.

PARTIAL NETWORK STATION.* A commercial television station that in "prime time" usually carries more than ten hours per week of programming offered by the three major television networks, but less than the 85 percent specified for "full-network stations."

PAY-TV (*also* SUBSCRIPTION TV; STV; TOLL TV). An independently programmed communications system charging subscribers for each program viewed. Distribution can be by encoded broadcast signal, wire, or cable channel, but the pay-TV operator cannot augment his offerings with programming from television broadcasts.

PENETRATION. The percentage of households in an area where cable service is available who have subscribed to the service.

PLANT. The physical equipment, or "hardware," of a cable system.

PRIME TIME.* Programming carried from 6 P.M. to 11 P.M., local time; except in the central time zone between 5 P.M. and 10 P.M., and in the mountain time zone where each station may decide whether the prime-time period shall be 6 P.M.–11 P.M. or 5 P.M.–10 P.M.

QUASI-LASER. A specialized microwave linkage to replace trunk coaxial cable. *See* AMC.

SERIES.* Two or more works centered on and dominated by the same individual or having the same cast of characters or a continuous theme or plot.

SIGNIFICANTLY VIEWED.* Viewing in other than cable television households of a station which constitutes a share of at least 3 percent of the total weekly hours, with a net weekly circulation of 25 percent; for an "independent," at least a 2 percent share, with a net weekly circulation of at least 5 percent.

SIPHONING. Charge of broadcasters that audience support of cable and pay-TV systems will allow them to outbid broadcasters for prime entertainment and sporting events, and therefore to deprive "free-TV" audiences of this premium programming.

SMALLER TELEVISION MARKETS.* All television markets not designated as "major," or top-100, markets.

SOFTWARE. A cable system's communication functions, including its programming and the information and data-retrieval services it offers, as opposed to its equipment.

SYNDICATED PROGRAMMING.* Any programming sold, licensed, or distributed to television stations in more than one market within the United States for noninterconnected television broadcasts. Live presentations are not included.

TERMINAL. The equipment at the subscriber end of the cable linkage. This term includes everything from a simple plate to which wires from the antenna outlet on the receiver are attached to sophisticated devices which might include keyboards, videotape recorders, and minicomputers.

TRANSLATOR. A low-powered relay device, licensed by the FCC, which receives a television signal on one channel and converts it to another channel, generally UHF, for retransmission without significantly altering its original characteristics. (The term "translator" now encompasses all spectrum-relay devices authorized by the commission, including VHF relays which previously would have been called "boosters.")

TRUNK. The main line of a cable system, usually including amplifiers as well as the coaxial linkages.

UHF (ULTRA HIGH FREQUENCY). A band of frequencies extending from 300 MHz to 3,000 MHz. Television stations assigned to channels 14–70 (previously through 83) are known as UHF stations and operate on frequencies ranging from approximately 470 MHz to 800 MHz.

UPSTREAM. A message flow from the subscriber terminal to the "head end" of a system.

UTILITY SERVICES. Cable functions not directly related to audience viewing, such as meter reading or security devices.

VHF (VERY HIGH FREQUENCY). A band of frequencies extending from 30 MHz to 300 MHz. Television stations assigned channels 2–13 are known as VHF stations. (Channels 2–6, from 54 MHz to 88 MHz; channels 7–13, from 174 MHz to 216 MHz.)

WHITE AREA. Area outside the normal coverage range of any broadcast service of a particular class. The term is usually used with reference to AM radio coverage.

WRIT OF CERTIORARI. Procedure by which a party in a judicial proceeding requests review of an adverse decision by the U.S. Supreme Court. The granting of such review is discretionary in most cases, and if the appeal is denied, the appellant customarily has no further legal recourse on that specific issue.

WRIT OF MANDAMUS. Procedure by which a party requests a court to compel a governmental official to perform an act he is required by law to perform.

For additional terms, see *CATV* (Special Edition), 17 February 1972, pp. 32–33; or *Dictionary of CATV Terminology*, Jones International Ltd., c/o National Cable Television Association, Inc., 918 Sixteenth St., N.W., Washington, D.C. 20006.

Notes

Notes

Chapter 1

1. While recent cable studies have continued to underestimate the force of the economic and political factors inhibiting innovation in the field of communications, a refreshing note of realism has been developing as the focus of wired-system research has shifted from abstract projections of cable functions to predictions based upon actual observation of system operation. Distance may have lent enchantment to the vision of cable as the messianic medium, and thus, although the long-term predictions of works such as Harold Barnett and Edward Greenberg's "A Proposal for Wired City Television," *Washington University Law Quarterly* 1968 (Winter 1968): 1, or the Electronic Industries Association's "The Future of Broadband Communication," FCC Docket 18397 (October 1969) pt. 5, may have generated the enthusiasm necessary to release CATV from its restraints, the more limited, and thus immediately realizable, ends considered by a series of Rand Corporation studies (cited in References) and typified by the Sloan Commission report, *On the Cable: The Television of Abundance* (New York: McGraw-Hill, 1971), could in the long run have greater influence upon the ultimate degree and extent of cable service.

2. In mid-1973 there were between 2,900 and 3,000 cable systems in operation, another 1,760 franchised but not yet in operation, and 1,600 additional franchise applications pending. While at least 75 systems were serving 10,000 or more subscribers, led by San Diego with 57,000, the average system still served only 2,240 homes. Some 175 systems reported offering more than twelve channels of service, but the industry average was 10.4 (*Television Factbook*, service vol. no. 42, 1972–73 [Washington, D.C.: Television Digest, 1972]; supplemented by "A Short Course in Cable, 1973," *Broadcasting*, 18 June 1973, p. 25).

3. This 25 percent estimate excludes any system simply classifying its automated weather or time service as "program origination." Thus, while more than 1,500 systems now have the capacity to offer this information, and some 375 advertise on their automated channel, this function was technologically possible in 1962 and therefore marks no advance in cable performance. Only the nearly 800 systems now originating programming on a regular basis (averaging ten hours a week) or offering more than twelve channels of service have progressed beyond the level of performance possible a decade ago (*Broadcasting*, 18 June 1973, p. 25).

4. An interim "freeze" was instituted on 1 April 1965 by FCC, "Notice of

Inquiry . . . in Docket 15971," 4 RR 2d 1679, with modifications in procedure but not in general effect in March 1966 and December 1968 (see chap. 7). It has been lifted under certain conditions by FCC, "Third Report and Order in Docket 18397," 24 RR 2d 1501 (1972). (For a discussion of docket numbers and FCC and RR citations, see References, under heading "Primary FCC Documents.")

5. The "public dividend" plan, (FCC, "Second Further Notice of Proposed Rulemaking in Docket 18397A," 24 FCC 2d 580 [1970]), was the first such proposal. This plan of June 1970 was abandoned in the face of widespread criticism (see chap. 8), but its general effect was carried forward by the "Third Report and Order," 24 RR 2d 1501.

6. TelePrompTer, after its merger with H and B American, became the largest single-system owner, but its 650,000 subscriber homes constitute only about 10 percent of the total cable audience, and thus only 1 percent of the 60 million television homes in the United States.

7. For an expression of this philosophy, see FCC, "Letter of August 5, 1971," 22 RR 2d 1755, p. 1760.

8. FCC, "Sixth Report and Order . . . ," 17 Fed. Reg. 3905 (1952). For a detailed criticism of basic commission planning with respect to audience coverages, see Martin Seiden, *An Economic Analysis of Community Antenna Systems and the Television Broadcasting Industry* (Washington, D.C.: Government Printing Office, 1965). More detailed information about the allocation of frequencies in the 30 MHz–960 MHz band can be found in the Office of Telecommunications Management study, *The Radio Frequency Spectrum of the United States: Use and Management* (Washington, D.C.: Office of Emergency Preparedness, 1969), although modifications by the FCC in February 1970 in Docket 18262, reallocating channels 70–81 to land mobile use, make its computations somewhat inaccurate. For a broader and more comprehensive analysis of general FCC allocation and assignment policies, see John M. Kittross, "Television Frequency Allocation Policy in the United States" (Ph.D. diss., University of Illinois, 1960).

9. The unduplicated-audience base of 25,000 was the absolute minimum projected by any feasibility study of network affiliation. The generally accepted minimum was actually 50,000 (U.S., Congress, Senate, Committee on Interstate and Foreign Commerce, *Network Broadcasting* [Barrow Report], 85th Cong., 2d sess., 1957 [Washington, D.C.: Government Printing Office, 1958]). Market coverage figures are from *Television Factbook,* service vol. no. 42, p. 58a.

10. All CATV figures prior to FCC mandatory-reporting requirements for cable in 1966 can only be estimates (these figures are from *Television Factbook,* service vol. no. 42, p. 79a). For an annual comparison of TV-CATV growth from 1952 through 1972, see Appendix A.

11. FCC, "In the Matter of Inquiring into the Impact of Community Antenna . . . on the Orderly Development of Television Broadcasting," Docket 12443, 18 RR 1573 (1959).

12. These specific grounds for restricting cable carriage of television signals are expressed in FCC, "Second Report and Order on Dockets 14895, 15233, and 15971," 2 FFC 2d 725 (1966), pp. 758 ff.

13. See "legislative proposals" following FCC, "Impact of Community Antenna," 18 RR 1753.

14. Jurisdiction was asserted by the FCC in "Second Report and Order," 2 FCC 2d 725. The judicial expression is from *Carroll Broadcasting v. Federal Communications Commission*, 258 F2d 440 (D.C. Cir., 1958). For an excellent overview of vacillating commission attitudes toward this issue, see Frank J. Kahn, "Economic Injury and the Public Interest," *Federal Communications Bar Journal* 23 (1969):182.

15. *Carter Mountain Transmission Corp. v. FCC*, 321 F2d 359 (D.C. Cir., 1962); cert. den. 375 US 951 (1963).

16. FCC, "First Report and Order on Dockets 14895 and 15233," 4 RR 2d 1725 (1965).

17. *Fortnightly Corp. v. United Artists . . .* , 392 US 390 (1968). See also *CBS v. TelePrompTer*, discussed in chapter 8.

18. FCC, "Notice of Inquiry and Notice of Proposed Rulemaking in Docket 18397," 15 FCC 2d 417 (1968).

19. See FCC, "Third Report and Order," 24 RR 2d 1501, p. 1760.

20. See Office of Telecommunications Management, Radio Frequency Spectrum. Also see U.S. Congress, House, Select Committee on Small Business, *The Allocation of Radio Frequency and Its Effect on Small Business*, H. Rept. 1978 (Washington, D.C.: Government Printing Office, 1968). For a comprehensive overview of spectrum management and use, see Harvey J. Levin, *The Invisible Resource: Use and Regulation of the Radio Spectrum* (Baltimore: Johns Hopkins Press, 1971).

In reality, not only this unfortunate pressure upon land mobile users but the entire "spectrum shortage" itself is primarily a creation of law rather then technology, for devices and techniques have already been developed which seem capable of extending the dimensions of this resource sufficiently to meet all existing needs. The problem, as Harvey J. Levin points out in "The Radio Spectrum Resource," *Journal of Law and Economics* (October 1968):437, is that "Mere physical availability of spectrum does not *ipso facto* mean technical usability, and technical usability does not necessarily imply economic usability. Nor need economic usability mean administratively sanctioned (effective) usability." Technology has expanded the technically usable portion of the spectrum dramatically during the past quarter of a century but a massive and continuing investment in equipment based upon past technology has discouraged regulatory action necessary to realize this new potential. As a result, while it can be argued that no spectrum shortage need exist, in a world governed by political rather than scientific law one does exist.

21. FCC, *Report of the Land Mobile Frequency Relief Committee* (Washington, D.C.: Government Printing Office, 1968).

22. These arguments are all advanced ably in Robert R. Nathan Associates, "The Social and Economic Benefits of Television" (29 April 1969), filed with the FCC on behalf of the National Association of Broadcasters.

23. The FCC, under *USCA*, title 47, para. 15, has the mandate not only to maintain communications service but also to make available "a rapid, efficient . . . service . . . with adequate facilities . . . ," a dual responsibility discussed more fully in chapter 2.

24. In 1970, the three major television networks were reported to have spent a combined total of $11 million each week for film programming. This comparison, while distorted by its omission of other costs involved in such cable

programming, simply suggests the magnitude of the revenues available through direct audience support.

25. For a description of some of the functions which might underwrite the costs of providing free television delivery service, see Electronic Industries Association, "Broadband Communication," FCC Docket 18397; Ben H. Bagdikian, *The Information Machines* (New York: Harper & Row, 1971); and Milt Bryan and Paul Maxwell, "That New World of Extras Is Technologically Today," *TV Communications*, June 1972, p. 128.

26. For a more comprehensive discussion of this point concerning the development of "free" broadcast programming, see chapter 3.

27. Herman W. Land Associates, *Television and the Wired City* (Washington, D.C.: National Association of Broadcasters, 1968) presents interesting empirical evidence that television usage increases only minimally as programming options expand. It argues, not only that people will not abandon professional programming for locally produced features, but that three channels of entertainment and news satisfy the needs of a majority of the population.

On the other hand, Daniel Boorstin, taking expanding usage as a "given," argues that increased programming options will only further fractionalize and isolate audiences, by reducing the commonality of shared viewing experiences and discouraging personal contacts even more than existing media ("Television," *Life*, 10 September 1971, p. 36). For a broader range of scholarly opinion on the social impact of increased public access to information, see Harold Sackman and Norman Nie, eds., *The Informational Utility and Social Choice* (Montvale, N.J.: APIFS Press, 1970).

The danger of two-way services invading subscriber privacy is discussed in Jerrold Oppenheim, "Watch Out for Big Brother Too," *Chicago Journalism Review*, August 1971, p. 8.

28. While this may seem an idealized objective for regulatory bodies, the necessity for such capacity in the field of communications innovation will be explained more fully in chapter 2. The damage resulting from the lack of such capacity in the past is described in Don R. Le Duc, "The FCC v. CATV et al.: A Theory of Regulatory Reflex Action," *Federal Communications Bar Journal* 23, no. 2 (Spring 1969):93.

29. In mid-1973, broadcasters were estimated to own about 37 percent of all cable television systems. While the FCC in its "Second Report and Order on Docket 18397," 19 RR 2d 1775 (1970), indicated its intention to compel television networks and television stations owning cable systems within their own markets to terminate such cross ownership prior to August 1975, this rule, even if strictly enforced, will not prevent broadcasters from expanding their cable holdings in other markets as a means of insuring their continued control of electronic mass communications. For a classic description of newspaper efforts to gain a foothold in the broadcast industry for a similar purpose, see Harvey J. Levin, *Broadcost Regulation and Joint Ownership of Media* (New York: New York University Press, 1960). The FCC's jurisdiction over cable television was affirmed in June 1968 by *United States v. Southwestern Cable,* 392 US 157.

30. For an excellent survey of these future distribution techniques, see U.S. News and World Report, *Wiring the World: The Explosion in Communications* (Washington, D.C.: U.S. News and World Report Books, 1971). Also see Ronald Brown, *Telecommunications: The Booming Technology* (Garden City, N.Y.: Doubleday, 1970); a more detailed and scholarly account of one

such innovation can be found in Q. B. McClannan and G. P. Heckert, "A Satellite System for CATV," *Proceedings of the IEEE* 58 (July 1970):987. For definitions of terms such as "trunk" and "microwave," see Glossary.

Chapter 2

1. *USCA*, title 47, para. 151 (chap. 652, title I, sec. 1, 48 stat. 1064).

2. Bernard Schwartz, "Crisis in the Commissions," in *The Politics of Regulation*, Samuel Grislov and Lloyd Musolf, eds. (Boston: Houghton-Mifflin, 1964), p. 25.

3. David Truman, *The Government Process* (New York: Knopf, 1951), p. 443.

4. Paul W. Cherington, Leon V. Hirsch, and Robert Brandwein, eds., *Television Station Ownership* (New York: Hastings House, 1971), p. 16.

5. Anthony Downs, *Inside Bureaucracy* (Boston: Little, Brown, 1967), p. 204.

6. Louis L. Jaffe, "The Effective Limits of the Administrative Process," *Harvard Law Review* 67, no. 7 (May 1954):1112.

7. Downs, *Inside Bureaucracy*, p. 204.

8. Ibid., p. 206.

9. Charles S. Hyneman, *Bureaucracy in a Democracy* (New York: Harper & Bros., 1950), p. xii.

10. Downs, *Inside Bureaucracy*, p. 99; also see Herbert Simon, *Administrative Behavior* (New York: Macmillan, 1957), for the same general view.

11. Robert H. Stern, "Television in the Thirties: Development, Control, and Government Concern," *American Journal of Economics and Sociology* 22, no. 3 (July 1963):361; ibid., no. 3 (July 1964):285–302.

12. Ibid., 22, no. 3 (July 1963):349.

13. The view that policy is central to equitable administration is developed in Emmettee S. Redford, *National Regulatory Commissions: Need for a New Look* (College Park, Md.: Bureau of Government Research, University of Maryland, 1959). The description of policy making is by an earlier advocate of this same view, James M. Landis, in his *The Administrative Process* (New Haven, Conn.: Yale University Press, 1938), p. 139. This chapter seeks only to establish an evaluative framework within which to view the forces shaping commission policy during the cable television era. For a more detailed analysis of the general structure of the FCC, see Erwin Krasnow and Lawrence Longley, *The Politics of Broadcast Regulation* (New York: St. Martin's Press, 1972); for a perceptive analysis of general commission allocation and assignment procedures with special emphasis upon UHF licenses, see John M. Kittross, "Television Frequency Allocation Policy in the United States," Ph.D. diss., University of Illinois, 1960); for commission reactions during the early days of television, see Robert H. Stern, "The FCC and Television: The Regulatory Process in an Environment of Rapid Technical Change," Ph.D. diss., Harvard University, 1951), or W. R. MacLaurn, "Patents and Technological Progress: A Study of Television," *Journal of Political Economics*, vol. 58 (April 1950), and for specific information about particular FCC commissioners, see either Lawrence W. Lichty, "Members of the Federal Radio Commission and the Federal Communications

Commission, 1927–1961," *Journal of Broadcasting*, vol. 6 (Winter 1961–62), or Walter Emery, *Broadcasting and Government* (East Lansing: Michigan State University Press, 1971), app. 2, "FCC Chronology and Leadership from 1934 to 1970," pp. 407–54.

14. Robert Cushman, *Independent Regulatory Commissions* (New York: Oxford University Press, 1941), p. 730.

15. Quoted in U.S., Congress, House, Committee on Interstate and Foreign Commerce, *Regulation of Broadcasting . . . : Study on H. Res. 99*, 85th Cong., 2d sess., 1958, p. 108.

- 16. President's Communication Policy Board, *Telecommunications: A Program for Progress* (Washington, D.C.: Government Printing Office, 1951), p. 195.

17. James M. Landis, *Report on Regulatory Agencies to the President-Elect*, printed for use of the Senate Committee on the Judiciary, 86th Cong., 2d sess., 1960 (Washington, D.C.: Government Printing Office, 1960).

18. Booz-Allen & Hamilton, *Organization and Management Survey*, for use of the Bureau of the Budget (Washington, D.C.: Government Printing Office, 1962), p. 239.

19. Leonard H. Marks, Roger Wollenberg, and Edward Morgan, "Revision of Structure and Functions of the Federal Communications Commission," *Federal Communications Bar Journal*, vol. 19, no. 1 (Fall 1964). This report was never officially adopted by the association.

20. President's Task Force on Telecommunications Policy, *Final Report* (Washington, D.C.: Government Printing Office, 1969), chap. 9, p. 24.

21. Alan Westin, "Inquiry into Our Watchdog Agencies," in Krislov and Musolf, *Politics of Regulation*, p. 16.

22. "Beelar-Dirksen Exchange," *Administrative Law Review* 12 (Winter 1959–60):134.

22. Ibid.

24. Louis J. Kohlmeier, Jr., *The Regulators* (New York: Harper & Row, 1970), p. 61; for a more comprehensive treatment of congressional influence on the commissioners, see Krasnow and Longley, *Politics of Broadcast Regulation*.

25. Bernard Schwartz, *The Professor and the Commissions* (New York: Knopf, 1959), pp. 203–4.

26. Cushman, *Independent Regulatory Commissions*, p. 682.

27. "Views of Nixon's New Communications Aide," *Broadcasting*, 16 February 1970, p. 38. For a more detailed discussion of the OTP role in the TV-CATV compromise of November 1971, see chapter 8.

28. Marver Bernstein, *Regulating Business by Independent Commission* (Princeton, N.J.: Princeton University Press, 1955), p. 87.

29. Herbert Simon, *Administrative Behavior* (New York: Macmillan, 1957), p. 388.

30. Perhaps the most famous exponent of this view is Charles E. Lindblom, whose articles "Policy Analysis," *American Economic Review* 48 (June 1958):298, and "The Science of Muddling Through," *Public Administration Review*, vol. 19 (Spring 1959), formed the basis for intelligent and pragmatic analysis of administrative behavior. To the extent that his evalua-

tion of policy formation describes the outer limits of administrative capacity, it also seems to provide strong justification for relieving regulatory bodies of this responsibility in the field of innovation or technology.

31. Schwartz, "Crisis in the Commissions," pp. 22–23.

32. President's Advisory Council on Executive Organization, *A New Regulatory Framework: Report on Selected Regulatory Agencies* (Washington, D.C.: Government Printing Office, 1971), p. 71. For a further elaboration of this point see Don R. Le Duc, "The FCC v. CATV et al.: A Theory of Regulatory Reflex Action," *Federal Communications Bar Journal* 23, no. 2 (Winter 1969):93–110.

33. Electronic Industries Association, "The Future of Broadband Communication," FCC Docket 18397 (October 1969), pt. 5, p. 23.

Chapter 3

1. These two descriptive definitions of alternative FCC objectives were prepared by the author from slightly more elaborate statements in Martin Seiden, *An Economic Analysis of Community Antenna Television Systems and the Television Broadcasting Industry*, Report to the Federal Communications Commission, February 1965 (Washington, D.C.: Government Printing Office, 1965).

2. Radio Act of 1927, 44 stat. 1162, sec. 81; Communications Act of 1934, 48 stat. 1064, *USCA*, title 47, paras. 151 and 307(a).

3. President's Task Force on Telecommunications, *Final Report* (Washington, D.C.: Government Printing Office, 1969), chap. 7, pp. 12–13.

4. Robert B. Summers and Harrison B. Summers, *Broadcasting and the Public* (Belmont, Calif.: Wadsworth, 1966) p. 38.

5. For expressions of early Radio Conferences opposing commercialization of radio through time sales, see Erik Barnouw, *A Tower in Babel: A History of Broadcasting in the United States to 1933*, vol. 1 (New York: Oxford University Press, 1966) pp. 105–14; 262–66. Also see Edward Sarno, "The National Radio Conferences," *Journal of Broadcasting* 13, no. 2 (Spring 1969):189.

6. Summers and Summers, *Broadcasting and the Public*, p. 38.

7. Ibid., pp. 42, 44.

8. John W. Spalding, "1928: Radio Becomes a Mass Advertising Medium," *Journal of Broadcasting* 8 (Winter 1963–64):31.

9. Barnouw, *Tower in Babel*, p. 200.

10. FCC, "Report and Statement of Policy re Commission en banc Programming Inquiry," 25 FR 7298 (3 August 1960).

11. Barnouw, *Tower in Babel*, p. 94.

12. Charles M. Adams, "Popular Delusions about Radio," *Popular Radio*, March 1927, p. 244.

13. Barnouw, *Tower in Babel*, pp. 206–7.

14. Summers and Summers, *Broadcasting and the Public*, p. 44.

15. All figures from U.S. Commerce Department, *Twentieth Annual Census, 1950* (Washington: Government Printing Office, 1955).

16. "Where Are the Broadcasters?" *Popular Radio*, April 1927, p. 397.

17. Institute of Radio Engineers, "The Clear Channel in American Broadcasting," in U.S., Congress, House, Committee on Broadcasting, *Hearings on H.R. 8210, . . .* , 87th Cong., 2nd sess., 1962, p. 91 (originally prepared in 1933).

18. FCC Engineering Department, "Report on Social and Economic Data," Docket 5072-A (1 July 1937), pp. 120–21.

19. Institute of Radio Engineers, "Clear Channel," p. 90 (see n.17 above).

20. President's Task Force on Telecommunications, *Final Report*, Chap. 7, p. 12.

21. Sydney W. Head, *Broadcasting in America*, 1st ed. (Boston: Houghton Mifflin, 1956), p. 150.

22. Described in more detail in "Public Responsibilities of Broadcast Licensees" (Blue Book) Report of the FCC, 7 March 1946. For more comprehensive descriptions of the FCC television allocation and assignment deliberations, see the sources cited in note 13, chap. 2, above.

23. FCC, "Sixth Report and Order," 17 Fed. Reg. 3905–4100 2 May 1952).

Chapter 4

1. The "Sixth Report and Order," 17 Reg. 3905–4100 (2 May 1952), assigned 2,053 television channels to 1,291 separate communities in the United States. In 1956, only 157 of the more than 1,500 UHF assignments had been used, even briefly, although total television broadcast earnings, before taxes, had increased during the three years from $55 million to $189 million. At that time 242 channels (80 VHF and 162 UHF) were allocated for noncommercial broadcasters. However, these allocations did little to broaden programming alternatives available to most audiences. One noncommercial station was on the air in 1953, 7 more joined it in 1954, 8 in 1955, 5 in 1956, 6 in 1957, 8 in 1958, and 7 in 1959—a total of 42 stations at the end of the decade. While the Educational Facilities Act of 1962 did aid in increasing that number to 156 by 1968, these stations were offering at that time an average of only 56 hours of programming a week, almost half of which consisted of duplicated programming. For year-by-year noncommercial totals, see Appendix A.

2. *Television Factbook*, service vol. no. 39 (Washington, D.C.: Television Digest, 1970) p. 58a. In 1959, UHF stations as a class reported broadcast revenues of $28 million and expenses of $28.5 million.

3. FCC, *Twenty-fourth Annual Report for the Fiscal Year 1958* (Washington, D.C.: Government Printing Office, 1958), p. 102.

4. For more detailed information on both the problems of designing early UHF transmitters and the lack of demand reflected in the fact that only 15 percent of all television receivers were factory equipped as late as 1957 to receive UHF signals, see U.S., Congress, Senate, Committee on Interstate and Foreign Commerce, *Network Broadcasting*, 58th Cong., 2d sess., 1957.

5. Ibid., p. 226.

6. U.S., Congress, Senate, Committee on Interstate and Foreign Commerce, *Television Inquiry, Television Allocations*, 86th Cong., 2d sess., 1960, pt. 8, p. 4587.

7. This half-million-dollar figure represents an average of the expenditures of non-network-owned stations during the period of 1954–56, much lower than but more typical of the average of the industry. In 1956, for instance, 459 television stations reported expenditures of $350 million, or an average of some $760,000 per station (*Television Factbook*, service vol. no. 39, p. 58a).

8. Sydney W. Head, *Broadcasting in America*, 1st ed. (Boston: Houghton Mifflin, 1956), p. 268.

9. "Local Live Production Pays Off," *Broadcasting*, 24 May 1954, p. 41. Hourly local production costs were estimated to range between $150 and $500, while syndicated film material in a smaller market could be leased for $100–$125 per program.

10. Head, *Broadcasting in America*, p. 266.

11. Based upon an analysis of *Broadcasting Yearbook* sources of programming data, 1957–69.

12. U.S., Senate, *Network Broadcasting*, p. 581. In 1950, local advertising revenues had constituted almost one third of television broadcast income, but by 1958, the local share was only 18 percent; national spot, 30 percent; and network, 52 percent.

13. Herman W. Land Associates, *Television and the Wired City* (Washington, D.C.: National Association of Broadcasters, 1968), p. 82.

14. U.S., Senate, *Network Broadcasting*, p. 207.

15. Ibid.

16. Martin Seiden, *An Economic Analysis of Community Antenna Systems and the Television Broadcasting Industry*, Report to the FCC (Washington, D.C.: Government Printing Office, 1965), p. 15.

17. Ibid., p. 14.

18. U.S., Senate, *Television Allocations*, p. 4603.

19. Although the FCC claimed that 90 percent of the nation could receive one television signal in 1956, this seems an exceedingly generous estimate in view of the less than three hundred communities then served by television stations. See "Text of the FCC Report and Order on Television Allocations," *Broadcasting*, 2 July 1956, p. 91.

20. Sources for this early CATV history include E. D. Lucas, Jr., "TV Cinderella," *Radio and Television News*, October 1954, pp. 47–49; Albert R. Kroeger, "Community Antenna Television: Friend or Foe?" *Television*, June 1962; J. E. Hastings, "CATV: Past, Present, and Future," *Electronic World*, August 1967, p. 23; and a personal interview with Archer S. Taylor, consulting engineer, Malarkey, Taylor and Associates, Washington, D.C.

21. *Clarksburg Publishing v. FCC*, 225 F2d 511 (1955), p. 517, n. 16.

22. Seiden, *Economic Analysis*, p. 50.

23. *Television Factbook*, service vol. no. 39, p. 78a.

24. Lucas, "TV Cinderella," p. 49.

25. U.S., Congress, Senate, *Licensing of Community Antenna Television Systems: S. Rept. 923 to Accompany S. 2653*, 86th Cong., 1st sess., 1959, p. 3.

26. Seiden, *Economic Analysis*, p. 96.

27. U.S., Congress, Senate, Committee on Interstate and Foreign Commerce, *Review of Allocation Problems of TV Service to Small Communities,* 85th Cong., 2d sess., 1958, p. 3490.

28. Ibid., p. 3498.

29. Commissioner Doerfer's speech was delivered to the National Association of Railroad and Utilities Commissioners (NARUC) in November 1955, and reprinted as "Community Antenna Television Systems," in *Federal Communications Bar Journal* 14 (1955):4–14.

30. FCC, "In the Matter of Amendment of Part 15 of the Commission's Rules Governing Restricted Radiation Devices," Docket 9288, 13 RR 1546(a) (1956).

31. FCC, "In the Matter Of J. E. Belknap and Associates," FCC-54-581 (1954).

Chapter 5

1. Archer S. Taylor, "Unauthorized Television Repeater Stations," NCTA comments on proposed FCC booster rules, in Docket 12116 (December 1957).

2. "Radiation from Community Antenna Systems," 13 RR 163 (1956). An increase in power for such translator facilities was authorized in Docket 12116, 17 RR 1763, during 1958.

3. Taylor, "Unauthorized Television Repater Stations."

4. U.S., Congress, Senate, Committee on Interstate and Foreign Commerce, Communications Subcommittee, *VHF Booster and Community Antenna Legislation: Hearings on S. 1739, S. 1741, S. 1801, S. 1886, and S. 2303,* 86th Cong., 1st sess., 1959 (hereafter cited as Hearings-1959), pp. 455–56.

5. U.S., Congress, Senate, Committee on Interstate and Foreign Commerce, *Review of Allocation Problems of Television Service for Smaller Communities,* 85th Cong., 2d sess., 1958 (hereafter cited as Hearings-1958), p. 3661.

6. Chapter 26, Laws of 1959, Public Laws of Montana; see also House Bill 208, 36th General Assembly, State of Montana.

7. Address of Warren F. Baker before the Sixth Annual Convention and Trade Show, National Community Antenna Television Association, Pittsburgh, Pennsylvania, 4 June 1957.

8. *C. J. Community Service, Inc. v. FCC*, 246 F2d 660 (1957), pp. 662–63.

9. Taylor, "Unauthorized Television Repeater Stations."

10. "The Booster Issue" (editorial), *Miles City Montana Star*, 9 March 1959, p. 8.

11. *Frontier Broadcasting v. Collier*, 16 RR 1005 (1958).

12. The memos are reproduced in greater detail in Hearings-1958, pp. 4142–46.

13. Ibid., p. 3480.

14. Ibid., p. 3507.

15. Ibid., p. 3556.

16. Ibid., pp. 3730–31.

17. Ibid., p. 3714.

18. Ibid., pp. 3650–51.

19. Ibid., pp. 3622.

20. Ibid., pp. 3542–53.

21. *Broadcasting*, 30 June 1958, p. 106.

22. Hearings-1958.

23. Ibid., pp. 48–49.

24. FCC, "In the Matter of Inquiry into the Impact of Community Antenna Systems, TV Translators, TV Satellites, and TV Repeaters on the Orderly Development of Television Broadcasting," Docket 12443 (hereafter cited as "First Report and Order," Docket 12443) 18 RR 1573, p. 1586.

25. Ibid., p. 1595.

26. *FCC v. Sanders Brothers Broadcasting*, 309 US 470 (1940).

27. The CATV complaint, *Palm Springs Translator*, 15 RR 70 (1957); the translator complaint, *Intermountain Microwave*, 16 RR 733 (1958); the broadcaster complaint, *Orchard Community TV Assn.*, 16 RR 944 (1958).

28. *Carroll Broadcasting v. FCC*, 258 F2d 440 (1958).

29. "First Report and Order," Docket 12443, p. 1604.

30. FCC 59-617, *Carter Mountain* application, 1959.

31. Hearings-1959, pp. 455–56.

32. Ibid., p. 511.

33. Ibid., pp. 542–43.

34. Ibid., pp. 576–77.

35. Ibid.

36. Ibid., p. 815.

37. U.S., Congress, Senate, *Licensing of Community Antenna Television Systems: S. Rept. 923 to Accompany S. 2653*, 86th Cong., 1st sess. (hereafter cited as Report-S. 2653), 1959, p. 12.

38. Ibid., p. 14

39. Hearings-1959, p. 1003.

40. Ibid., p. 999.

41. Report-S. 2653, p. 27.

42. Hearings-1959, pp. 1089–91.

43. U.S., Congress, Senate, S. 2653, *Congressional Record*, 17 May 1960, p. 10417.

44. Ibid., p. 10418.

45. Ibid., p. 10421.

46. Ibid., p. 10430.

47. S. 1044 and H.R. 6840 (identical bills), 87th Cong., 1st. sess., 1961.

48. "It's a Federation Now" (editorial), *Broadcasting*, 16 March 1959, p. 186.

49. Hearings-1959, p. 577.

Chapter 6

1. Martin Seiden, *An Economic Analysis of Community Antenna Television Systems and the Television Broadcasting Industry*, Report to the Federal Communications Commission (Washington, D.C.: Government Printing Office, 1965), p. 82.

2. *Televison Factbook*, service vol. 39, no. 2. Northeastern states include Connecticut, Maine, Massachusetts, New Hampshire, Vermont, New Jersey, and Pennsylvania; East South Central—Alabama, Kentucky, Mississippi, and Tennesee; Mountain—Arizona, Colorado, Idaho, Nevada, New Mexico, Wyoming; West South Central—Arkansas, Louisiana, Oklahoma, and Texas.

3. Seiden, *Economic Analysis*, p. 10.

4. Albert R. Kroeger, "CATV Revisited," *Television*, September 1962, p. 20.

5. Seiden, *Economic Analysis*, p. 31.

6. Ibid.

7. Ibid., p. 58.

8. Ibid., p. 28, explains this concept of "cash flow" in greater detail and provides a table illustrating the cash-flow ratios of various systems. This concept of the value of cash flow is challenged by Edward Schaefer's "Cable TV: Is State Regulation Really Necessary?" *Public Utilities Fortnightly*, 3 July 1969, p. 27.

9. "Big Money in Cable," *Television Digest*, 23 November 1964, p. 1.

10. U.S., Congress, House, Committee on Interstate and Foreign Commerce, Subcommittee on Communications and Power, *Regulation of Community Antenna Television: Hearings on H.R. 7715*, 89th Cong., 1st. sess., 1965 (hereafter cited as Hearings-1965), pp. 138–39.

11. "Should FCC Have CATV Control?" *Broadcasting*, 22 June 1964, p. 27.

12. "CATV Accord Comes Apart," *Broadcasting*, 24 December 1964, p. 33.

13. "What to Do with Community Television," *Broadcasting*, 23 March 1964, p. 61.

14. Hearings-1965, p. 41.

15. *Carter Mountain*, FCC-59-617 (1959).

16. *Carter Mountain*, FCC-61-D-74; for the initial action in the Carter Mountain case, see chap. 5, p. 100.

17. *Carter Mountain*, Docket 12931, 22 RR 193.

18. *Carter Mountain Transmission v. FCC*, 321 F2d 359 (C.A., D.C., 1963), p. 361. The court in expressing this philosophy cited *Federal Power Commission v. Transcontinental Gas Pipe Lines Corp.*, 365 US 1 (1961), which affirmed FPC denial of a request to transport natural gas for what was deemed an "inferior use," burning the gas to fuel industrial heaters. This appears to have been the first case in which an agency was granted the right to look beyond a legitimate industry function to its ultimate result.

19. *Business Radio*, FCC-1285, pt. 10.

20. FCC Public Notice, Report 1256: "Business Radio Service for TV Relay to CATV Systems."

21. *Common Carrier*, Docket 15233; *Business Radio*, Docket 14895.

22. "Community Antenna Relay Stations," Docket 15586 (29 July 1964).

23. Hearings-1965, p. 82.

24. "Wisconsin Public Service Commission," 7 RR 2054 (1951).

25. See "New Mexico," 10 RR 2058; "Utah," 14 RR 2063; "Arizona," 12 RR 2094.

26. *Television Transmission Inc. v. Public Utilities Commission (California)*, 301 P2d 862 (1956).

27. *Community Television Systems of Wyoming* (Wyoming, D. Ct., 1958) overturning *Cokerville Radio*, 17 RR 435, 11 RR 204.

28. Wisconsin Statutes, chap. 196, 1950.

29. Pennsylvania Statutes, H.B. 1456, 835, 91; West Virginia, H.B. 397; Arizona, H.C.R. 12; Montana, S.B. 184; Washington, S.B. 425.

30. Maryland Statutes, H.B. 186; New Hampshire, H.B. 268; Oregon, H.B. 1546; Arkansas, H.B. 309; California, A. 2743; Oklahoma, H.B. 914; Utah, H. 914; Vermont and Mississippi, no statute numbers.

31. Laws of Connecticut, chap. 289, sec. 16-330-333.

32. Hearings-1965, pp. 368-69.

33. For a complete description of this Connecticut experience plus other experiences in Nevada and New York see Michael R. Mitchell, *State Regulation of Cable Television*, memorandum R-783-MF (Santa Monica, Calif.: Rand, 1971).

34. For a discussion of the CATV-telephone controversy, see chap. 7, pp. 160–63.

35. For a survey detailing some of the variances in franchise agreements, see Seiden, *Economic Analysis*, pp. 44–45.

36. Hearings-1965, pp. 368–69.

37. A general description of these proceedings is contained in chap. 4.

38. U.S., Congress, Senate, Committee on Interstate and Foreign Commerce, *VHF Booster and Community Antenna Legislation: Hearings on S. 1739 ... S. 2303*, 86th Cong., 1st. sess., 1959 (hereafter cited as Hearings-1959), p. 810.

39. *Intermountain Broadcasting v. Idaho Microwave*, 196 F. Supp. 315 (S.D., Ida., 1961); *Cable Vision v. KUTV*, 211 F. Supp. 47 (S.D., Ida., 1962), 335 F2d 348 (9th Cir., 1964), cert. den. 379 US 989 (1965).

40. *Cable Vision v. KUTV*, case no. 3546, in the U.S. District Court for the District of Idaho, Southern District; summons dated 3 September 1959.

41. *Intermountain*, 196 F. Supp. 315, pp. 325–26.

42. Ibid.

43. *Associated Press v. International News Service*, 248 US 215 (1918).

44. *Intermountain*, 196 F. Supp. 315, p. 327.

45. *Intermountain*, 379 US 989; Circuit reversal at 335 F2d 348 (9th Cir., 1964).

46. *Sears Roebuck v. Stiffel Co.*, 376 US 225 (1964); *Compco Corp. v. Day Brite Lighting Co.*, 376 US 234 (1964).

47. *Cable Vision*, 335 F2d 348.

48. "The Wire Mire: The FCC and CATV," *Harvard Law Review* 79 (1965):375–76.

49. Seiden, *Economic Analysis*, p. 61.

Chapter 7

1. "Carter Mountain Transmission," 32 FCC 459 (1962); affirmed, *Carter Mountain Transmission Corp. v. FCC*, 321 F2d 359 (1963).

2. "Appendix to Reply Comments of the National Association of Broadcasters," FCC Dockets 14895 and 15233 (1964), pp. 1, 2.

3. Martin Seiden, *An Economic Analysis of Community Antenna Television Systems and the Television Broadcasting Industry*, Report to the Federal Communications Commission (Washington, D.C.: Government Printing Office, 1965), p. 71.

4. Ibid., p. 64.

5. Ibid., p. 74.

6. NCTA comments, Docket 15971; see *NCTA News Letter*, 20 April 1965.

7. "In the Matter of Amendment of Subpart I, Part 21, to Adopt Rules and Regulations to Govern the Grant of Authorizations in the Domestic Point to Point Microwave Radio Service for Microwave Stations Used to Relay Television Signals to CATV," in "First Report and Order," 38 FCC 683 (23 April 1965), p. 700.

8. *Carroll Broadcasting v. FCC*, 258 F2d 440 (D.C. Cir., 1958), p. 443.

9. "The Wire Mire: The FCC and CATV," *Harvard Law Review* 79 (1965): 389.

10. *United States v. Southwestern Cable*, 392 US 157 (1968).

11. "FCC Given Hotfoot on CATV," *Broadcasting*, 1 March 1965, p. 64.

12. "Five Ways to Control, Contain, or Cut," *Broadcasting*, 8 February 1965, p. 24.

13. Seiden, *Economic Analysis*, p. 5.

14. "The Rifts over CATV Widen," *Broadcasting*, 12 April 1965, p. 53.

15. "First Report and Order" (see n. 7 above): "In the Matter of Amendment of Part 24, 74 (Proposed Subparts J and 9) to Adopt Rules Relating to the Distribution of Television Broadcast Signals by CATV, and Related Matters", "Notice of Inquiry and Notice of Proposed Rulemaking" (hereafter cited as Notice of Inquiry-1965), 1 FCC 2d 453 (23 April 1965).

16. U.S., Congress, House, Committee on Interstate and Foreign Commerce, *Regulation of Community Antenna Television: Hearings on H.R. 7715*, 89th Cong., 1st sess., 1965 (hereafter cited as Hearings-1965), p. 32.

17. Ibid., p. 135.

18. Notice of Inquiry-1965, p. 500.

19. Hearings-1965, p. 31.

20. Ibid., p. 29.

21. Ibid., p. 33.

22. Ibid., p. 46; for exchange between Commissioners Henry and Cox, see pp. 66–72.

23. Ibid., pp. 49–50.

24. "Harris Stakes His Claim to CATV," *Broadcasting*, 3 May 1965, p. 67.

25. "In the Matter of Amendment of Subpart I, Part 91, to Adopt Rules and Regulations to Govern the Grant of Authorization to the Business Radio Service . . . to Relay Television Signals to CATV," Docket 14895; "Amendment of Subpart I, Part 4, to Adopt Rules and Regulations to Govern the Grant of Authorizations in the Domestic Public Point-to-Point Microwave Service . . . to Relay Television Signals to CATV," Docket 15233; "Amendment to Parts 21, 74 and 91, to Adopt Rules and Regulations Relating to the Distribution of Television Broadcast Signals by CATV and Related Matters," Docket 15971, in "Second Report and Order," 6 RR 2d 1717 (17 March 1966).

26. "Second Report and Order" (Federal Register), p. 4546.

27. Ibid., p. 4562.

28. Ibid., p. 4548.

29. The practical effect of the "full complement of network station" rule was to extend protection to 97 of the top 100 markets, as ranked by ARB, on the basis of net weekly circulation of the largest station in each market.

30. U.S., Congress, House, Committee on Interstate and Foreign Commerce, Subcommittee on Communications and Power, *Regulation of Community Antenna Television: Hearings on H.R. 12914, H.R. 13286, H.R. 14201*, 89th Cong., 2d sess., 1966 (hereafter cited as Hearings-1966), p. 276.

31. "Community Antenna TV Systems Brought under FCC Jurisdiction," *Wall Street Journal*, 16 February 1966, p. 2.

32. Ibid.

33. Hearings-1966, pp. 5–9; for Commissioner Cox's criticisms, pp. 815–16.

34. Ibid., pp. 139–40.

35. Ibid., pp. 306–7.

36. "Bill Sanctioning FCC Regulation of CATV Slowly Gains Ground in House Committee," *Wall Street Journal*, 6 June 1966, p. 3.

37. "How Much Interference?" *Barron's*, 13 November 1967, p. 3; data on system size from *Broadcast Management/Engineering*, July 1967.

38. "Wired for Growth," *Barron's*, 30 June 1969, p. 3.

39. Ibid.

40. Ibid.

41. *United States v. Western Electric Co. and American Telephone and Telegraph*, Civil Action 17-49 (D.N.J. 1956).

42. "AT&T Gets a Letter from FCC on CATV," *Broadcasting*, 4 October 1965, p. 46.

43. *California Water and Telephone*, 5 FCC 2d 229; *Associated Bell Systems*, 5 FCC 2d 357; affirmed *General Telephone of California*, 13 FCC 2d 448, 413 F2d 390 (1969), cert. den. 396 US 888; for other actions see 6 FCC 2d 434, 34 Fed. Reg. 6290 and 21 FCC 2d 307, 22 FCC 2d 746.

44. Jules Tewlow, "CATV Revisited," *ANPA Research Institute*, R.I. Bulletin 970, September 1968, pp. 371–72.

45. *General Telephone*, Docket 17333.

46. "End Run; Unable to Beat CATV, the Big Broadcasters Have Started to Join," *Forbes*, 1 August 1968, p. 26.

47. "Wired for Growth," *Barron's*, 30 June 1969, p. 1.

48. *United Artists Television Inc. v. Fortnightly*, 149 USPQ 758 (S.D., N.Y., 1966).

49. *Uproar Co. v. NBC*, 8 F. Supp. 358 (D. Mass., 1934); modified 81 F2d 373 (1st Cir); cert. den. 298 US 670 (1936).

50. *Z Bar Net v. Helena Television*, 125 USPQ 595 (1960).

51. *Buck v. Jewell La Salle*, 283 US 191 (1931). As an historical side-light, the Freemont, West Virginia, community antenna system was the system accused by broadcasters of causing the first television station casualty in the conflict between cable and broadcasters; its refusal to carry the signal of UHF station WJPB-TV, Freemont, in 1954 put that station out of business (see chap. 5).

52. "House Approves Copyright Overhaul Bill; CATV Section Dropped," *Wall Street Journal*, 12 April 1967, p. 3.

53. *Fortnightly Corp. v. United Artists*, 392 US 390 (1968).

54. *Black Hills Video v. United States*, 399 F2d 65 (8th Cir., 1968); *Buckeye Cablevision v. FCC*, 387 F2d 220 (D.C. Cir., 1967); *Southwestern Cable v. FCC*, 378 F2d 118 (9th Cir., 1967).

55. "Notice of Inquiry and Notice of Proposed Rulemaking in Docket 18397," FCC 68-1176 (12 December 1968), para. 3.

56. "San Diego U Sees CATV as Help, Not Hindrance," *Broadcasting*, 6 September 1965, p. 63. KAAR-TV became KCST in November 1965. KJOG-TV, the complaining UHF station, never went on the air, and KCST, the UHF station favoring cable penetration in San Diego, finally seems to have succeeded in gaining FCC support to replace the Mexican ABC affiliate now providing local service in the San Diego market. See "Beginning of the End for XETV-ABC Association," *Broadcasting*, 5 June 1972, p. 36.

57. *Midwest Television*, 13 RR 2d 698.

58. *Buckeye Cablevision v. FCC*, 387 F2d 220, p. 222.

59. *United States v. Southwestern Cable*, 392 US 157 (1968).

60. *Midwest Television*, 13 RR 2d 698, p. 700.

61. *Black Hills Video v. United States*, 399 F2d 65 (1968).

62. "New Sweep of FCC Powers," *Broadcasting*, 17 June 1968, p. 23.

63. Federal Communications Commission, *Thirty-fourth Annual Report for the Fiscal Year 1968* (Washington, D.C.: Government Printing Office, 1968) pp. 112, 135.

64. "FCC Doesn't Want CATV Research," *Broadcasting*, 15 January 1968, p. 56.

65. *FCC Annual Report to Congress, 1968*, as reported in *CATV Weekly*, 8 February 1968, p. 10.

66. "Notice of Inquiry and Notice of Proposed Rulemaking in Docket 18397," FCC 68–1176 (12 December 1968).

67. Ibid., para. 43.

68. "Amendment . . . to Docket 18397," FCC 69-54, 17 January 1969.

69. Dissent of Robert T. Bartley, in "Notice of Inquiry," p. 1.

70. Jack Gould, "TV: A Decade of Turmoil Is Promised by the FCC," *New York Times*, 16 December 1968, p. 95.

71. Jack Gould, "At Least and at Last: A Beginning," *New York Times*, 22 December 1968, p. 14.

72. "What the Notice Is All About," *Broadcasting*, 23 December 1968, p. 62.

73. U.S., Congress, House, Committee on Interstate and Foreign Commerce, Subcommittee on Communications and Power, *Regulation of Community Antenna Television: Hearings on H.R. 10510*, 91st Cong., 1st sess., 1969.

74. Wayne Green, "CATV Industry Seen Switching Strategy in Copyright Negotiations," *Wall Street Journal*, 2 June 1969, p. 3.

75. "The Wording of a Compromise," *Broadcasting*, 2 June 1969, p. 24.

76. "Wrecking Crew Hits Cable Compromise," *Broadcasting*, 16 June 1969, p. 44.

77. Christopher Lyden, "Cable TV Picture Brightens," *New York Times*, 21 December 1969, p. 3:1.

78. "First Report and Order on Docket 18397," 17 RR 2d 1570.

79. Robert I. Shayon, "Signals, One, Two, Three," *Saturday Review*, 6 September 1969, p. 75.

80. Lyden, "Cable TV Picture Brightens," p. 3:1.

81. "Where the CATV Homes Are in US," *Broadacsting*, 6 April 1970, p. 81.

82. Basic ownership breakdown, from Edward Schaefer, "Cable TV: Is State Regulation Really Necessary?" *Public Utilities Fortnightly*, 3 July 1969, p. 27.

83. FCC, *The Economics of the TV-CATV Interface* (Washington, D.C.: Research Branch, Broadcast Bureau, 1970).

Part IV Introduction

1. As one example of the rapid pace of communications innovation, the issue of *Broadcasting*, 7 February 1972, which outlines (p. 17) the FCC's "Third Report and Order," ushering in the major-market cable era, also contains (p. 67) proposals for a domestic satellite system far more effective than existing coaxial point-to-point lines; the system has been projected as being capable within fifteen years of delivering signals directly to each television home.

2. Melvin De Fleur, *Theories of Mass Communication*, 2d ed. (New York: McKay, 1970), p. 7.

3. "Third Report and Order on Docket 18397," 24 RR 2d 1501.

Chapter 8

1. For some examples of these criticisms, see Leonard Chazen, "The Price of Free TV," *Atlantic Monthly*, March 1969, p. 59; "Wired for Growth: If Official Interference Ends, Cable TV Could Fulfill Its Promise," *Barron's*, 30 June 1969, p. 3; "CATV on a Leash," *Economist*, 29 June 1968, p. 40.

2. "Notice of Proposed Rulemaking in Docket 18397A," 24 FCC 2d 580.

3. U.S., Congress, House, Subcommittee on Communications and Power, *Regulation of CATV*, 89th Cong., 1st sess., 1965, p. 41. Also see chap. 6, p. 122.

4. U.S., Congress, Senate, Committee on Commerce, *Nominations—1969: On Nominations of Dean Burch to Be Chairman, Federal Communications Commission; Robert Wells to Be Member of the Federal Communications Commission*, 91st Cong., 1st sess., pp. 5–6.

5. For broadcast background and former ownership interests of Commissioner Wells see ibid., p. 17.

6. For R. E. Lee's own statements concerning his commitment to UHF broadcasting, see "UHF and CATV," *Television Age*, 25 March 1968, p. 58; and "FCC's Lee Says CATV to Stay as Is until UHF Builds," *Variety*, 5 February 1969, p. 44. Lee, who joined the commission in 1953, was active in efforts to support and extend this service from that time onward.

7. Commissioner Johnson's philosophy concerning cable television seemed to shift from time to time during this era. From his article, "CATV: Promise or Peril," *Saturday Review*, 11 November 1967, and his statements to cable groups, he seemed sympathetic to their interests; yet he concurred in the notice of December 1968 and cast the deciding vote in the Midwest Video case (13 RR 2d 698), overturning the hearing examiner's decision (see chap. 7) and imposing stringent "Second Report and Order" restraints upon San Diego CATV systems after *United States v. Southwestern Cable*.

8. Chairman Burch crusaded against "footnote 69" restrictions so diligently that when "Third Report and Order" (24 RR 2d 1501) was published, citation jumped from footnote 68 to footnote 70 with the comment, "There is no footnote 69" (p. 1561).

9. For a synopsis of these comments see ibid., p. 1519, para. 30.

10. Ibid., esp. para. 27.

11. "Second Report and Order on Docket 18397," 19 RR 2d 1775.

12. For cross ownership of radio and CATV, and of newspapers and CATV, see Docket 18891, 23 FCC 2d 833.

13. For a somewhat unsympathetic summary of the proceedings, see "At FCC: A Spectacular on Cable TV," *Broadcasting*, 15 March 1971, p. 50.

14. "Notice of Intent," 22 RR 2d 1755 (5 August 1971).

15. For a chart prepared by the FCC in its "Third Report" clarifying these importation rules, see Appendix B.

16. Minor changes in the definitions of "substantial viewing," in determining "local signals," and of "leapfrogging" are described later in this chapter.

17. The OTP was not technically a "new force," since the office evolved from a study during the Truman administration. However, after its reorganization in 1970, it began to broaden its base of operation. See U.S., Congress, House, Committee of the Whole House, *Approving Reorganization Plan No. 1 of 1970 (Telecommunications)*, 91st Cong., 2d sess., 1970.

18. "Critique '71," *CATV*, 3 January 1972, p. 30.

19. Ibid., p. 37.

20. "Notice of Intent," 22 RR 2d 1755 (5 August 1971), p. 1760.

21. For the full statement of the OTP compromise agreement, see Appendix C.

22. "Out of the Trenches for Cable," *Broadcasting*, 15 November 1971, pp. 16, 17.

23. For a more complete examination of this rationale, see Harvey C. Jassem, "The Selling of the Compromise, 1971; or, Cable Television Goes to the City" (Masters thesis, Ohio State University, 1972).

24. "The FCC Delivers on Cable," *Broadcasting*, 7 February 1972, p. 17.

25. Ibid., p. 18.

26. For the full text of this debate, see U.S., Congress, Senate, Subcommittee on Communications, *Overview of the Federal Communications Commission*, 92nd Cong., 2d sess., 1972, pp. 152–70.

27. *CBS v. TelePrompTer*, 173 USPQ 778 (1972). Ironically, this case, decided by the court on the basis of stipulated facts involving only one issue —whether five representative TelePrompTer systems were "performing" broadcast programming because of their other broadband functions—was decided in favor of TelePrompTer by Judge Constance Baker Motley, who in 1971 found Irving Kahn of TelePrompTer guilty of bribery and perjury on charges arising out of negotiations for a franchise in Johnstown, Pennsylvania, in 1966. In March 1973 the U.S. Second Court of Appeals reversed this decision on the question of cable copyright liability for "distant signals," remanding the case to the District Court for further proceedings in line with its determination that cable carriage of such signals constituted copyright infringement. See *Broadcasting*, 12 March 1973, p. 12. Cable interests were considering an appeal from this decision as this book went to press. *United States v. Midwest Video*, 406 US 649 (1972), was appealed rather reluctantly on behalf of the FCC by the solicitor general. The lower court decision challenging FCC authority was 441 F2d 1322 (8th Cir., 1971).

28. *CBS v. TelePrompTer*, 173 USPQ 778, p. 781.

29. "McClellan Moves to Prolong Life of Copyright Law," *Broadcasting*, 26 June 1972, p. 46.

30. "First Report and Order," Docket 18397, 17 RR 2d 1570. As a result of the challenge in 441 F 2d 1322 (n. 27 above), the cablecasting rule was suspended pending final resolution of this controversy.

31. 441 F 2d 1322, p. 1328.

32. *United States v. Midwest Video*, 406 US 649, p. 656.

33. Ibid., pp. 4626–34.

34. Ibid., pp. 4634–36.

34. For Kahn charges in Johnstown, Pennsylvania, affair, see note 27 above. For more detailed charges of improper influences in cable franchising, see New Jersey and New York hearings listed in References.

36. In "joint venture" agreements the crucial question is not what percentage a local group owns in a local system, but what degree of autonomy that system has within the interlocking ownership structure of the multisystem owner.

37. Some of these problems are discussed in Thomas Freebairn, "Public Access in New York City: An Interview with Theadora Sklover," *Yale Review of Law and Social Action* 2, no. 3 (The Cable Fable) (Spring 1972): 227. See also "Funding Problem Plagues N.Y. Public Access Cable," *Broadcasting*, 19 June 1972, p. 18, and "Open Access: What Happens?" *Broadcasting*, 1 May 1972, p. 46.

38. While the FCC does retain authority under its certification procedures to review nonbroadcast service functions, the prime purpose for delegation initially was to avoid a burden of supervision beyond the commission's capacity. Thus, careful scrutiny of such functions seems highly unlikely.

39. "The Coming Box Office in Cable TV," *Broadcasting*, 22 May 1972, p. 21.

40. For a more detailed analysis of two-way functions, see Walter S. Baer, "Interactive Television Prospects for Two-Way Services on Cable," memorandum R-888-MF (Santa Monica, Calif.: Rand, 1971).

41. These figures are from a study prepared in 1968 by Complan Associates of Suffern, New York, for the President's Task Force on Telecommunications Policy.

42. U.S., Congress, Senate, S. Rept. 772, 69th Cong., 1st sess. (1926).

43. President's Advisory Council on Executive Organization (Ash Commission), *A New Regulatory Framework* (Washington, D.C.: Government Printing Office, 1971), p. 4.

44. Studies commissioned by the president include: *President's Committee on Administrative Management* (Brownlow Committee), 1937; U.S. Commission on Organization of the Executive Branch of the Government, *The Independent Regulatory Commissions: Task Force Report* (Hoover Commission), 1949; U.S. Commission on Organization of the Executive Branch of Government, *Task Force on Legal Services and Procedures* (2d Hoover Commission), 1955; James Landis, *Report on Regulatory Agencies to President-Elect*, 1960; U.S. Bureau of the Budget, *Study of Federal Communications Organization*, 1968; President's Task Force on Telecommunications Policy, *Final Report*, 1968; and the Ash study (cited in n. 43 above).

45. For a discussion of the investigation from the staff counsel's point of view, see Bernard Schwartz, *The Professor and the Commissions* (New York: Knopf, 1959).

46. Connecticut Statutes, title 16, chap. 289 (1963–65); Nevada, sec. 711 (1967); Rhode Island, title 39-19-1 (1969); Vermont, title 30, para. 501 (1969); Hawaii, sec. 440G (1970); and Massachusetts (see *NCTA Bulletin*, 22 November 1971, p. 1). Early in 1972, Illinois's attempt to assert jurisdiction under existing PSC statutes has been overturned, but New York has enacted legislation modeled after is moratorium.

47. *TV Pix v. Taylor*, 304 F. Supp. 459; affirmed 396 US 556 (1970).

48. *Florida Lime v. Paul*, 373 US 132; cited with approval in *Head v. Board of Examiners*, 374 US 424 (1963).

49. *Greater Fremont v. City of Fremont*, 302 F. Supp. 652 (1968).

50. See Michael R. Mitchell, "State Regulation of Cable Television," memorandum R-783-MF (Santa Monica, Calif.: Rand, 1971), for an interesting historical background on state controls in Connecticut and Nevada. Unfortunately, since the relationship between cable and state has broadened, the common carrier approach used in this study limits its usefulness for future analysis of state cable control.

51. Rhode Island Statutes, title 39-19-6 (1969).

52. In the case of *Illinois Broadcasting v. City of Decatur*, 238 NE 2d 261, a cable franchise was considered a vested right, with any attempt to impair the contract by subsequent legislation deemed unconstitutional.

While, in the 1950s, the doctrine of "mutual mistake" might have allowed avoidance of a franchise granted a community antenna system "in perpetuity," construction relying upon the promise of the franchising unit might "estop" the unit from avoiding a more recent contract. These questions would turn initially on state law, but the federal government could play a role in ending such a franchise simply by denying carriage of broadcast signals to all systems not complying with certain minimum franchise conditions, as it now proposes to do under its certification procedures.

53. The classic case limiting the power of a state legislature to impair an existing contract right is *Dartmouth College v. Woodward*, 4 Wheat 518, 4 L. Ed. 629 (1819).

54. A recent attempt to broaden local franchise vision is described in *Cable Communications in the Dayton Miami Valley* (Santa Monica, Calif.: Rand, 1972). This effort, despite excellent planning, seems destined to be challenged severely by both the urban and the suburban areas it proposes to link.

55. Somewhat ironically, in the end it may be that the state rather than the federal government will be the only force capable of enforcing the "local service" goal which has traditionally been given highest priority by the FCC. If wired dissemination should end the justification for spectrum-based federal program controls, states might still retain sufficient authority to attain these ends, simply because state police power has generally been accorded greater regulatory scope in areas of public welfare than federal police power (see *Jacobsen v. Massachusetts*, 197 US 11 [1905]).

References

References:
An Annotated List
of Cable Sources

More than six thousand articles, studies, and reports examining various aspects of community antenna, CATV, or cable-TV activity have appeared in print during the past quarter of a century. An exhaustive listing of all publications concerning cable communications would simply duplicate the function of existing bibliographies and indexes; hence, this list has been designed to isolate and annotate only those major sources of broadest dimension; the significant studies are described in some detail, while the reader is offered access to the more particularized treatments through the research guides cited below.

Research Guides

Cable articles can be found through the H. H. Wilson Company publications *Business Periodical Index,* s.v. "CATV or Television: Broadcasting, Community Antenna"; *Index to Legal Periodicals,* s.v. "Television"; *Readers' Guide to Periodical Literature,* s.v. "CATV or Television: Broadcasting, Community Antenna"; *Social Sciences and Humanities Index,* s.v. "CATV or Television: Broadcasting, Community Antenna"; or through *Topicator* (Thompson Bureau), s.v. "Cable TV," "NCTA," or "Copyright."

Cable Bibliographies

Douglass, Edward. "New Communications Technologies and Public Policy." Mimeographed. Urbana: Department of Radio and Television, University of Illinois, 1972. An excellent series of bibliographies covering regulatory actions, cable studies, and treatises examining the impact of communications technology upon society. Prepared for seminar use, these references have sufficient scope and breadth to be useful for a wide range of research interests.

Gompertz, Kenneth. "A Bibliography of Articles about Broadcasting in Law Periodicals, 1965–1968." *Journal of Broadcasting,* vol. 14, no. 1, pt. 2 (Winter 1969–70), s.v. "Community Antenna Television" and "Copyright." This comprehensive and well-indexed guide fur-

265

nishes nearly all the important articles analyzing legal issues involving cable during the period covered.

Le Duc, Don R. "A Selective Bibliography on the Evolution of CATV: 1950–1970." *Journal of Broadcasting* 15, no. 2 (Spring 1971): 195–235. This topically organized reference includes more than one thousand of the most significant reports, governmental actions, and articles during this era arranged in chronological order under headings such as "Economics and Ownership," "Intermedia Competition," and "Regulation."

Molends, Michael H. "Educational Implications of CATV." Mimeographed. Greensboro: School of Education, University of North Carolina, 1971. A fairly complete annotated reference for educational and cultural uses of cable covering the period 1968–71.

Office of Telecommunications Policy. "Cable Television Bibliography," Staff Research Paper. February 1972. An extremely limited and uneven list of sources of value only as a secondary reference for checking other sources.

"Preliminary Checklist of Materials on the Legal Aspects of CATV." *New York Bar Record*, October 1966, pp. 494–505. An excellent collection of early articles dealing with cable regulation and franchising.

Research Center in Economic Growth. "Studies in the Economics of Mass Communication," compiled by Bruce Owen, David Grey, James Rosse. Stanford, Calif.: Stanford University, 1970. A mammoth, well-indexed compilation of articles involving the economics of mass media, with a fairly extensive list of cable citations.

Texts

Phillips, Mary Alice Mayer. *CATV: A History of Community Antenna Television*. Evanston, Ill.: Northwestern University Press, 1972. This work is less a history than a chronicle of a few early community antenna systems, linked to a rather generalized outline of cable regulation during the past decade. Part 1, dealing with these pioneer systems, is far stronger than the analytical and projective sections following.

Price, Monroe, and Wicklein, John. *Cable Television: A Guide for Citizen Action*. Philadelphia: Pilgrim Press, 1972. An action handbook, designed not to survey or to analyze cable systems but to reform them through effective citizen involvement in all stages from franchising to processing of complaints. Although published prior to the "Third Report and Order," much of the material covering such topics as "public access" remains valid and is covered more comprehensively in this text than in any other source.

Sloan Commission on Cable Communications. *On the Cable: The Television of Abundance.* New York: McGraw-Hill, 1971. This report seems to be an instance in which the whole is not equal to the sum of its parts. More than twenty studies and reports were synthesized into this generalized overview of the evolution of cable communication and its probable course of development through 1985. Some of the studies are excellent in themselves, but in attempting to encompass them all within a single text, the report tends toward a superficiality which limits its overall effectiveness. In essence a good primer, but not the perceptive study the underlying research should have produced.

Smith, Ralph Lee. *The Wired Nation: Cable TV, the Electronic Communications Highway.* New York: Harper & Row, 1972. This expansion and updating of Smith's often cited "Wired Nation" article of 1970 provides a useful introduction for those unfamiliar with cable television and the issues it is raising and will raise in the future.

Tate, Charles, ed. *Cable Television in the Cities: Community Control, Public Access, and Minority Ownership.* Washington, D.C.: Urban Institute, 1972. Another action primer, but with a greater emphasis upon minority participation than the Price-Wicklein handbook, and more detailed instruction on how to insure such rights.

Major Cable-Related Trade Publications

Broadband Communications Report [Biweekly], Broadband Information Services, Inc., 274 Madison Avenue, New York, New York 10016. A newsletter covering the political, financial, and technological aspects of two-way networks, interactive home terminals, electronic mail, closed-circuit video, and other advanced communications techniques.

Broadcasting [Weekly], Broadcasting Publications, Inc., 1735 DeSales Street, N.W., Washington, D.C. 20036. The trade journal of the broadcast industry, now with a special section devoted to cable in each issue.

Broadcast Engineering [Monthly], Interec Publishing Corp., 1014 Wyandotte Street, Kansas City, Missouri 64105. A publication treating the technical problems of broadcast and cable electronic engineering, usually on the basis of individual case studies.

Broadcast Management/Engineering [Monthly], Broadband Information Services, Inc., 274 Madison Avenue, New York, New York 10016. A magazine devoted to station and system operational techniques which carries a substantial number of articles on cable management and service.

Cablecasting: Cable TV Engineering [Bimonthly], C. S. Tepfer Publishing Company, Inc., 607 Main Street, Ridgefield, Connecticut 06877. Official journal of the Society of Cable Television Engineers, which covers the technical problems of cable system operation.

Cable/News [Weekly], Cable Communications Corp., 5700 North Portland, Oklahoma City, Oklahoma 73112. An excellent trade magazine oriented toward small systems.

Cable Tech [Monthly], Cable Tech, P.O. Box 1475, Englewood, Colorado 80110. The official journal of the National Cable Television Institute, treating basic maintenance problems involved in operating a cable system.

CATV [Weekly], Communications Publishing Corp., 1900 Yale Street, Englewood, Colorado 80110. The general trade journal of the cable television industry.

Communications Investor [Biweekly], Paul Kagan Associates, Inc., 3930 Sally Lane, Oceanside, New York 11572. A newsletter analyzing the financial position and potential of corporations engaged in communications.

Educational & Industrial Television [Monthly], C. S. Tepfer Publishing Company, Inc., 607 Main Street, Ridgefield, Connecticut 06877. A publication emphasizing closed-circuit and videotape aspects of training and educational uses of cable technology.

Electronic News [Weekly], Fairchild Publications, Inc., 7 East Twelfth Street, New York, New York 10003. Reports emphasizing the common carrier aspects of advanced communication systems.

Electronics World [Monthly], Ziff-Davis Publishing Co., 1 Park Avenue, New York, New York 10016. An excellent collection of articles on evolving technology, explaining communication developments in clear terms.

ETV Newsletter [Bimonthly], C. S. Tepfer Publishing Company, Inc., 607 Main Street, Ridgefield, Connecticut 06877. A newsletter covering educational uses of cable television as well as educational broadcast operation.

Television Digest [Weekly, with cable and TV addenda], 2025 Eye Street, N.W., Washington, D.C. 20006. The most detailed treatment of weekly events in the cable and electronic industries.

TV Communications [Monthly], Communications Publishing Corporation, 1900 West Yale Street, Englewood, Colorado 80110. A journal of increasing stature, now beginning to cover broad trends in cable communications.

VideoPlay Report [Biweekly], C. S. Tepfer Publishing Company, Inc., 607 Main Street, Ridgefield, Connecticut 06877. A newsletter featuring in-depth analysis of cassette development for future communication systems.

In addition to these industry-oriented trade journals, a number of "underground," or antiestablishment, publications have emerged from time to time during the past few years. Unfortunately, most of these efforts focusing either on experimental videotape concepts or the general venality of those operating traditional cable systems have turned out to be only "occasional papers" that have vanished as casually as they have appeared. One exception may be *Radical Software* (Raindance Corporation, Suite 1304, 440 Park Avenue South, New York, New York 10003), which has reappeared a sufficient number of times to be considered at least a semipermanent voice for both types of "underground" viewpoints, while the cable reports of Jerrold Oppenheim in the *Chicago Journalism Review* (192 North Clark Street, Chicago, Illinois 60611) stress the corruptive influence of big business on cable communications, and the need to protect subscriber privacy.

Those interested primarily in video experimentation and public access channels can find more detailed information in *Magnetoscope* (Video White Light, P.O. Box 298, Planetarium Station, New York, New York 10024); or by contacting the Washington Community Video Center (Federal City College, Washington, D.C.); New York University's Alternate Media Center; or Theodora Sklover's Open Channel.

Also of value is an excellent monthly collection of informal articles on various aspects of program origination in a publication sponsored by the National Film Board of Canada, *Access*, Challenge for Change/Société Nouvelle, P.O. Box 6100, Montreal, 101, Quebec.

Primary FCC Documents

FCC docket numbers provide the broadest access to all information relevant to a particular topic. In Pike, James, and Fischer, Henry, *Radio Regulation* (hereafter cited as RR), Current Service (2d ser.), vol. 1, each docket report is located in its digest system (p. 5:287); and proposed rules relating to the docket are listed (p. 1:51). FCC and RR citations have been used interchangeably in this section. For a table converting FCC citations to their RR equivalents, see RR, Current Service, vol. 1, p. 6:301.

13 RR 1546a. "Rules and Regulations Incidental to Restricted Radiation Devices." Subpart D, pt. k5, Docket 9288. 11 July 1956. First FCC rules pertaining to community antenna.

18 RR 1573. "In the Matter of Inquiring into the Impact of CATV ... on the Orderly Development of Television Broadcasting." Docket 12443, 13 April 1959. Report and order finding no immediate economic damage to television caused by CATV operation.

22 RR 193. "Carter Mountain Transmission." Docket 12931, 16 February 1962. Commission finding that threat of economic impact to TV station justifies restraints upon microwave service to competing CATV system.

4 RR 2d 1677. "First Report and Order on Dockets 14895, 15233." 25 April 1965. FCC asserts control over microwave-served CATV systems.

4 RR 2d 1725 (also see 5 RR 2d 1583, 5 RR 2d 1655). "Notice of Inquiry and Proposed Rulemaking on Docket 15971." Imposed freeze upon additional microwave importation to top-100 markets' CATV systems, pending rules.

6 RR 2d 1717 (see also 7 RR 2d 1570, 7 RR 2d 1627). "Second Report and Order on Dockets 14895, 15233, and 15971." 8 March 1966. FCC asserts general CATV jurisdiction.

15 FCC 2d 417. "Notice of Inquiry and Notice of Proposed Rulemaking in Docket 18397." FCC imposes retransmission consent upon importation rights and opens new round of cable investigations.

17 RR 2d 1570. "First Report and Order on Docket 18397." Makes cablecasting mandatory for systems of more than thirty-five hundred subscribers; allows advertising.

22 FCC 2d 50. "Notice of Proposed Rulemaking in Docket 18892." Sets up inquiry on proper roles of federal, state, and local governments in cable control.

23 FCC 2d 833. "Notice of Proposed Rulemaking in Docket 18891." Sets up inquiry on cross-media ownership of cable and proper policy in this field.

24 FCC 2d 580. "Second Further Notice of Proposed Rulemaking in Docket 18397-A." Proposes "public dividend" plan coupling importation right with payment to ETV.

25 FCC 2d 38. "Notice of Proposed Rulemaking in Docket 18894." Sets up inquiry on technical standards for cable signal carriage.

19 RR 2d 1775. "Second Report and Order on Docket 18397." Establishes restrictions upon ownership of cable systems by either network or colocated TV station.

22 RR 2d 1755. "CATV Regulation Report to Congress." Letter of 5 August 1971 setting up general provisions to be included in cable regulation proposed by FCC.

24 RR 2d 1501. "Third Report and Order on Docket 18397." Comprehensive major-market cable rules setting importation, nonbroadcast, and technical standards.

Congressional Deliberations Involving Cable

A number of Congressional hearings and reports have treated some aspect of the cable question, but this list attempts to cite only major sources of such material. Documents have been cited by the numbers and sessions of the Congresses producing them (e.g., 85.2 indicates 85th Congress, second session). They may be obtained from the Government Printing Office, Washington, D.C. 20402.

U.S., Senate, Committee on Commerce

(85.2) *Review of Allocation Problems of Television Service to Smaller Communities.* 1958.

(85.2) *The Problems of Television Service for Smaller Communities: FCC Staff Report* (Cox). December 1958.

(86.1) *VHF Boosters and CATV Legislation: Hearings on S. 2653.* 1959.

(86.1) *Licensing of CATV: Report on S. 2653.* September 1959.

(92.1) *Community Antenna Television Problems.* 1971.

U.S., Senate, Committee on the Judiciary

(91.1) *Revisions of Copyright Act of 1909: Hearings on S. 543.* 1969.

U.S., House, Committee on Interstate and Foreign Commerce (Including Subcommittee on Communications and Power)

(89.1) *Regulation of CATV: Hearings on H.R. 7715.* 1965.

(89.2) *Regulation of CATV: Hearings on H.R. 12914, H.R. 13286, H.R. 14201.* 1966.

(91.1) *Regulation of CATV: Hearings on H.R. 10268, H.R. 10510.* 1969.

U.S., House, Committee on the Judiciary

(89.2) *Proposed Amendments of Copyright Act of 1909: Hearings on H.R. 4347, H.R. 5680, H.R. 6831, H.R. 6835.* 1966.

Primary Legal Decisions Affecting Cable Development

Cable Vision v. KUTV. 335 F2d 348 (9th Cir., 1964); cert. den. 379 US 989 (1965). Denied broadcaster right to prohibit CATV carriage of its network programming on the basis of station's exclusive affiliation contract with network.

Carter Mountain Transmission Corp. v. FCC. 321 F2d 359 (D.C. Cir., 1962); cert. den. 375 US 951 (1963). Affirmed FCC authority to restrict microwave service to CATV system if end result of increase in service would be adverse effect on competing local broadcaster.

CBS v. TelePrompTer. 173 USPQ 778 (1972). Held that even modern microwave importation and nonbroadcast augmentation by cable systems did not change the nature of cable usage; carriage of signal still did not constitute "performance" (see *Fortnightly* below). In March 1973 the U.S. Second Circuit Court of Appeals reversed this decision on the question of cable copyright liability for use of "distant" broadcast signals, remanding the case to the District Court for further proceedings applying this standard of copyright liability. See *Broadcasting,* 12 March 1973, p. 12. This question remains unresolved as this book goes to press.

Fortnightly Corp. v. United Artists Television. 392 US 390 (1968). Held CATV to be essentially a reception rather than a broadcast service, so that carriage of TV signals did not constitute a "performance" which would make a CATV system liable for copyright infringement.

Intermountain Broadcasting v. Idaho Microwave. 196 F. Supp. 315 (S.D., Idaho, 1961). Denied broadcaster right to charge cable system for carriage of programming broadcast by his station, or to restrict cable usage on the basis of "unfair competition."

TV Pix v. Taylor. 304 F. Supp. 549 (D., Nev., 1968), affirmed 396 US 556 (1970). Recognized right of state to control all aspects of domestic CATV operation not preempted by federal control.

United States v. Midwest Video. 406 US 649 (1972). Upheld FCC right to compel cablecasting as an ancilliary power of its right to control cable as an auxiliary broadcast service (see *Southwestern Cable* below).

United States v. Southwestern Cable. 392 US 157 (1968). Affirmed FCC authority to regulate CATV as an adjunct of the agency's general power over electronic mass media.

General References

Publications devoted to cable television have tended to be limited in scope, with each typically focusing on only one of the predominant issues emerging during each period. Perhaps this restricted range of commentary reflects the rapid evolution of the medium, the centrifugal force of its transition driving writers toward narrow areas of certitude within a process still largely in flux. Whatever the reason, the quantity of cable literature available is far more imposing than its quality, and thus the purpose of this annotated list is to isolate the relatively few broad-scaled and perceptive studies of cable which might otherwise be obscured by the sheer bulk of publication in the field. While this compilation does not purport to cite every useful study relevant to cable communication conducted during the past quarter of a century, it should, when used in conjunction with the chapter notes and the basic materials listed earlier in this section, furnish access to sufficient information and analysis to provide a substantial foundation for understanding the nature of the cable challenge and its implications for future communications functions in our society.

History

It may sound grandiloquent to speak of the "history" of a field still emerging after only a decade of nationwide attention, but cable lacks not only a comprehensive treatment of its transition from antenna to communications complex, but even a collection of chronicles to form the foundation for such a study in the future. As in broadcasting, the best work has been done in economic and regulatory historic analysis relating to existing problems, while the process by which individual systems evolved in service and function—the essence of historic research —has been generally overlooked. Mary Alice Mayer (Phillips) interviewed a number of cable "pioneers" in the process of writing her dissertation, "An Historical Study of the Issues and Policies Related to the Educational Application and Utilization of Community Antenna Television" (Northwestern University, 1969), and the author contacted a more limited group of early cable leaders in preparing his dissertation, "Community Antenna Television as a Challenger of Broadcast Regulatory Policy" (University of Wisconsin, 1970), but such basic data remain in short supply.

At present the three most useful historical overviews have been written by proponents of the industry, a Jerrold Electronics official and two former NCTA general counsels.

Hastings, Jerry F. "CATV: Past, Present, and Future." *Electronics World,* August 1967, p. 23. A brief outline of cable growth patterns from the mid-1950s and projected through 1970, together with an explanation of CATV operation and its competitive strength as a communications system.

L'Heureux, Robert. "CATV Industry: Its History, Nature, and Scope." *TV & Communications,* June 1965, p. 25; July 1965, p. 72; August 1965, p. 55; September 1965, p. 39; October 1965, p. 35; December 1965, p. 30; January 1966, p. 36. The most extensive and authoritative treatment of community antenna and CATV evolution yet published.

Smith, E. Stratford. "The Emergence of CATV: A Look at the Evolution of a Revolution." *Proceedings of the IEEE* 58 (July 1970) :967. A well-organized but basically legally oriented analysis of federal regulatory influences upon cable growth.

Two early regulatory histories of exceptional merit are:

Palmer, John; Smith, James; and Lake, Edwin. "CATV: Survey of a Regulatory Problem." *Georgetown Law Journal* 52 (Fall 1963): 136. "Wire Mire: The FCC and CATV." *Harvard Law Review* 79 (December 1965):366.

Other more recent studies of similar focus include:

"The FCC and Regulation of CATV." *New York University Law Review* 33 (March 1968):117.

Huntley, Robert E., and Phillips, Charles, Jr. "Community Antenna Television: Some Issues of Public Policy." *Alabama Law Review* 18 (Fall 1965):296.

Le Duc, Don R. "The Cable Question: Evolution or Revolution in Electronic Mass Communications." *Annals of the American Academy of Political and Social Science* 400 (March 1972):127.

Shampton, John. "The Childhood of CATV." *Ohio State Law Journal* 30 (Spring 1969):382.

For early economic information about the cable industry, the two best sources are:

"CATV's 16-Year Growth Pattern." *Television Digest*, supp., 27 February 1967. An extensive compilation of annual expansion data describing the period 1950–66.

Seiden, Martin. *An Economic Analysis of Community Antenna Systems and the Television Broadcasting Industry.* Report to the Federal Communications Commission. 12 February 1965. Washington, D.C.: Government Printing Office, 1965. This broad-based survey and extensive analysis of booster and cable impact upon broadcast stations contains much basic information obtainable from no other source. Out of print at the Government Printing Office, this report should be available in most law libraries and is reproduced in U.S. Congress, Senate, Hearing before the Subcommittee on Communications of the Committee on Commerce, *Progress Report from the FCC, 1965* (89th Cong., 1st sess., 1965). Much of this information is contained in Seiden's recent text, *Cable Television USA: An Analysis of Government Policy* (New York: Praeger, 1972).

Economics

Studies in cable history and cable economics offer an interesting contrast in source problems, for while the medium's two decades of transition are generally covered in a pro forma "out of the foothills of Pennsylvania came community antenna" paragraph, its economic implications are often analyzed far too minutely by researchers seeking legal rather than scholarly evidence. This is not to disparage the entire body of economic literature sponsored by competing communications entities, but simply to point out that such findings, no matter how scrupulously derived, will often be influenced by the structure of analysis imposed by the funding organization.

In 1965 Franklin M. Fisher attempted the first extensive economic study of this type, and his decision to reject imperfect existing data and create a model to illustrate his theories has been followed by most recent researchers, although each element of the model he constructed has been challenged by subsequent investigators.

Fisher, Franklin M. "The Impact of CATV Competition on Local Television Stations." *NAB Appendix: Dockets 14895 and 15233.* 1965. Lacking precise empirical evidence, Fisher assigned a projected economic value to each television household in a broadcaster's market, measuring loss of revenues in terms of households viewing other channels via cable.

Fisher, Franklin M., and Ferral, V. E. "CATV and Local Television Station Audiences." *Quarterly Journal of Economics* 80 (May 1966) :227. A description of the basic techniques used in the NAB study, with modifications suggested by later research.

Three later abstract model studies have tended to question the severe economic impact projected by Fisher's work.

Park, Rolla Edward. *Potential Impact of Cable Growth on Television Broadcasting.* Memorandum R-587-FF. Santa Monica, Calif.: Rand, 1970. A projection that CATV penetration would pose little threat to major-market television stations but might be damaging to smaller-market operators.

———. *Cable Television and UHF Broadcasting.* Memorandum R-595-MF. Santa Monica, Calif.: Rand, 1971. On a less extensive analytical framework, cable penetration is projected as aiding rather than injuring major-market independent UHF stations.

Federal Communications Commission. *The Economics of the TV-CATV Interface.* Washington, D.C.: Research Branch, Broadcast Bureau, 1970. A study finding that broadcaster projections of damage caused by cable competition were grossly overstated. In response to this staff paper submitted in Docket 18397-A, twenty-one television stations filed a brief with the FCC questioning the accuracy of the commission's Research Branch paper. Included were an analysis by Seiden (Appendix D) and assessments by Fisher and Gerald Kraft (Appendix E) alleging significant errors in the findings of the agency staff, and, by implication, errors in the Rand reports as well. (This brief can be found at the FCC, 1919 M Street, Washington, D.C. 20554).

Such divergence among studies employing similar analytical techniques appears to indicate that efforts to isolate a single determinant within a process this complex and irrational still remain beyond the present state of the art of economic analysis. Perhaps for this reason the studies which have focused primarily upon the economic potential of communications without attempting to focus on the specific aspect of intermedia competition have generally been more successful. Among the best works in this area are:

Barnett, Harold, and Greenberg, Edward. "On the Economics of Wired City Television." *American Economic Review*, 50 (June 1968):503. A broad outline of possible profitable functions cable communication systems can perform in the future.
Goodfriend, H. E., and Pratt, F. T. "Community Antenna Television." *Financial Analysts Journal*, March 1970, p. 48. A much more specific but sound evaluation of the present and future economic factors which should dictate capital investment patterns in cable.
Ohis, J. C. "Marginal Cost Pricing: Investment Theory and CATV." *Journal of Law and Economics* 13 (October 1970):439. A fascinating framework for analyzing the profit potential of cable functions.

The debate among scientists and engineers about the technological potential of cable communication systems has been far less acrimonious, but projections concerning the ultimate functions of future media are still far from uniform. In part, this reflects the reality that science in itself will not dictate the shape of future systems, but rather economic and political forces unknown in these equations. Television broadcasting today could be far more effective in delivering signals if released from the constraints imposed by law and its accompanying financial structures; so all technological projections must be viewed as only tentative in nature, dependent upon variables beyond the control of the scientist. Among the most comprehensive of the recent studies are:

Baer, Walter S. *Interactive Television: Prospects for Two-Way Services on Cable*. Memorandum R-888-MF. Santa Monica, Calif.: Rand, 1971. An excellent overview of the technological aspects of two-way systems, with a discussion of the economic potential and policy questions raised by such functions.
Industrial Electronic Division, Electronic Industries Association. "The Future of Broadband Communications." Comments before the FCC.

In Docket 18397, 28 October 1969, pt. 5. An exciting and imaginative analysis of public and private communication systems which can evolve from existing and developing technology in the field.

Schafly, Hubert. *The Real World of Technological Evolution in Broadband Communication*. Report prepared for the Sloan Commission on Cable Communications (New York), September 1970. A more pragmatic analysis of the technological and economic potential inherent in developing communications technology.

U.S. News and World Report, *Wiring the World: The Explosion in Communications* (Washington, D.C.: U.S. News and World Report Books, 1971). A layman's guide to potential electronic media functions made possible by evolving technology.

Ward, John E. *Present and Probable CATV/Broadband Communications Technology*. Report prepared for the Sloan Commission on Cable Communications (New York), June 1971; revised January 1972. A detailed description of existing and evolving communications delivery services. A condensed version of this report is contained in Appendix A of the Sloan Commission's *On the Cable: The Television of Abundance* (New York: McGraw Hill, 1971).

Rand recently announced plans to issue a new series of cable studies. For further information on these publications, contact Communications Dept., Rand Corporation, 1700 Main Street, Santa Monica, California, 90406.

Social

Predicting the probable social consequences of various mass media functions seems of prime importance, since advance planning is essential if future communications expansion is to be guided to any extent by societal needs. Unfortunately, the literature in this area has tended thus far to be either philosophical in nature or extremely problem oriented, with no cohesive program or policy yet emerging to provide such guidance. Two of the best general studies of this type have been:

Baran, Paul. "On the Impact of New Communications Media upon Social Values." *Law and Contemporary Problems* 32 (Summer 1969):244. An interesting theory of social change based upon expanding media options, with basic suggestions for more constructive operation of such media.

Goldhamer, P., and Westrum, R., eds. *The Social Effects of Communications Technology*. Santa Monica, Calif.: Rand, 1970. A collection of articles on social effects of communications upon education, political behavior, economics, government, and culture in general with suggestions advanced for further research in this field.

Since the more particularized treatments of media effects upon social values are so diverse in nature, they have been listed for ease of location under the general type of dedicated channel access they involve.

Social-Government Channel

Brown, Marie D., ed. "Cable TV and the Black Community." *Black Politician*, vol. 2, no. 4 (April 1971). A complete issue devoted to techniques for reaching Black constituencies, and to the influences cable may have upon political campaigns in Black communities.

Dordeck, Hubert, and Lyle, Jack. *Access by Local Political Candidates to Cable Television: A Report of an Experiment*. Santa Monica, Calif.: Rand, 1971. A report of increased voter awareness created by unlimited time given local candidates on a cablecast channel in Hawaii.

de Sola Pool, Ithiel, and Alexander, Herbert. *Politics in a Wired City*. Report prepared for the Sloan Commission on Cable Communications, September 1971. A series of proposals for using the expanded message capacity of cable systems for increasing citizen involvement in the political process.

Shelton, Don. "Time for a New City Hall Communicator." *Nation's Cities*, March 1971, p. 27. A short informal essay on the necessity for local governments to explain their problems and needs to their citizens.

Social-Educational Channel

Association for Educational Communications and Technology. "Position Paper on Community Antenna Television." *Audiovisual Instruction*, November 1971, p. 56. Proposals for future educational access to cable; also includes an excellent background in prior access to broadcast facilities and suggests techniques for improving access in view of cable's greater capacity.

Hill, Roger W., Jr. "Educational Considerations of CATV: Cablecasting, Telecommunication." *Educational/Industrial Broadcasting*, November 1969, p. 57. A solid, pragmatic approach to educational uses of cable facilities.

Shafer, Jon. *A Cable TV Guide for Educators*. St. Paul, Minn.: Educational Research and Development Council of the Twin Cities Metropolitan Area, 1972. An excellent outline of the particular tactics school administrators should use in gaining maximum educational benefits from cable.

Public Access Channel

Crichton, Judy. *Toward an Immodest Experiment in Cable Television: Modestly Produced*. Report prepared for the Sloan Commission on

Cable Communications (New York), March 1971. A modest but detailed paper describing the production of specialized programming for low-income groups.

Freebairn, Thomas. "Public Access in New York City: An Interview with Theodora Sklover." *Yale Review of Law and Social Action* 2, no. 3 (Spring 1972):227. A brief but fairly definitive discussion of the problems involved in and the hopes emerging for public access programming, based upon the New York experience.

Pepper, Robert. "Citizen Rights and the Cable." Mimeographed. Report for a seminar conducted by Professor Charles Sherman, University of Wisconsin, Spring 1972. An exceptional study outlining legal guarantees necessary for effective public access, safeguards essential to protect subscribers against loss of privacy through cable linkage, and other issues of citizen's rights of equal concern today.

Legal

In areas involving regulation and copyright, cable literature is so rich and deep that the basic problem is not one of discovery but of limitation, to impose some standard of selectivity upon citation. Because the FCC's "Third Report and Order" has altered the legal status of major-market cable systems drastically, only those articles offering an extensive analysis of past regulatory patterns or whose comments have not been affected by this rule-making proceeding have been included. For other articles now primarily of historical interest, see the *Journal of Broadcasting*'s legal bibliography cited above under the heading "Cable Bibliographies."

Federal Regulation

Boteen, Michael. "CATV Regulation: A Jumble of Jurisdictions." *New York University Law Review* 45 (October 1970):816. An extremely useful outline of the problems inherent in the several levels of cable regulation, with emphasis on the difficulty of achieving cohesive policy within this pattern of federalism.

Chasen, Leonard, and Ross, Leonard. "Federal Regulation of Cable Television: The Visible Hand." *Harvard Law Review* 83 (June 1970):1820. An excellent analysis of federal governmental influences upon cable growth, with primary emphasis upon signal restrictions and copyright controls.

Johnson, Leland. *The Future of Cable Television: Some Problems of Federal Regulation.* Memorandum RM-6199-FF. Santa Monica, Calif.: Rand, 1970. A broad overview of federal regulation of cable and issues involved in such regulation.

President's Task Force on Communications Policy. *Final Report.*

Washington, D.C.: Government Printing Office, 1968. A massive
study of federal communications priorities, including cable policies.
A list of the research papers used in this report can be obtained from
the National Technical Information Service, Springfield, Virginia.

Other useful but somewhat less comprehensive studies include:

Comanor, William S., and Mitchell, Bridger M. "The Costs of Planning: The FCC and Cable Television." *Journal of Law and Economics* 15, no. 1 (April 1972):177.
Le Duc, Don R. "The FCC v. CATV et al.: A Theory of Regulatory
Reflex Action." *Federal Communications Bar Journal* 23, no. 2
(Spring 1969).
McGowan, John J. "Competition, Regulation, and Performance in Television Broadcasting." *Washington University Law Quarterly*, Fall
1967, p. 499.
Sucherman, Stuart P. "Cable TV: The Endangered Revolution." *Chicago Journalism Review*, May–June 1971, p. 13.

State Regulation

Barnett, Stephen. "State, Federal, Local Regulation of Cable Television." *Notre Dame Lawyer* 47 (April 1972): 156. A study advocating a strong state role to fill in the gaps in federal control and to add
enlightenment to local franchising efforts.
Cable Television Information Center. "An Annotated Outline of an
Ordinance for Use in Considering a Process for Local Regulation of
Cable Television," 12 May 1972. Mimeographed. CTIC Office, 2100
M Street, N.W., Washington, D.C. An extensive compilation of
existing franchise provisions organized under general topics each franchising unit should consider when drafting its own ordinance. Annotated.
Center for Analysis of Public Issues. *Crossed Wires: Cable Television in
New Jersey*. Princeton, N.J.: CAPI, 1971. A comprehensive survey
of franchising practices in New Jersey. Indicates the need for broad
policy guidance at the state or federal level. Also see a more recent
study by this organization, *Public Access Channels: The New York
Experience*. Princeton, N.J.: CAPI, 1972.
City of Detroit. *Cable Television in Detroit: A Study in Urban Communications*. Detroit, Mich.: City Clerk's Office, 1972. A major
examination of urban communication needs. Recommends municipal
ownership as the best possible solution in this instance.
Mitchell, Stephen. *State Regulation of Cable Television*. Santa Monica,
Calif.: Rand, 1971. A historical study of the Connecticut and
Nevada experiences with some suggestions for strengthening state

control. Somewhat dated now in view of the general tendency of recent statutes to range beyond common carrier controls at the state level.

Muth, Thomas. "State Interest in Cable Television Regulation." Ph.D. dissertation, Ohio State University, 1973. A massive analysis of state rights to regulate various aspects of modern broadband communications systems.

New York State Public Service Commission. *Regulation of Cable Television by the State of New York.* Report to the commission by Commissioner William K. Jones. Albany: New York State Public Service Commission, 1970. A detailed study of the problems of cable regulation in New York. Concludes with the recommendation that the Public Service Commission assert jurisdiction.

Wisconsin, the Governor's Blue Ribbon Task Force on Cable Communications. "Cable Communications in Wisconsin: Analysis of Proposed Recommendations." Mimeographed. Madison, Wisc.: Cable Commission, 27 East State Capitol Building, 1972. An extensive preliminary draft, based upon ten major public hearings held throughout the state. Offers a comprehensive overview of possible regulatory alternatives available for cable control. These proceedings should provide an incentive for other states to attempt similar surveys, since the total budget of this office for its comprehensive efforts in fact finding and policy formulation was only $28,000.

Copyright

"CATV and Copyright Liability: The Final Decision." *Commercial Law Review,* December 1968, p. 401. A lucid explanation of the implications of the *Fortnightly* decision for cable carriage of broadcast signals.

Finkelstein, H. K. "Music, CATV, Educational Broadcasting, and Juke Boxes." *Iowa Law Review* 52 (February 1968):870. An excellent background on the alliances of the 1960s which prevented Congress's attempts to revise the copyright laws from succeeding.

Krasilovsky, M. W. "The Copyright Dilemma." *Television Quarterly* 7 (Fall 1968):33. A description of copyright laws as a mechanism for controlling distribution of programming, and of the inability of copyright to protect the local broadcaster's signal.

Ross, Leonard. *The Copyright Question in CATV.* Report prepared for the Sloan Commission on Cable Communications (New York), April 1971. A clear description of territorial exclusivity as it pertains to protection of copyrights and broadcast markets.

For the most recent thought on cable copyright issues, see the annual review of copyright law and federal deliberations in *Copyright Law*

Symposium, a yearly compendium of studies available in most law libraries.

Other Areas of Cable Reference

For sources treating broader issues such as media monopoly or federal communications innovation policy, or more specific topics such as cablecasting in particular communities, see notes following the appropriate chapters in this text or the readers' guides cited above under the heading "Cable Bibliographies." The effort to collect sources yielding the maximum amount of generalized information has left this compilation somewhat restricted in both philosophical breadth and empirical detail. It is hoped, however, that this basic body of material may serve at least as a point of departure for researchers interested in either type of specialized knowledge.

Index

Index

285